Praise for *The Business of Sharing*

"A remarkable book, a sweeping view of a fascinating new economy in which peer-to-peer exchange will be central, written to be simultaneously very intelligent and very readable. Alex Stephany is a rare author, combining the experiential insight of a successful entrepreneur with the longer range vision of a deep thinker. If you want to get a head start on seeing the future of business, and understanding how you will play an increasing role in creating it, read this book. And after you do, share it with a friend."

Arun Sundararajan, Professor and Rosen Faculty Fellow, Stern School of Business, New York University

"*The Business of Sharing* is a great book about history being made today in the sharing economy. Alex Stephany puts together a thorough, insightful, thoughtful, and entertaining account of what is transpiring today and what will undoubtedly be here to stay."

Alfred Lin, Partner, Sequoia Capital

"Alex offers an engaging and informative narrative on the business of 'sharing' that has emerged in recent years. From the perspective of an insider, he brings valuable insight to the waves this industry is creating both inside and outside of itself."

Lily Cole, Founder, Impossible.com, and actor

"*The Business of Sharing* is an excellent read for any entrepreneur. Alex gives a great overview of the sharing economy: from how it works to the current key players in the market and the stories, such as my own, of founders who launched businesses that rely upon the sharing economy. The sharing economy is still in its infancy and I look forward to watching it mature."

Martin Varsavsky, Founder, Fon, and serial entrepreneur

"Alex Stephany writes a compelling and incisive guide to how sharing economy dynamics make businesses and communities agile, innovative, and powerful. Read this book. Because by the end you'll understand how the sharing economy has unleashed a complex and massive shift in the way business is done."

Lisa Gansky, Entrepreneur and author of *The Mesh*

"Many have written about the sharing economy, but Stephany brings the rare insight of a CEO at the forefront of this economy. By tying in the perspectives of all its key players—founders, investors, corporates, and governments—Stephany not only gives a practical guide to anyone looking to get involved, but also provides a holistic picture that only a person who has spent countless hours balancing the diverse needs of these demanding stakeholders could fully appreciate or articulate. Superbly written, this is a fascinating and must-read book for anyone interested in how business and society are now changing hand-in-hand."

Shelby Clark, Founder, RelayRides, and Executive Director, Peers

"To live within our means we must share more, but learning to share is difficult, especially when some people have much more than others. As more of us squeeze into cities, into less and less space, unless we share better we will be squeezed out by our junk. Alex Stephany reveals how more sharing can happen, in both the marketplace and beyond. Entertaining, informed, and provocative."

Danny Dorling, Halford Mackinder Professor of Geography,
University of Oxford

"Covering all aspects of the sharing economy, this is the most comprehensive—and by far the best—book written on this topic. It provides an extremely informative and insightful look into how corporations and independent businesses can successfully partner in this progressive movement. Alex has provided excellent models for rewiring the future of business and, as a business leader in the sharing economy, adds insights and wisdom for all that are looking to participate in this modern movement. This is a delightful must-read."

Mick McCabe, Chief Strategy Officer, Leo Burnett USA

"Stephany's excellent contribution to this field stands out as it focuses on the commercial side of the sharing economy as much as the social. In my view, neither can be sustained without the other."

Giles Andrews, Co-founder and CEO, Zopa

The Business of Sharing

Making it in the New Sharing Economy

The Business of Sharing

Alex Stephany

palgrave
macmillan

First published 2015 by
PALGRAVE MACMILLAN

Palgrave Macmillan in the UK is an imprint of Macmillan Publishers Limited, registered in England, company number 785998, of Houndmills, Basingstoke, Hampshire RG21 6XS.

Palgrave Macmillan in the US is a division of St Martin's Press LLC, 175 Fifth Avenue, New York, NY 10010.

Palgrave Macmillan is the global academic imprint of the above companies and has companies and representatives throughout the world.

Palgrave® and Macmillan® are registered trademarks in the United States, the United Kingdom, Europe and other countries.

ISBN: 978–1–137–37617–6

This book is printed on paper suitable for recycling and made from fully managed and sustained forest sources. Logging, pulping and manufacturing processes are expected to conform to the environmental regulations of the country of origin.

A catalogue record for this book is available from the British Library.

A catalog record for this book is available from the Library of Congress.

Typeset by Aardvark Editorial Limited, Metfield, Suffolk.

For my parents, for everything
And for you, more than a number in this new economy

Contents

List of Figures

x

Foreword

It won't be long before most of the global population is online. We have just begun to see the Internet's impact when it comes to how we live and who governs us. One need only look at the use of smartphones and social media during the Arab Spring or the frightening use of similar technologies in the spread of ISIS to understand how our world will be molded by the Internet and its organizing principles: scale, transparency, and speed. And at the root of it all—connectivity. The most promising trend arising from this global, mobile, and social connectivity is what thought leaders have started calling the "sharing economy."

Picked up by the world's media, this economy is empowering citizens to get goods and services from each other and to get more out of their own assets and time. In fact, the sharing economy's impact on how we consume and its ability to fuel economic growth may be the most profound change of all that the Internet will bring. That is why Alex Stephany's superb book is so timely.

Along with consumption, this is about labor. We are at the beginning of a major reorganization of who does work and how they do it. The last decade has seen the rise of global Internet companies whose profits have primarily benefitted wealthy people. The next two decades may bring greater rewards to global participants in this connected network. Those with specialist technical skills can participate in global projects. Those with extra space in their homes or cars that are sat idly—or even simply time on their hands to grab some groceries for a neighbor—are finding new opportunities. *The Business of Sharing* is a major new book on this economic and social revolution.

Above all, it is also the first ever book on the subject written by someone working on the frontline of this new economy. As CEO of one of the UK's best-known sharing economy businesses, Alex brings razor-sharp insights on the challenges and opportunities for us all in this fast-changing landscape.

And throughout this fascinating journey, as a trusted insider in this world, Alex takes the reader along with him, from the boardroom of Silicon Valley's most prestigious venture capital firm, Sequoia Capital, to inside the home of the British Prime Minister, 10 Downing Street, and beyond.

This book will offer you unparalleled access to the founders, the funders, the big businesses, the workers, and the governments who must somehow make sense of these upheavals. Chapter by chapter, Alex looks at all the key stakeholders in this new economy. Practically, the book lets readers dive into the chapters that most relate to their own careers and aspirations.

I have spent my career in two of these camps: as a founder of companies with past exits behind me and now as a venture capitalist. I've been able to look at business from these perspectives. In *The Business of Sharing*, Alex views this important new economy from 360 degrees. But more than that, this structure serves to pull out the complex collaborations and tensions at play in an economy that affects everyone, from a single mother needing to sell her crib to make rent money, to the world's biggest conglomerates.

This is no one-sided propaganda piece for this new economy. Alex discusses the frightening risks and dangers that come with these upheavals. And make no mistake—change this dramatic will create millions of losers. As he points out, it could even undermine morality itself by placing a monetary value on deeds once done for free. Meanwhile, Alex describes how governments will have to intervene in the strife between special interest groups who have everything to lose and those with everything to gain.

If you're new or nearly new to the subject, you owe it to yourself to understand how the global, mobile, social Internet and the collaborative economy will impact you or your children—because its impact will be felt far beyond the world of technology and startups.

The Business of Sharing is a fast and thrilling read. Thank you, Alex Stephany, for bringing us this brilliant first-hand account of one of this century's most important trends.

Mark Suster
Partner, Upfront Ventures
@msuster/www.bothsidesofthetable.com

Acknowledgments

I'm very grateful to Anthony Eskinazi for supporting this project and everyone at JustPark; I couldn't ask for a more fun and talented bunch of teammates. I'd also like to thank Lisa Gansky, April Rinne, and Arun Sundararajan of NYU for providing feedback on the manuscript, as well as some of the finest entrepreneurs and investors anywhere who have given their time to this book: investors like Robin Klein, Fred Wilson, Jeff Jordan, and Mark Suster who kindly wrote the foreword, and entrepreneurs like Giles Andrews, Nate Blecharczyk, Nicolas Brusson, Manish Chandra, Robin Chase, Shelby Clark, Lily Cole, Jeff Lynn, Fred Mazzella, Alex Mittal, Naval Ravikant, James Reinhart, Roo Rogers, Andy Ruben, Martin Varsavsky, Jamie Wong, and others. Thank you to some amazing friends too for their comments—Berger, FitzGerald, Ellie Ereira —and in particular my great pal Alex Feldman for his detailed and predictably insightful mark-up of the manuscript. Thank you also to Tamsine O'Riordan at Macmillan for asking me to write this book and my agent Viv Schuster at Curtis Brown. Finally, thank you to the best sibs imaginable and my wonderful Mum and Dad to whom this book is dedicated.

The Billion Dollar Moustache

It was 2 am in San Francisco. Leather-jacketed hipsters were crowding into the taco joints and I could hear drum rolls coming from a bar somewhere down the dirty boulevard. And a car with a fluffy pink moustache was headed straight for me.

The car pulled up. I walked round to the driver's side and he lowered his window. He had the same dark, gelled hair and nervous smile as his photo. There was no question that it was him.

"Alex?" he said.

I nodded and we bumped fists. Then I got into the front seat.

Four minutes earlier, I had taken out my iPhone and opened an app called Lyft, one of the US's fastest growing tech startups. On the screen was a map of the Mission District, car icons dotted around the gridironed streets. I pressed the green button, big enough for fingers far drunker than mine, and the app had showed me a thumbnail photo of my driver, Eddie. Before I knew it, a car icon was edging across the screen of my iPhone as the real thing sped towards me through the dark streets.

Lyft is a peer-to-peer taxi service. It provides software that lets people register as taxi drivers and—once "background checked and personality screened" by the startup—operate a taxi business from their smartphone. It also doles out giant pink moustaches for their drivers to attach to their cars. Lyft's army of drivers includes retirees, PhD students, and actors. *As for the people running this strange new breed of taxi company?* Forget dead-eyed men behind safety glass. Think Stanford-educated "data scientists" scribbling algorithms on whiteboards (with the occasional break for ping pong).

Lyft is just one of a new wave of companies (see the Appendix) powering the so-called "sharing economy." This is an economy built on people sharing assets, often ones that they already own. The sharing unlocks value in the downtime of those assets. Lyft taps into the downtime of two types of assets: cars that, on average, sit and rust for 23 hours a day,[1] and their owners' spare time. This economy is not only empowering people to share their cars with strangers. Today, people are sharing everything from their hard-earned cash and expensive apartments to their beloved pooches. It is an economy that is already estimated to be worth over $15 billion a year.[2] And it's growing like wildfire.

Of course, there is nothing new about renting belongings or sharing assets. Every city dweller is used to communal parks, gyms, and public transit. What *is* new, however, is the application of technology to many old as well as new forms of shared consumption. The Internet and smartphones are fueling the growth of huge and liquid online marketplaces where these shared assets and their owners live. Through these online marketplaces and the energies of millions of everyday entrepreneurs, entire sectors are being opened up to the sharing treatment.

The business I run, JustPark, allows property owners to share their parking spaces. Before the Internet, the odd person would stand in their driveway holding a sign if they happened to have a desirable parking spot near a sports ground. But to have over a million people globally parking in other people's driveways would have been unthinkable a decade ago. The 1960s saw the birth of the timeshare when it made sense to share expensive and infrequently used assets like holiday homes. Now we can monetize things as inexpensive as the drills and hammers used to build them.

Eddie passed me his iPod and said, "You choose."

He was an off-duty paramedic, driving for Lyft to make some extra cash. He seemed to be enjoying the novelty of driving people who were not likely to do him the discourtesy of dying in the back. As for me, I was struck by the bizarre sensation that the stranger taking me home actually cared about me—even a tiny little bit.

"Are you British?" asked Eddie.

"I'm from London," I told him.

"Awesome!" he said. "I'm going this year for the first time. Any recommendations?"

"What kind of stuff are you into? Do you like the theatre? Museums? There are literally hundreds of galleries. And ..." Off I went, well aware that my advice would be inferior to what he could find on websites like TripAdvisor and Yelp and that he would probably go to them anyway and, besides, who was I to compare with the collective wisdom of online communities millions strong?

We pulled up outside Cara's apartment. I knew Cara little better than Eddie. I was staying in her duplex in San Francisco's trendy SoMa neighborhood, blocks of former factories and sweatshops that are now turning out startups. I had rented Cara's place through the hip poster child of the sharing economy, Airbnb. In choosing to spend my holiday in someone else's home, I was not alone. Over 17 million travelers have already used Airbnb to book stays in strangers' spare rooms and apartments.[3] Founded in only 2008, the startup is valued at over $10 billion.

So it was that instead of picking up my key from a hotel night porter, I delved into my pocket for Cara's spare keys and unlocked her front door. I collapsed onto her sofa, wondering if JustPark could ever reach the same kind of scale as Airbnb. Would we get 10 million users? *100 million?* It made my head spin. Could a business, *our* business, one owning nothing more than laptops, whiteboards, and a remote control monster truck, also be worth billions? Could we create as much value? That morning, Cara had told me how her Airbnb income had supported her when her working hours were cut, and had given her the economic freedom to write a book. "I feel so utterly grateful," she had said.

As these companies have gained traction, so the money has come pouring in. Lyft was only founded in 2012 but, in the rich soil of Silicon Valley, has already raised $330 million of venture capital and is valued at over a billion dollars. *A billion dollar pink moustache. Really?* The skeptical Englishman in me cannot be silenced. *What if Lyft is as full of hot air as its logo's green balloon?* But that is small fry. Another San Francisco taxi startup, the better-known Uber, has raised venture capital at a valuation of $40 billion. Weeks after one of its fundraisings, James Surowiecki, author of *The Wisdom of Crowds* wrote, "The flood of new money into all these new businesses feels like a mini-bubble in the making."[4]

My brother Paul, a fund manager in the City of London, would say so. He has invested in far less valuable companies that are highly profitable or have decades of cutting-edge R&D. Consider one of the sharing economy's success stories, Chegg, a textbook resale marketplace. Had you delved into its listing prospectus, you would have found warnings of the weak economic fundamentals that characterize many sharing economy marketplaces. "We have a history of losses," read the prospectus ($170.4 million to be precise) "and we may not achieve or sustain profitability in the future ..." Chegg floated in 2013 at a valuation of over a billion dollars. Its shares currently trade at half their initial public offering (IPO) price. Zipcar, the sharing economy's largest ever acquisition at $500 million, was bought by Avis Budget for less than half of its IPO price after it too never turned a profit.

Those are the sharing economy's success stories. Many a sharing economy company has fallen by the wayside altogether. Loosecubes was a marketplace for shared office space backed by the mighty Accel Partners venture capital firm. It folded in 2012. A year later, WhipCar, a UK car-sharing service, followed suit. It plastered posters all over the London Underground but failed to grow revenue. *There is logic in these business models but are they ahead of their time?* Generally, we don't like strangers driving our cars or sleeping in our beds. We exhibit to varying degrees what I call the "Goldilocks Complex": an instinctive displeasure at the thought of strangers eating our metaphorical porridge, sleeping in our literal beds, or using our belongings. It is in the interests of almost every company to preserve the Goldilocks Complex. Between them, they spend around half a trillion dollars each year on marketing to get us to buy, not share.[5]

Surely, too, the excitement about sharing economy businesses is artificially high in the echo chamber of Silicon Valley. As Marcus Wohlsen writes in *Wired*, "Digital utopianism runs through Silicon Valley like water down the Mississippi. But the rhetoric reaches even higher levels than usual when the tech cognoscenti start talking about 'the sharing economy'." British author Carole Cadwalladr writes in *The Guardian*, "In San Francisco – where Airbnb is one of the sun kings of the startup scene ... the 'sharing economy' has the kind of resonance that 'free cake' or 'hot sex' has for the rest of us."

I was bedding down in the epicenter of this new world where thousands of evangelical sharers believe that this new economy will add value in the world beyond the one of fund managers and stock exchanges. For them, sharing can turn cities of individuals into networks of communities. It can reduce our destructive and unsustainable consumption of natural resources. It can cull the materialism and greed that brought us to the verge of global financial catastrophe. For them, the sharing economy is nothing short of social, environmental, and economic salvation.

Back in 2011, I did not join JustPark, then a tiny three-person startup, because it was part of the sharing economy. I joined because I thought that we could solve a big problem: parking in major cities. Three years later, I found myself at the start of a different journey: to find out if the sharing economy was all it was cracked up to be. During that journey, I watched zealots and cynics banging their drums every passing day on blogs and Twitter, and in half the world's newspapers. In *The Business of Sharing*, I want to let readers decide for themselves whether the sharing economy is real-world substance or media hype: hot stuff or hot air.

Today, the sharing economy may have San Francisco as its beating heart but it has become a global movement. In writing this book, I talked to entrepreneurs from the Philippines to Belgium, venture capitalists from Silicon Valley to Israel, and politicians from London to Seoul. But above all, I met the customers of the many businesses that crowd beneath the umbrella of the sharing economy: people inviting strangers into their kitchen for dinner in Barcelona and crowdfunding farms in Bulgaria. Some were daring and brave, and others were on the wacky side of visionary. But most of them, I suspect, were not so very different from you.

The next morning, I was due to meet one of the architects of this new movement. I decided to give myself an extra 15 minutes in bed. I could always take a Lyft.

Notes

1   Shoup, Donald, *The High Cost of Free Parking* (American Planning Association, 2005). A report by the UK's RAC Foundation found that UK cars are parked for 96.5% of the time: http://www.racfoundation.org/assets/rac_foundation/content/downloadables/spaced_out-bates_leibling-jul12.pdf.

2   *The sharing economy: how will it disrupt your business?* Megatrends: the collision; PricewaterhouseCoopers research, August 2014. A team at PricewaterhouseCoopers,

including PwC Chief Economist John Hawksworth, market-sized the sharing economy at $15 billion in August 2014 and predicted it would grow to a $335 billion market by 2025: http://pwc.blogs.com/northern-ireland/2014/08/uks-sharing-economy-could-be-worth-9-billion-a-year-by-2025.html.

3   At the time of writing in September 2014, over 17 million guests had stayed in Airbnb spare rooms and apartments, growing at the rate of approximately 1 million a month. https://www.airbnb.co.uk/about/about-us.

4   Surowiecki, James, Uber Alles, http://www.newyorker.com/magazine/2013/09/16/uber-alles-2.

5   Around $0.5 trillion of global advertising spend in 2014 was forecast by Magna Global, a unit of New York Stock Exchange-listed Interpublic: http://news.magnaglobal.com/article_display.cfm?article_id=1578.

Architects
Building on New Ground

The bay glittered in the hot morning sun and the seagulls wheeled above me. I was waiting in line for my ferry at San Francisco's grand Ferry Building. As weekend shoppers browsed the organic farmers' market, I was nervously planning out my lunch appointment with Lisa Gansky across the bay.

Gansky is a successful entrepreneur with two exits behind her. In 1993, she co-founded Global Network Navigator, the first website offering clickable ads, which she sold to AOL. Her second business, Ofoto, a photo-sharing service, was almost as pioneering. She grew Ofoto to over 50 million users before selling it to Eastman Kodak in 2001. I had read in *Fast Company* that Gansky had made "tens of millions" from her exits.

Now it seemed like she had set out to save the world through sharing. Among her many angel investments in the sharing economy are RelayRides, which lets people rent each other's cars, Scoot Networks, a Zipcar for scooters, and Science Exchange, a website for researchers to book experiments at shared laboratories. But I was there to talk to Gansky about her visionary book, *The Mesh: Why the Future of Business is Sharing*. She was meeting me off the ferry in Vallejo at midday, presumably in some kind of electric Batmobile. I was at the ferry building 45 minutes early. Missing the ferry was not an option.

Better safe than sorry, I checked with the guy in front of me that I was in the right queue for Vallejo.

"*Vallejo?*" he blurted. "*That's* the ferry for Vallejo."

I followed his gaze. A white ferry was pulling away from the pier. "No!" I cried involuntarily.

People gathered round to assist the distressed foreigner. The next ferry to Vallejo was not until the late afternoon, long past my slot with Gansky. I had flown from London and this was a meeting I had to make. I felt sick.

"Try and catch it at Pier 41," suggested someone. "It's picking up folks there."

According to Google Maps, Pier 41 was 31 minutes' walk. I had 14 minutes and neither Lyft nor Uber could save me: the seafront road was gridlocked with traffic. So I ran. 1.5 miles down the Embarcadero. I arrived at Pier 41, sweat pouring off me. I charged up to an official stood in front of a gangplank beneath a sign that read "SAUSALITO."

"Vallejo?" I panted.

He nodded at another white ferry in front of us, pulling away from its moorings.

"I NEED TO GET ON THAT BOAT!" I yelled.

"Sorry. I took the sign down."

"PLEASE! I'VE JUST RUN…"

The growl of the ferry's engines cut out. It drifted away a few more meters before slowly re-docking. They must have spotted me.

"*I ain't never seen that before*," murmured the man. "Must be your lucky day."

He unchained the gates and I ran down the gangplank, throbbing with gratitude. They slammed the ferry doors and, as the engines powered back up, I dragged myself onto the sundeck. Soon, San Francisco's sparkling skyscrapers and the vast spans of the Bay Bridge were disappearing into the cloudless sky. We passed Alcatraz Island. The former prison was hunched on its rock, an unrepentant hulk of concrete. The thought of those who suffered inside in solitary confinement sent a shiver down my spine. I had never felt freer. I had never felt more thankful to be part of a connected and collaborative world.

Definitions: so what is the sharing economy?

I went to a geeky school. I was taught that if you wanted to understand something the answer could be found in the many heavy volumes of the *Oxford English Dictionary* in the school library. Find that word or that concept in the *Oxford English Dictionary* and you would find the end of the scotch tape (or "Sellotape," as we Brits call it). But the OED does not have a definition of the sharing economy. These days, I go to Wikipedia for my definitions. Indeed, the Wikipedia project itself, radically participatory and iterative, is to the sluggish centralized authority of the OED what the sharing economy is to the old economy. At least for now, Wikipedia defines the sharing economy as:

> A sustainable economic system built around the sharing of human and physical assets. It includes the shared creation, production, distribution, trade and consumption of goods and services by different people and organizations. These systems take a variety of forms but all leverage information technology to empower individuals, corporations, non-profits and government with information that enables the distribution, sharing and reuse of excess capacity in goods and services.

I define the sharing economy more abruptly:

> The sharing economy is the **value** in taking **underutilized assets** and making them **accessible online** to a **community**, leading to a **reduced need for ownership** of those assets.

(Even more abruptly, I say the sharing economy is the value in redistributing excess to a community, or getting "slack to the pack.")

My definition has five main limbs.

1 Value

Sharing economy platforms create reciprocal economic value. Usually, they are revenue-generating e-commerce sites, or have the potential to be revenue-generating. Sometimes, the revenue motive appears incidental or exists only to make the service sustainable. For example, it is free to swap books on BookMooch. Users get points by mailing their old books to someone else and redeem points by requesting someone else's books. This earns the website precisely nothing. However, BookMooch is able to make revenue from its visitors when they click on Amazon affiliate links for second-hand books that are not available on their website.

Sometimes, goods and services in the sharing economy are changing hands through a gift economy. On yerdle, people gift their unwanted objects, but the users will be monetized later on, most likely through the purchase of credits. As the title suggests, my focus in this book is on the *business* of sharing. While TeamUp! Against Cancer, a marketplace that connects cancer victims with local volunteers, is a great philanthropic initiative, I will be looking in more detail at a business like TaskRabbit, a marketplace where people get paid for doing chores and the platform earns commission.

2 Underutilized assets

In the sharing economy, the assets on platforms can be anything from yachts to baby clothes to dogs. BorrowMyDoggy is a UK startup that matches up dog owners with dog-less dog lovers, with both parties paying an annual subscription. Dog owners get a break from looking after their canine. Non-dog owners get the novelty of having a dog on demand. Alien as it would appear to their doting owners, even dogs can be viewed as assets. Services in the sharing economy, such as mowing someone's lawn or helping them to set up a blog, are usually the output of intangible assets like time and expertise.

The value in all of these assets is in their so-called "idling capacity": the periods of time when extra value could be extracted from them. Idling capacity is a notion that was first systematically studied and measured in the context of industrial processes. The sharing economy applies the same ruthless logic of how best to run an aluminum smelter to all of our assets. That means turning an asset's downtime into revenue, whether that asset is a bicycle or the time of someone who could be riding that bicycle to deliver a package.

3 Online accessibility

For utilization to increase, these assets need to be made accessible. "Sharing" in the context of the sharing economy has become shorthand for "making accessible," a process that happens once assets are listed online. Making accessible can mean selling, for example through the peer-to-peer (P2P) e-commerce pioneer and granddaddy of the sharing economy, eBay.

It can mean renting such as through Airbnb, gifting as we just saw with yerdle, or even swapping. On Swapz, you can find exchanges such as a DJ offering to play for free in return for some maintenance to his van.

4 Community

But making underutilized assets accessible is not enough: the assets need to move within a community. Community means more than just supply and demand. In successful sharing economy businesses, communities of users engage with each other above and beyond their transactional needs. They trust each other. They are values-based and, as we will see, police these values from internal threats and defend them from external ones. Often, these communities are built around interest groups. On SabbaticalHomes.com, the people swapping homes are all university academics. On a website like DogVacay, where dog owners board their dogs with ordinary people rather than at kennels, the community is chatty on social media and united by a love of dogs.

Community is often the decisive difference between a sharing economy business and a traditional rental one like CORT, the world's largest supplier of rental furniture. Although CORT has the potential to be a sharing economy business, there is no sense of the community behind the business: no reviews, profiles, ability for users to message each other, or customer stories. The people and small businesses who rent the furniture are effectively invisible. CORT'S owners, Warren Buffett's Berkshire Hathaway conglomerate, must view previous renters of their furniture as unfortunate reminders of its unpalatable second-handness rather than a strength to be leveraged.

5 Reduced need for ownership

Once people can access assets within a community, it leads to a reduced need to own those assets. Rise Art is a website that lets people rent fine art. If you move house often or do not want to stare at the same art for years on end, it makes sense to rent paintings. Or consider how each shared Zipcar can take 17 other cars off the road.[1] This makes Zipcar fundamentally different from a traditional rental car business like Alamo. While Alamo's core business is supplying supplementary cars at airports, Zipcar deploys its cars around cities, reducing the need to own them in the first place. One consequence of such business models is that goods become services. As Arun Sundararajan, a professor at New York University and the sharing economy's leading academic, notes, "Sharing economy businesses are spawning a range of efficient new 'as-a-service' business models in industries as diverse as accommodation, transportation, household appliances, and high-end clothing."

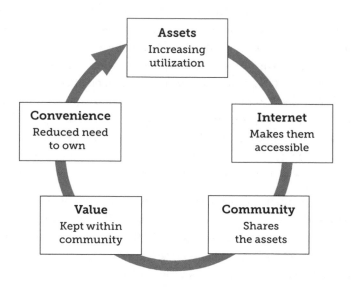

FIGURE 1.1 The sharing economy: increasing asset utilization

The two sharing models

If the end-user merely accesses the inventory, then who owns it? Sharing economy companies come in two flavors. Some are business-to-consumer (B2C). Others are P2P. Consider the differences between Zipcar's business model and that of another car rental business, RelayRides. Zipcar is a B2C business that buys and maintains a fleet of new vehicles that it rents to drivers. RelayRides, on the other hand, is a P2P marketplace that allows individuals to rent out their own cars to other drivers. Although their ends may be similar—providing convenient access to a car—their means differ in two ways. On a P2P marketplace, the inventory is already out there, making RelayRides a leaner business model. Furthermore, the provider of the service is not a company but a person. If there is an issue with my Zipcar booking, I contact their customer service team. If there is a problem with my RelayRides car, my first port of call is the individual owner.

This is not to say there is anything unprofessional about having to deal with an individual rather than a company. Sellers on P2P platforms are not incorporated businesses as we know them but micro-entrepreneurs, often running highly slick operations. Instead of a corporate brand, they leverage their personal brand through a profile page. Instead of a Yellow Cab taking me downtown, it is Eddie. Instead of a Hilton hotel checking me in, it is Cara. The buyers too are often more than passive consumers, as I felt by getting to know Eddie and Cara. As we will see, in this new economy "consumers" can also be lenders or investors. Thus, I avoid the term "consumer-to-consumer" or "C2C" when talking about P2P marketplaces. Sharing economy ventures that are B2C can create astonishing efficiencies. But P2P ones are blurring the once-neat divide between business and consumer, in the process transforming society itself.

Drawing a line

It is a mystery as to who first used the term "sharing economy." Perhaps it is appropriate that its ownership is shared. But it has left the term without a guardian and vulnerable to loose definitions. The term's definition has also been stretched by countless startups trying to jump on the sharing economy bandwagon. *Why would a startup want to do that?* Firstly, sharing economy companies carry extraordinary moral clout. They are coolly collaborative and linked to the local and sustainable. That can make the first major challenge many startups face—attracting talent and potentially co-founders to work for little or nothing—a lot easier. Secondly, sharing economy businesses benefit from disproportionate amounts of positive PR that can reel in a startup's first customers. Thirdly, the hype around the sharing economy helps stoke racy company valuations that let startups raise finance with less dilution of the founders' shareholdings. Little wonder that many entrepreneurs try to pin a sharing economy ribbon to their startup's scruffy lapel.

One consequence of the loose definition of the sharing economy has been the impossibility of accurately market-sizing it. Some companies have only one foot in the sharing economy, adding further layers of complexity.

People auctioning unwanted second-hand goods on eBay are certainly getting "slack to the pack." However, 75% of eBay's marketplace revenue comes from merchants selling new, fixed-price goods.[2] Attempts have indeed been made to market-size the sharing economy, with estimates ranging from $3.5 billion to the low tens of billions,[3] a large range that reflects the porous boundaries of the term. Nonetheless, while there will always be gray areas and not every sharing economy company will meet each of my five criteria, it is time to rein in the definition of the sharing economy. If the sharing economy is to know what it is, it must be ready to say what it is not. Entrepreneurs and journalists should be unafraid to draw a line. So that is my definition, at least for now. Please disagree with me by tweeting @alexmstephany. Words are worth wrestling over.

When sharing is not sharing

You would be forgiven for reading my definition of the sharing economy and thinking, *this has nothing do with sharing: this is about renting and selling!* If so, you would not be the first person to find the term confusing if not downright misleading. Martin Varsavsky, the founder of Fon, stressed to me, "Renting is not always sharing. Renting is renting." In a thinly veiled dig at Airbnb, Ed Kushins, the founder of home-swapping platform HomeExchange has said, "Sharing is sharing and not paying."[4] At least the rental of assets involves them being used by multiple parties but, as we noted, "sharing" can also apply to the sale of goods. Either way, "sharing" carries none of its usual sense of joint, usually equal, use or ownership.

Those hoping that the sharing economy has anything to do with the redistribution of money or the end of private property will be sorely disappointed: this economy is capitalism distilled. As the left-leaning online magazine *The New Inquiry* puts it, "The sharing economy's rise is a reflection of capitalism's need to find new profit opportunities in aspects of social life once shielded from the market." Some go further and accuse the term of being downright duplicitous: a collective attempt by entrepreneurs to put a moral gloss on their cutthroat businesses. The meaning of sharing, according to John Harvey, a researcher on the digital economy at the University of Nottingham in the UK, should be "wrestled back from the jaws of those using it to profiteer."

According to this version of events, if the entrepreneurs and their PR teams who propagate the term are guilty of wanton deception, millions of people around the world and thousands of journalists are also stupid enough to be deceived. But by no means every mainstream journalist plays ball. I asked the BBC's Chief Technology correspondent, Rory Cellan-Jones, what he thought of the term. "Everyone loves a label," Cellan-Jones told me, before pausing as if to give himself one last chance to wrap his head around the term. "But I can't work out where this word 'sharing' came from. It's incredibly Californian and bullshitty."

Why then am I using the term "sharing economy" time and time again in this book? In part, I do so because this term has come to dominate discourse on the subject. The genie is out of the bottle. It would be near-impossible to dislodge the term without the risk of fracturing a growing movement of people who largely have no problem with the term, and who are building something that—for the most part, as we will see—is a social and economic good. But I also understand the term "sharing" in the fundamental sense that this is an economy that, in its truest guise, is built on shared experiences. This new wave of companies is helping us to realize what the great English poet John Donne knew in the 17th century, that "No man is an island."

Other "economies"

Clouding the scene still more are a range of overlapping terms. While the sharing economy is by far the most popular one, a number of similar terms are used almost interchangeably. I sometimes call it the "we-conomy," especially in relation to its P2P businesses and their implications. Others such as Jeremiah Owyang, the founder of consultancy Crowd Companies, call it the "collaborative economy." Arun Sundararajan of New York University prefers the term the "peer economy." Sarah Lacy, editor-in-chief at *PandoDaily* and the Queen of West Coast tech journalists, does too. "The sharing economy is great marketing but this phrase is getting people in trouble," she told me. "The 'peer-to-peer economy' is really a better way of thinking about it."

There are also more distantly related economies. In the 1970s, Swiss sustainability expert Walter Stahel predicted the emergence of what he termed the "Performance Economy." This economy would be built on the sale of services rather than products. Companies would make more profit by reusing their inventory. Customers would save money by paying only for what they actually needed. Between them, they would divide the spoils of smarter asset utilization. Stahel, who also founded the Product-Life Institute in Geneva to promote the environmental benefits of extending the useful lives of goods, anticipated the success of a business like Rent the Runway. Over five million American women turn to the New York startup to rent designer dresses for special occasions. Rent the Runway owns, dry-cleans, and repairs the dresses itself, economically incentivized to make them last as long as possible.

The "service-life extension of goods" advocated by Walter Stahel would become a core tenet of yet another related "economy": the "Circular Economy." As the sharing economy promotes the efficient use of goods by consumers, this economy does the same for the raw materials that go into making them. It does so by advocating virtuous cycles that involve the reuse of waste. The Circular Economy's key thinkers are designer William McDonough and chemist Michael Braungart, and its key work is their book, *Cradle to Cradle: Remaking the Way We Make Things*. These days, the Circular Economy's best-known champion is record-breaking round-the-world sailor, Dame Ellen MacArthur. Her foundation's website points to examples like intelligent design in 60,000 ton Maersk container ships that tags every steel section as a different grade. When the ships are finally sent to the breaking yard, they can be recycled into new, higher quality ships.

If the Circular Economy relates to the environmental side of the sharing economy, the Experience Economy relates to its social angle. In 1970, futurist Alvin Toffler published *Future Shock*. The six million-selling work predicted an "experiential industry" emerging from the postindustrial economy. Toffler influenced consultants Joseph Pine and James Gilmore, who coined the term "Experience Economy," the supposed successor to the services economy. Well-run businesses could move up the value chain by offering experiences: after all, economic value was less about the product than the experience of that product, *how* rather than *what* was consumed. In the Experience Economy, goods and services are mere props and employees just actors in the theatre of customer experience. Pine and Gilmore conclude that, "Businesses must learn to stage a rich, compelling experience." In the sharing economy, the most successful brands unite utility with these rich social experiences.

Back to Lisa Gansky, author of The Mesh

Gansky did not meet me off the ferry in an electric Batmobile after all. But it was exciting nonetheless to sit beside her in her open top MINI Cooper and head north through Napa's rolling wine country, the wind in our faces and the sun reflecting in her wooden-framed sunglasses. Our destination was an upscale French restaurant with pristinely laid tables under vines. The hostess greeted Gansky like a celebrity. As we sat down, Gansky told me how, in 2007 after selling Ofoto, she did some maths. She calculated that she could have rebuilt Ofoto from scratch for 5% of the $60 million of venture capital she had raised for it in 1999 and 2000. "Share platforms" like oDesk for off-shored rather than permanent labor and Amazon Web Services for hosting websites in the cloud had slashed the cost of launching a business.

Gansky saw how these share platforms would slash the costs of doing many other things too. The data on these platforms would shine a light on the vast amounts of waste in underutilized physical and human assets. It could be waste in the form of a neighbor's garage full of supposed junk or, less tangibly, underutilized intellectual property. And waste is valuable. Gansky points out that there is up to 30 times more gold in a ton of old mobile phones than in a ton of gold ore.[5] In *The Mesh*, Gansky predicted a flowering of new businesses that would capture the value in this waste, through what she visualizes as a "meshing" of goods, talent, and services. As for the "Mesh customers," Gansky writes in her "Mesh Manifesto" that they get "convenient service that is customized and timely, without the burden of buying, maintaining, insuring, storing, and disposing of more stuff."

Gansky argues that businesses built on share platforms will outperform traditional businesses based on the sales and ownership model. "Mesh businesses" that provide shared goods time and again to customers enjoy more touch points with them than traditional businesses do. These touch points let Mesh businesses build valuable customer relationships. In the process, Mesh businesses collect data that allows them to better refine their offerings. Since Mesh businesses are based on sharing goods, they can also use "tryvertising," acquiring customers by letting them cheaply sample goods. It is easier for Spinlister, a P2P bike-sharing startup, to get people on its bikes given the low cost of bike rental than it is for a bike manufacturer selling new ones. "Every Mesh transaction," writes Gansky, "is an opportunity to deliver on the promise you make to your customers—to give them convenient access to customized goods and services."

Several times over lunch Gansky brought up Netflix, a Mesh business that she clearly admires. In her book, she recounts the tale of how Netflix slayed Blockbuster by creating an online share platform for its inventory of DVDs. Netflix's multiple touch points and vast amount of user data allowed it to build an addictive recommendation engine to help users decide what to watch next. As they reach scale, Mesh businesses also benefit from network effects whereby each new unit added into the network creates more value than the previous one: Netflix edged unassailably ahead of Blockbuster in part because the more customers it acquired, the more social content it owned in the form of online reviews, attracting yet more customers. A shared plate of local oysters came and went as Gansky told me that had she predicted that millions of people would be taking vacations in each other's apartments 10 years ago, she would have been called "a crazy Californian."

Remembering how to share

As Gansky knows well, the behavior that she was predicting was in many ways not new. At the root of many sharing economy transactions is an old-fashioned neighborliness that is verging on quaint. People are putting up guests in spare rooms through websites like Roomorama and letting them pitch tents in their gardens through CampinmyGarden.com, neighborly forms of behavior that are now being rediscovered en masse. When Brian Chesky described his new business "AirBed & Breakfast"—later to be re-named Airbnb—to his mum, she was horrified. "Are you crazy?" she said, terrified at the thought of opening her home to strangers. Then Chesky explained the startup to his grandfather. "Of course," replied the old man. "That's how I used to travel when I was a boy." When his grandfather crossed America, he would knock on strangers' doors and ask to sleep in their barn. Things have gone full circle: there are now hundreds of barns to rent on Airbnb.

We forgot how to share and are only now remembering. *What explains this generational amnesia?* Chesky's mum grew up in the 1950s' zenith of consumerism. America had emerged from World War II with its economy strengthened as the world's only superpower. In the decades that followed, food prices plummeted with the advent of factory farming and the use of pesticides and fertilizers on an industrial scale. With cheaper food came disposable income that was spent on cars, washing machines, and other status symbols that no one wanted to share. But Chesky's grandfather grew up in a time before families had jumped into their Ford Model Ts and fled to the suburbs. He knew an America before people had put up fences around their houses and wanted to own one of everything. As Pulitzer prize-winning author Tina Rosenberg writes in *The New York Times*, "Before World War II, the shared economy was most of the economy."

Now sharing is back in town, quite literally. A generation of "new urbanists" is moving back into downtown areas, once again embracing crowded, diverse neighborhoods and a shared existence. Unlike Mrs Chesky's generation, Chesky and younger members of Generation Y are at home with the everyday reality of sharing in crowded cities, whèther those shared amenities are co-working spaces or one of the over 500 bike-share schemes around the world. William Strauss and Neil Howe, the first to define the "millennial" generation as those born between 1982 and 2004, probe this generation in *Millennials Rising: The Next Great Generation*. According to Strauss and Howe, this new generation will grow up with a strong sense of civic duty and with old-fashioned values, much like the generation that grew up during the Great Depression and fought in World War II.

We forgot the shared ownership structures of cooperatives too. Now there are over 30,000 cooperatives with 1 billion members globally,[6] a greater number of people than are working for multinationals. These models are far older than Chesky's grandfather. The first cooperative dates back to 1769 when, in a humble cottage in Scotland, weavers sold discounted oatmeal. Gansky harks back further, likening 21st-century share platforms to medieval guilds that were united around plying a trade. One could go yet further back to the evidence that pre-Neolithic tribes held land in common. According to Professor Russell Belk at York University in Toronto, "Not only is sharing critical to the most recent of consumption phenomena like the Internet, it is also the oldest type of consumption." Sharing is not new; it's déjà vu. It has nothing to do with Communism or Karl Marx, who would feel ambivalent about the sharing economy's enrichment of the propertied class. Sharing is deeper and older than ideology, too deep to have been snuffed out by suburbs and the postwar materialism.

We are sharing again. *But why now?*

The world's town square

When Pierre Omidyar released an unknown little website called eBay, he made a test listing of a piece of junk: a broken laser pointer. To Omidyar's amazement, someone tried to buy it. Omidyar messaged the potential buyer to explain that the laser pointer was actually broken beyond repair. The buyer messaged back: it transpired that he collected broken laser pointers. In that instant, Omidyar realized that, with the reach of the Internet, a buyer could be found for anything and that eBay could become a gigantic business. As we will see, sharing is growing on the back of convergent trends across technology, society, and the economy. But before any of that matters, sharing requires the matching of haves and wants, known in business studies as "the coincidence of wants." The Internet is the most powerful tool yet invented to match up these haves and wants.

In the past, the upper limit of potential customers for a marketplace was the number of people who could physically fit into the town square. The marketplace in Europe's largest town square, for example, in Kraków in Poland, drew merchants and buyers from miles away for centuries. These days, the number of buyers and sellers in any online marketplace is effectively uncapped. With almost no constraint on supply and demand, marketplaces can more easily achieve liquidity, to the benefit of everyone trying to do business. Broadband penetration is ever-rising too. "Only 3% were online when I started AOL," notes Steve Case, who has invested part of his $1.5 billion fortune in sharing economy businesses. According to the Pew Research Centre, 87% of Americans today use the Internet, at least occasionally.[7]

Alongside the Internet's vast scale come hugely shrunken transaction costs. Consider the cost in 1995 of selling a pram that your toddler had grown out of. You would have to pay to advertise the pram in shop windows or the classified sections of newspapers. You would have to spend time visiting local shops and phoning newspaper offices. After all that cost and time, you would have only a small chance of finding a buyer. Perhaps the deal would fall through when a reader of the short classified ad turned up to discover that one of the pram's wheels was rusty. The only time that sharing such low-value goods worked well was between people who were already connected: family and friends, or colleagues if free ads could be placed on communal noticeboards. Online marketplaces, however, let sellers list items for free, with full descriptions and photos, and in minutes.

Developers for sharing economy businesses are busy making online marketplaces function still better. They are collecting shared assets in vast structured databases and building bespoke tools for their management, rental, and sale. They are allowing users to easily make and receive payments online, solving another friction point. Payment gateways like Braintree's Marketplace and Balanced Payments are built specifically for marketplace payments. Moving money online is especially useful when payments are small: no one wants a fistful of dimes. Online payments also create the illusion of taking money out of the equation, vital for transactions that people would rather see as neighborly. When Chesky stayed with early Airbnb hosts, he noted an awkward moment when they asked for their money. Counting out cash into someone's hand—someone who might have become a friend over the course of a few days living together—soured the entire experience. Clunky offline sharing transactions can now feel seamless online.

The Internet: sharing in its DNA

If you were prone to exaggeration (*not that anyone working in technology ever is, of course*), you could say that the Internet itself is built on sharing. Its entire foundation is a client–server model that works on sharing and replication. Servers store information in the form of files and share them with "clients": software that allows people all over the world to access the same content at the same time.

The Internet would also be unrecognizable without the culture of open source: freely available shared code. Apache, the world's most popular web server, was assembled by a motley crew of geeks whose shared "open source" product is more widely used than one made by Microsoft. Open source Android is the world's most popular mobile operating system and is based on Linux, more open source software. The world's most popular database, MySQL, is again open source, as is the backbone of the world's most popular content management system, WordPress. Scripting languages like PHP and Python are distributed under open source licenses, and developers often share code for others to use on repositories like GitHub, the Great Library of Alexandria for code. Open Hub, a directory of open source projects, lists over 3 million people now working on a staggering 700,000 collaborative projects. It is almost impossible to imagine the Internet having evolved any other way.

Open source is far more than just useful. For many programmers, there is nothing more sacrosanct. Legendary programmer and open source advocate Richard Stallman says, "to understand the concept [of open source], you should think of 'free' as in 'free speech,' not as in 'free beer'." Many programmers still live by the "hacker ethic" defined by Steven Levy in his 1984 classic *Hackers*. The hacker believes that common good comes from unfettered access to computers and decentralized collaboration. These are values that are dear to anyone building a P2P sharing economy business. In fact, Internet access itself is now being shared. Fon is a Madrid-headquartered company that allows its members to share their own wireless capacity and has grown to become the world's largest wifi network.

Mobile, mobile everywhere

And then came the smartphone. To all intents and purposes, it came on January 9th , 2007 with the unveiling of the iPhone. "Today, Apple is going to reinvent the phone," proclaimed Steve Jobs to a sea of adoring fans at Macworld. He was as good as his word. Less than a decade later, people carry smartphones everywhere except the shower (although Sony and Samsung sell waterproof models). Smartphones make it easier than ever to transact on online marketplaces. Within the palm of our hand is access to all the visible idling assets in the world. Peter Diamandis, the founder of the XPRIZE and Singularity University, puts it powerfully, "A Masai warrior on a cellphone in the middle of Kenya has better access to knowledge than President Reagan did 25 years ago." The smartphone is becoming a more potent catalyst to sharing with the roll-out of 4G and superfast fiberoptic networks. "We now have hundreds of millions of consumers who are carrying in their pockets powerful computers that are always connected to high-speed networks," says Arun Sundararajan of New York University. "That makes it possible for people to rethink the way they consume."

Americans spend more time on smartphones than desktop devices. Each year, the gap widens. According to comScore, desktop traffic in the US grew by only 15% in the 3 years leading up to May 2013. However, the overall time spent online practically doubled due to the growth in smartphone and tablet usage.[8] In 2010, Eric Schmidt announced that Google was going "mobile first" when it came to thinking about its products. By September 2013, Google announced that over a billion Android devices had now been activated.[9] Fast forward to 2014 and Schmidt said, "The trend has been mobile was winning; it's now won." For young people today, the Internet is unthinkingly "mobile first." As Twitter's CEO Dick Costolo joked in his Commencement speech at the University of Michigan, "When I was your age we didn't have the Internet in our pants. We didn't even have the Internet *not* in our pants—that's how bad it was."

Aside from its sheer ubiquity, mobile has other specific advantages over desktop. Companies can send SMSs or "push notifications" from smartphone applications straight to users' pocket, bringing further efficiencies to two-sided marketplaces. When on JustPark a driver makes a request to rent out a parking space, that property owner receives an SMS. It takes them seconds to text a reply accepting the booking. Then there is GPS. A phone knows where you are, vital for apps that are location-specific. If you want to rent a Car2Go car, the app shows you the nearest vehicle. If you hail a taxi with Lyft, the GPS tells the driver where you are while the GPS on the driver's phone gives away his location, allowing you to track his progress right to you. Finally, smartphones have high-quality cameras that turn each phone into a nimble listing tool, whether that means adding your driveway to JustPark or selling your dress on a P2P fashion marketplace like Poshmark.

Sharing 2.0: the social web

When I was 16, I lived briefly on a Kibbutz. I can remember the communal storeroom, laden with everything from bread to batteries, to which every family had a key. "From each according to his ability, to each according to his need," goes the saying of 19th-century French socialist Louis Blanc. Each family on the Kibbutz took from the storeroom according to their need. It blew my teenage mind. The community seemed a utopian model for how we could all live. Cleaners earned the same as doctors and everyone was bronzed and athletic, certainly compared to us weedy English kids. But later, it seemed obvious that the Kibbutz model of sharing would only work in tiny, self-contained communities where everyone knew and trusted everyone. Sharing economy interactions such as giving strangers the keys to your home require similar levels of trust. In order for them to work, something needed to make hundreds of millions of people knowable and human. That something was social media and, above all, Facebook.

Today, there are over 1.3 billion Facebook users, pouring their private lives online at the rate of 350 million photos a day and with ever-lower privacy settings. By 2015, Facebook's population will probably be bigger than China's.[10] Meanwhile in China, where Facebook is banned, locals are embracing other social networks like RenRen, Sina Weibo, and the rampantly successful WeChat. Then there is YouTube, Twitter, LinkedIn, and Pinterest. Of course, inconceivably vast amounts of other personal information are crawled and made accessible via Google. Every day, Google answers over 3.5 billion searches[11] and, in the interests of making informed decisions, we have all become professionals at ~~stalking~~ researching people online. We are all, wherever we live in the world, just URLs away from each other.

Sharing reborn, "Sharing 2.0" as I call it, is turbo-charged by this highly social Internet. With people's lives led increasingly online, we can often know more about a potential counter-party on the other side of the world than we might about our next-door neighbor. And vice versa. Marketplaces surface this data by encouraging users to log in with their social media profiles. They also ask users to write profiles so that Jeff, an optician who likes blues music, *House of Cards*, and baseball, feels less of a stranger. Platforms further increase trust by verifying users' phone numbers, bank accounts, and even passports to keep the bad guys out. Above all, they create trust through review systems—staples of online marketplaces since they were pioneered by eBay. Sharing behaviors are usually not new but trust at scale is. The world is fast becoming the "global village" that Canadian media theorist Marshall McLuhan prophesied in the 1960s. Half a century on, the same kind of trust that exists in a tight-knit Kibbutz can be replicated in the vast online communities of sharing economy companies.

Into the vacuum: online communities

Here in Britain, traditional community institutions have been eroded, especially in cities. "The average Londoner knows just one neighbor," notes actor Lily Cole and founder of gifting platform Impossible. "We've lost something fundamentally human and we don't even realize it." A mere 800,000 people attend church on Sundays while the number of people living alone has doubled in the last 40 years.[12] Britain is not unique. In *Bowling Alone*, Harvard professor Robert Putnam portrayed an America in social decline. Putnam charted the decay of America's "social capital," the value stemming from human interaction and cooperation. Drawing from over half a million interviews, he showed how Americans were spending less time with friends and families and belonging to fewer civic organizations. When Putnam was writing in the 1990s, more Americans were ten-pin bowling than ever, yet the bowling leagues were in decline: people were bowling alone. In part, Putnam blamed technologies like TV for "individualizing" our lives. If technology was part of the problem, it is now part of the answer. Perhaps it is the only answer.

Online communities that bridge the online and offline worlds have helped fill these social vacuums, providing a much-needed sense of belonging. Although technology changes, people have not. The sharing economy taps into the near-universal enjoyment people take in meeting strangers and broadening their social circles. I loved meeting Cara, my Airbnb host. For Cara too, the benefits of hosting are social as well as financial. "I've met so many interesting people," she told me. "One guest was a Buddhist monk who left me fruit and a book on Zen philosophy." Some sharing economy businesses are even more skewed to this social upside. Inspired by the success of Airbnb, a clutch of new startups is taking the same model to dining. Feastly in the US and EatWith in Israel let homeowners cook dinners for locals and foreigners. The primary lure is not the home-cooked meal but a social and cultural interchange. Sometimes, a community facilitates relationships that never come to fruition, to use the gaming jargon "IRL" or "in real life." A platform like Threadflip allows women to trade fashion advice and physical clothes from other's virtual wardrobes. These women often feel like friends but will never meet in the flesh.

Sharing economy businesses cherish this communal aspect of their businesses. A truism of many a sharing economy CEO is that their startup's most valuable asset is their community. They hire "Community Managers," a ubiquitous job at sharing economy startups, to build a cohesive community whose members want to engage—and spend money—with each other time and again. Boatbound, for example, a "pier-to-pier" boat rental marketplace, has what it calls "the Ahoy culture." It asks boat owners and renters to greet each other with an "Ahoy!" and to snap and share photos of themselves as Captains with their Boatbound captain's hat. Props like that or the Lyft pink moustaches may be fun but are more than mere gimmicks. They say: "*You belong.*" In *Sacred Economics*, Charles Eisenstein narrates a history of money from ancient, socially vital gift economies to our present-day alienation. It is possible that community-based commerce could help us return to our less alienated roots.

Tired of owning

While I was writing this book, I moved into a new flat. I found myself wasting time and money filling my space with objects: drinks coasters, an armchair I never use, a juicer ... On reflection, none of it added to my happiness. I was living out the somber warning of philosopher Bertrand Russell that "It is the preoccupation with possessions, more than anything else that prevents us from living freely and nobly." Russell's intuition was hardly novel. Boethius explored the same sentiment in the 6th century in *The Consolation of Philosophy*. Material wealth, realized the deposed, once-mighty Roman consul, is not freedom but stress and damned hard work. Russell and Boethius were from a wealthy aristocratic elite. These days, "disownership" is an aspiration for a growing number of plebs like me. Lynn Jurich is the CEO of SunRun, a company that installs domestic solar panels, giving homeowners access to clean energy without having to buy the panels. According to Jurich, "The new status symbol isn't what you own—it's what you're smart enough *not to own.*"

Sharing can mean sacrificing absolute quality and certainty: will the second-hand sweater feel as soft as the new one? Will the Airbnb host be on time to hand over their keys? But it remains a paradox that sharing can help us to lead a richer life. That richness means having what we want but only when we want it. That may mean the richness of driving the right vehicle for the right occasion by borrowing one through a platform like Dutch car-sharing service SnappCar, whose slogan is "*De ideale auto lenen*"—borrow the ideal car. That may mean the richness of being able to choose from millions of tracks rather than filling your home with bulky CDs. Kevin Kelly, the co-founder of *Wired*, put it best: "access trumps ownerships." More and more, we aspire to an Apple-like simplicity in idealized, clutter-free lives. Silicon Valley's most prominent "superangel"—an angel investor with a network and expertise comparable to those of a venture capital fund—is Ron Conway. According to Conway, this preference for access rather than ownership constitutes "a seismic shift in the American dream."

These dreamers are mostly young. Generation Y, dubbed "the asset-light generation" by venture capitalist Mary Meeker, is acutely sensitive to the tediousness of owning things. For this generation, the "Goldilocks Complex" of possessive ownership is wearing off. As Tomio Geron writes in *Forbes*, "the ascendant economic force in America [has] been culturally programmed to borrow, rent and share." In particular, millions of young people are abandoning their thirst to own cars. According to the chief economist of Edmunds.com, the proportion of new cars bought by Americans aged 18 to 34 dropped from 16% in 2007 to 12% in 2013.[13] "When I grew up," says Neal Gorenflo of *Shareable*, "the car was freedom; now it's a ball and chain. Freedom is an iPhone." David Karp, the founder of Tumblr, and a man worth $200 million by the age of 25, is Generation Y to a tee. He owns almost nothing. His 1,700 square foot apartment in Brooklyn is empty apart from a TV, sofa, and bed. "I'm always so surprised when people fill their homes up with stuff," he says. When Karp needs stuff, he can access it.

The recession: broke and sharing

September 15th, 2008. I was watching from inside my shiny glass tower in Canary Wharf the day that Lehman Brothers collapsed. Through the floor-to-ceiling windows of the corporate law firm where I worked, I saw bankers walking out of Lehman's revolving doors clutching files and family photos, economic refugees in well-cut suits. The party was over. Logically, it had to end *some* time; we all knew that deep down. And though there was some talk that it was a free bar—*get your order in quick before it shuts!*—we could have guessed that a nasty bill would be coming our way. More than half a decade later, we are still living with the hangover.

The anger was aimed at the bankers but many of us were also to blame. With the relaxation of consumer credit conditions around the turn of the millennium, everyday people had binged beyond their means. Between 1998 and 2010, America had more than 1.1 cars per driver: it had become a country with millions more cars than drivers.[14] Meanwhile, self-storage, often a pre-landfill purgatory for excess belongings, swelled to a gargantuan $22 billion industry in the US, twice what Americans spend each year on movie tickets.[15]

For women like Mrs Chesky, ownership was a sacred part of the American Dream. But when the bubble burst, ownership would become a living nightmare. Millions of consumers were left holding too much of everything: from second homes to furniture and designer shoes. Cash-poor and frightened, many of them suddenly had the financial impetus to make money from their own excess. *And sharing economy companies made sure that there was a steady flow of PR telling them how.* What made the impact of the recession so profound from the standpoint of the sharing economy was that it erupted on a world that at no point in human history had become so full up with stuff that was unneeded, unopened, unwanted, and unused: in short, unnecessary.

There was business to be done. Ordinary people became hustlers, putting their goods to work on platforms like Sweden's aptly named Getrid. They started renting out their bedrooms and getting such good yields that some of them even took on extra properties. Some began renting out their cars on RelayRides. Some drove people around town on Lyft. Some started teaching their skills on platforms like Skillshare. Slowly but surely, an alternative economic model began to rise from the wreckage of the credit crunch. It was during the recession that millions of people saw the waste—and opportunity—in their own lives. "When the crisis hit," says Nathan Blecharczyk, co-founder of Airbnb, "there were people in desperate need of alternative solutions. We were one of those solutions."

Blecharczyk recalls with pride one of the first letters from a customer that the company received. It reads:

> Hi Airbnb,
> I'm not exaggerating when I say you literally saved us. My husband and I just married this past May, after having lost both of our jobs and our investments in the stock market crash last year. We slowly watched our savings dwindle to the point where we didn't have enough to pay our own rent. You gave us the ability to keep our home, travel together and have the peace of mind knowing that we were going to be able to make it through this challenging time in our lives.

Financial pressure hit both sides of online marketplaces at once, also leading consumers to try innovative, low-cost options. Again, this played into the hands of sharing economy startups, whose first claim to fame was usually that they were cheaper than the traditional alternatives.

The human brand advantage

It was not only purchasing power that the credit crunch eroded: it was faith in many large companies themselves. In April 2009, *The Economist* reported that "This recession has triggered a wholesale reappraisal by shoppers of the value that their habitual brands deliver." More than that, the crisis led many consumers to doubt the moral integrity of big business as a whole. Every year, The Boston Consulting Group (BCG) releases its "Global Consumer Sentiment Survey." Based on interviews with over 12,000 people, the report is a barometer for how consumers view the world. In its 2010 survey, BCG found that the majority of consumers in the US and Europe and more than 40% of consumers in Japan said that the credit crunch "increased their distrust of big businesses."[16]

Unsurprisingly, the financial sector fared even worse. 2008 saw two banking scandals of colossal proportions. In the US, Bernie Madoff was exposed for his huge $65 billion Ponzi scheme. Meanwhile in Europe, Jérôme Kerviel became known as the most destructive rogue trader in history for illegally accruing losses of $6.9 billion while at Société Générale. By 2011, thousands would take to the streets as part of the Occupy movement that started in Manhattan's Zuccotti Park and spread to over 900 cities around the world. The discontent was not restricted to the activists and anarchists. The Financial Trust Index, an initiative of two professors at the Chicago Booth School of Business and Kellogg School of Management, found in March 2009 that only 19% of Americans trusted their bank.[17]

At the same time, social media and trust between strangers was on the rise. Increasingly, we were looking to individuals for more than just recommendations: we were looking for the products and services themselves. In 2008 before the credit crunch, Etsy, a handmade goods marketplace, was selling around $5 million of products a month. By 2013, Etsy had surpassed $1 billion of annual revenue. This was not e-commerce as we knew it: buyers can see the faces and read the stories behind the million-plus individuals who now sell through the Etsy platform. The sharing economy has allowed individuals to step into the breach of our declining trust in big brands. "Because we've been able to engender trust between individuals," says Airbnb co-founder Joe Gebbia, "the role that a brand can play isn't as important any more."

Gansky writes in her "Mesh Manifesto" how share platform brands like Airbnb "are more trustworthy because they have to be." The downturn plus the rise of the social web created fertile ground for alternative human-centric models. Rather than trusting your savings to JPMorgan Chase, a P2P service like Lending Club began to look increasingly viable. Rather than buying a car from General Motors, a startup like Getaround showcased trustworthy individuals willing to make their cars available for less hassle and at a fraction of the cost. Some companies—including of course, General Motors—had found themselves on the ropes during the crisis. Some had not. But once the dust had settled, many an incumbent found itself with millions of new potential competitors: us.

More people, bigger cities

Every day, there are 200,000 more people on this planet. Twenty-five years ago in 1990, we were 5 billion. Today, with malaria on the wane, falling infant mortality, and increased life expectancies, including for sufferers of HIV and AIDS, we are over 7 billion.[18] Alongside this population explosion is another major demographic shift: mass urbanization. We have been scattered and dispersed for almost all of human existence, but these new people are overwhelmingly city dwellers. Two centuries ago, a mere 3% of the global population lived in cities. In 2007, the United Nations announced that for the first time in human history more people lived in cities than in the countryside.[19] Primarily, this shift has been driven by urbanization in the developing world. When I lived in China in 2000, I remember the sea of poor Chinese men encamped on bamboo mats at major train stations. With only a few yuan, they were starting their lives anew, seeking work in cities just as the English rural poor did centuries earlier during the world's first industrialization.

Sharing is thriving on this urban density. More people means more demand for shared goods and services. For many crammed into cities, a sharing lifestyle has become almost a practical imperative. As Emily Badger of *The Atlantic Cities* explains, "That means more people living in apartments instead of detached homes. That means using a car-share instead of individually owning cars. That means using public parks instead of private backyards—all simply because there just won't be enough space in crowded cities for everyone to individually own all of these things." Jonas Singer is the founder of Union Kitchen, a shared cookery space for 52 food startups that I visited in Washington DC. "We're all living in slightly smaller spaces," he says. "A lot of the sharing economy just has to do with the number of people living per square foot of land." Good sharing services also grow by word of mouth, something that happens quickly in dense urban areas.

The majority of sharing businesses leverage the potential of large concentrations of people and asset value in cities. Nonetheless, sharing is happening outside of cities too. MachineryLink taps into the idling capacity in valuable farm machinery by providing 270 rental combine harvesters to farmers. The service relies on the migration of grain harvests across the North American continent, starting in Northern Texas before finishing up in the Pacific Northwest. Furthermore, services that do not require physical interaction can actually favor the countryside. Online workers on a labor marketplace like London-based PeoplePerHour are incentivized to locate themselves outside the largest cities where the cost of living is usually high. Social commerce companies that require only the mailing of goods between users can also provide valued companionship for users in more remote rural areas.

/ ... And a whisker of concern about the planet

Earth Overshoot Day "celebrates" the day each year when we move beyond our annual amount of sustainable consumption. From that day onwards, the planet is operating with an ecological deficit, using more resources than it can produce and emitting more CO_2 than it can absorb. Each year, the day moves forward. In 1992, it was October 21st. By 2014, it had advanced to August 19th. The message is clear: our consumption is unsustainable—especially in the west where Americans comprise 5% of the global population but use a fifth of its energy.[20] As Danny Dorling, Professor of Geography at Oxford University, writes, "no amount of new wind power or other changes to how we produce energy or grow food, build homes or travel, will solve our growing problems of overconsumption and greed without our changing how we behave and what we wish for. We who consume most have to consume less."[21]

The ecological harm begins with the polluting extraction of raw materials and lasts for centuries after we bin the finished goods. In between are badly designed business systems that cause the permanent loss of what environmentalist and entrepreneur Paul Hawken calls "natural capital": essentially, the productive and regenerative value in natural ecosystems. "We are cutting and mining and hauling and trashing the place so fast," says the writer of 'The Story of Stuff' Annie Leonard, "that we're undermining the planet's very ability for people to live here." The result is a scary mess of our own doing. Thirteen of the 14 warmest years since records began in 1850 have been in the 21st century.[22] Climate change causes appalling de-speciation; the WWF estimates that at least 10,000 species become extinct each year.[23] Perhaps our biggest problem, however, concerns our fundamental requirement: water. Over a billion people live in conditions of extreme water shortage while our consumption of water increases at double the rate of population growth.[24]

Sharing economy startups often emphasize the green arguments for their services. Zipcar, for example, talks up the green credentials of car-sharing to boost its bottom line. But the vast majority of consumers are indifferent to living in a giant chemistry experiment with deeply uncertain results. When asked "What do you think is the most important problem facing this country today?" in a series of 2014 Gallup polls, fewer than 2% of US voters put "Environment/pollution."[25] Repeated surveys confirm that the environment is a fringe concern when it comes to the adoption of sharing services. A 2013 survey by The People Who Share found that five times more people said their use of sharing services was primarily motivated by making and saving money than by environmental concerns.[26] What some would say should be the strongest driver is actually the weakest.

Botsman and collaborative consumption

Lisa Gansky's book was published just days apart from a competing title: *What's Mine Is Yours: How Collaborative Consumption Is Changing the Way We Live.* Its authors were Rachel Botsman and Roo Rogers. Botsman, a brainy Oxford alumna, has since become the movement's public intellectual and the voice most strongly associated with the sharing economy. Roo Rogers is a green entrepreneur, strategy consultant, and son of world-renowned British architect Richard Rogers. Botsman and Rogers would come to popularize a new term for much of what Gansky was describing: "collaborative consumption." Botsman defines collaborative consumption as:

> An economic model based on sharing, swapping, trading, or renting products and services, enabling access over ownership that is reinventing not just what we consume but *how* we consume.

Botsman and Rogers did not invent the term "collaborative consumption"— it was coined by two academics, Marcus Felson and Joe L. Spaeth, in a 1978 paper on car-sharing. But in Botsman's words, "we gave it a lot of fuel."

In *What's Mine Is Yours*, Botsman and Rogers organize collaborative consumption businesses into three categories. Firstly, there are "Redistribution Markets." These redistribute goods from places where they are not wanted to ones where they are. reCrib, for example, is a Redistribution Market for second-hand, out-grown baby clothes. The second category of sharing economy business is "Collaborative Lifestyles." When people adopt collaborative lifestyles, they might be using a co-working space rather than a conventional office. They might be gardening someone else's garden through Landshare, a UK website that match-makes keen gardeners looking for land to grow produce with owners of unused land. The third subset of collaborative consumption is what Botsman and Rogers call "Product Service Systems." These allow people to get the benefit of assets while leaving the hassle of ownership to a company. Thus, through a service like Car2Go, members access a car when they need one.

I Skyped with Rachel Botsman at her Sydney home. Botsman described to me how when she first picked up on these trends, she soon realized she was onto something huge. "You know when you learn a new word and you start to see it everywhere?" she said. "It was like that." Thousands of press releases and startups later and with the benefit of hindsight, the trend seems obvious. But this says more about the authors' prescience. "Once we defined it," says Botsman, "other collaborative consumption enthusiasts started coming together and it created a very strong community." What now pleases Botsman most about *What's Mine Is Yours* is that they identified a taxonomy that remains valid 4 years on. Thousands of builders of this community now carry Botsman and Roger's torch. Among them are Neal Gorenflo in the US and Antonin Léonard in France.

Neal Gorenflo and *Shareable*

I met Gorenflo at Hacker Dojo, a co-working space in Mountain View in Silicon Valley where Pinterest started out. Hacker Dojo: picture a lofty metal hangar filled with programming books, giant inflatable dinosaurs, a table tennis table, and gaggles of geeks. This being Mountain View, Google leaves its trace: across the road is the airfield where Larry Page and Sergey Brin land their private jets. Here too, on Fairchild Drive in the 1950s, was the factory of the famous Fairchild semiconductor company, the granddaddy of the semiconductor industry. Fairchild pioneered the integrated circuit, putting the "silicon" in Silicon Valley. In its wake, Fairchild left a startup, founded by former employees, called Intel, a venture capital firm, Kleiner Perkins, that would become one of the Valley's greatest, and hideous amounts of contamination. Before Hacker Dojo could open, the Environmental Protection Agency had to excavate megatons of toxic soil from an area that, pre-Fairchild, was a land of rolling greenery known for its fruit trees. Fairchild's innovations would turn electronics into cheap throwaway items, something Gorenflo is trying to fix from the very same spot half a century later.

I had not seen him since we co-hosted a sharing economy party at South by Southwest, the world's largest tech conference in Austin, Texas. Gorenflo is bearded, almost priestly in appearance. With a boyish glint in his eye, sneakers, and rucksack, he belies his 40-something years. But back in 2004, Gorenflo did not wear sneakers to work. He was working for DHL on their global strategy and living in Brussels. His mission: "to make DHL the best box-mover in the world." One Saturday afternoon, Gorenflo went on a jog. As he ran through a parking lot, he unexpectedly started to cry. He fell to his knees, suddenly grasping the meaninglessness of his life, and wept. "On paper," Gorenflo told me, looking shaken at the memory, "I was a success. But in that moment I saw that I was alone and that my life was a solo performance. I projected forward and anticipated this mountain of regret. But I was *not* alone. There were millions of people like me, disconnected from themselves and others." There on the tarmac, Gorenflo made "a vow" to find a "world with community." He got up and returned to his hotel where he penned a letter of resignation. Then he took the first flight home.

Back in San Francisco, Gorenflo found his kindred spirits. His epiphany would lead him to co-found *Shareable*, a "nonprofit news, action and connection hub for the sharing transformation." *Shareable* is the online playbook for sharing everything from baby food and housing to skills and solar panels. "Business has spent centuries making buying really easy," says Gorenflo. "We're just at the beginning of making sharing easy." Gorenflo describes himself as "super pragmatic" and wants people to make real changes to their lives. Shareable.net hosts articles like "12 Agrihoods Taking Farm-to-Table Living Mainstream" and "Why Driving for Lyft is Good for the Soul." Gorenflo has also co-edited an anthology of first-hand tales from the sharing economy. Against the backdrop of uncertain labor conditions and ever-depleting resources, *Share or Die* describes how to thrive through — *no prizes for guessing* — sharing.

OuiShare: sharing à la française

Inside a gigantic bell tent draped with red velvet in a Parisian park, people sat listening to speakers and tweeting in the dimness. The talks covered subjects like the use of crypto-currencies in the sharing economy and "Open Source Beehives: A Solution to the Global Bee Crisis." Beside the stage, an artist frantically captured the talks in cartoon form. A houseboat on the canal Saint-Denis served as another stage, while in the gardens, entrepreneurs and sharing enthusiasts from around the world cheerfully networked and proposed collaborations. For lunch, we had to exchange a cardboard meal ticket for a bowl of salad provided by The Food Assembly, an organization of local food cooperatives. Later, at the closing party on the festival's third day, branded OuiShare condoms were passed around on trays. Judging by the look of the 4 am dance floor, the contraceptives assisted in some other forms of sharing. It added up to a very French and bohemian take on the sharing economy.

The people behind the festival were OuiShare: "a think and do-tank with the mission to empower citizens, public institutions and companies to create a collaborative economy." OuiShare started with the frustration of one Antonin Léonard. While at business school, Léonard was bored by the "rigid capitalistic view of the world". There *had* to be an alternative — one Léonard had glimpsed while "couchsurfing" through Brazil for 6 months. Inspired by *Shareable* and the writings of Botsman and Gansky, Twitter soon became his "best professor" as he began to share ideas with kindred spirits from around the world. Léonard, who speaks four languages, wondered if he could join up the dots of light in this global movement while fulfilling his dream to "live free and travel the world." So "without knowing a thing about how to run a blog," Léonard started a blog about the collaborative economy. It led to a torrent of interest from traditional media. He was drinking Mojitos on the beach in Sri Lanka when a British tourist suggested the name for his new collective: "OuiShare", a pun on "We."

With three co-founders, OuiShare was born. The key part of their distributed model is a network of "Connectors" scattered around the globe from Buenos Aires to Budapest. Ouishare's Connectors support local initiatives between startups, local governments, and corporates to catalyze a transition to a sharing economy. In Berlin, I caught up with Thomas Dönnebrink, OuiShare's Berlin Connector. I needed the free wifi but it was not in the spirit of OuiShare that I suggested meeting in Starbucks. Dönnebrink, dressed in a simple linen shirt, asked for a water. Nor was it in the spirit of OuiShare when I returned with Evian. But as the local Connector, Dönnebrink welcomed me warmly to his sharing parish. He was planning the OuiShare tour of Germany, involving panel events in major cities with entrepreneurs like the founders of Carpooling.com. Dönnebrink was also assisting Columbia University with some related research. One by one, Connectors like Dönnebrink are making connections to move this economy forward.

Building for selfish sharers

Like many working in this new economy, Dönnebrink believes the sharing economy is already changing the world but that it can use all the help it can get. In this same spirit, Gansky and Botsman are more than theoreticians and architects: they are hands-on builders of this new economy. Both women run their own online content hubs: Gansky's Meshing.it and Botsman's CollaborativeConsumption.com to guide users to online resources. Both women often take to the stage too, not least at TED. Above all, Gansky and Botsman catalyze the catalysts: the entrepreneurs. When I met Roo Rogers in his Post-it strewn office in Downtown Manhattan, he told me, "Rachel [Botsman] wanted to start a global movement." That remains her work. In the sharing economy, even the architects roll up their sleeves to build a new reality, even if—with no one quite sure what is now emerging—they are building to slightly varying plans.

Yet in whatever precise form it takes, the great edifice being built remains dizzyingly ambitious. Sharing as we knew it has never worked. Marxism, scaled up to millions of people in Russia, China, and Cambodia, bore no resemblance to its ideals. Sharing led to grotesque corruption. Worse still, it led to gulags, a Cultural Revolution, and the Killing Fields. Nor has sharing truly ever worked in its most benign forms. The Kibbutz model does not work at scale. The Burning Man festival is at scale: a desert encampment of 70,000 people where money is banned and goods move only through gifting. But that model of sharing only lasts as long as the supplies. The "Burners" share only consumption and not the responsibility of production, heaving everything they need from the outside world in a desert traffic jam of trucks and RVs.

The sharing economy has a very different ethos from that of Burning Man. It is not sharing for morality's sake, the "share nicely" that you hear parents teach their toddlers at any kindergarten. The sharing economy is sustainable because it is anchored firmly on self-interest and free market principles. While sharing traditionally left people with less, sharing in this economy is a market-based transaction that leaves people with more—most often, in the form of money. Yet the implications of this new economy are far more profound than enabling millions of people to cash out: "99% of the population are driven by self-interest," says Botsman. "The self-interest piece can hook people in but that is not what keeps them engaged in this economy."

So what does keep people engaged? The answer might just change the world.

Notes

1   Carplus Annual Survey of Car Clubs 2013/14. The report estimated that each shared car in London defers or prevents the purchase of 17 other cars: http://www.carplus. org.uk/resources/annual-survey-of-car-clubs/annual-survey-201314/. Other research puts this number in different markets in a range starting at 9–13, in a report by transportation academics Elliot Martin and Susan Shaheen, and rising to as many as 32, a less plausible outlier from research firm AlixPartners.

2   "Our marketplace is 75% brand new, fixed price sales, and 25% auction," as confirmed to me by email from eBay's UK press team on August 18th, 2014.

3   Kusek, Kathleen, *The Sharing Economy Goes Five Star* (Forbes, July 2014). Forbes has market-sized the sharing economy at $3.5 billion: http://www.forbes.com/sites/ kathleenkusek/2014/07/15/the-sharing-economy-goes-five-star/.

4   Ed Kushins' talk at OuiShare Fest 2014, "The Road to an Active Collaborative Community is Paved with Trust," Paris, May 6th, 2014.

5   A tonne of ore from a gold mine produces 5 grams of gold on average. By contrast, a tonne of discarded mobile phones can yield 150 grams of gold or more, according to a study by Japanese recycling firm Yokohama Metal Co Ltd: http://www.reuters.com/ article/2008/04/27/us-japan-metals-recycling-idUST13528020080427.

6   Over a billion people now work for cooperatives according to Washington's Worldwatch Institute: http://www.worldwatch.org/membership-co-operative- businesses-reaches-1-billion-0.

7   Data taken from Pew Research Center, a nonpartisan fact tank that has been conducting surveys on Internet use since 2000: http://www.pewinternet. org/2014/02/27/part-1-how-the-internet-has-woven-itself-into-american-life/.

8   Fulgoni, Gian, *The Digital World in Focus*, 2013, slide 36: http://www.slideshare.net/ mhmoo/com-score-thedigitalworldinfocusdma2013.

9   In December 2013, Google SVP Sundar Pichai shared the breaking news of Google passing the milestone of a billion Android activations in a Google+ post: https://plus. google.com/+SundarPichai/posts/NeBW7AjT1QM.

10   Statista suggests that Facebook's population may overtake China's by 2015, counting only "active users" who log in at least once a month: http://www.statista.com/ chart/1836/facebooks-user-growth/.

11   Internet Live Stats visualizes real-time Google searches: http://www.internetlivestats. com/google-search-statistics/.

12   Church of England figures, Statistics for Mission, 2012: https://churchofengland.org/ media/1936517/statistics%20for%20mission%202012.pdf.

13   Quoted in *Airbnb And The Unstoppable Rise Of The Share Economy* by Tomio Geron (*Forbes*, January 23rd, 2013): http://www.forbes.com/sites/ tomiogeron/2013/01/23/airbnb-and-the-unstoppable-rise-of-the-share-economy/.

14   Sivak, Michael, *Has Motorization in the US Peaked?* (University of Michigan, Transportation Research Institute, June 2013): http://deepblue.lib.umich.edu/ bitstream/handle/2027.42/98098/102947.pdf.

15   Quoted by David Ferrell in *Self-storage industry grows into a colossus* (*Buffalo News*, February 13th, 2013): http://www.buffalonews.com/20130218/self_storage_ industry_grows_into_a_colossus.html.

16   A New World Order of Consumption, *BCG Perspectives*, 2010: https://www. bcgperspectives.com/content/articles/consumer_products_retail_new_world_order_ of_consumption/?chapter=4.

17   The Financial Trust Index is calculated quarterly on a sample of 1,000 American adults. Its mission is to "monitor the level of trust Americans have in banks, the stock market, mutual funds, and large corporations, and to regularly assess how current events, policy and government intervention might affect this trust." http://www.financialtrustindex.org/resultswave2.htm.

18   Data taken from non-profit research body, World Population Balance: http://www.worldpopulationbalance.org/faq.

19   The world goes to town, *The Economist*, May 3rd, 2007: http://www.economist.com/node/9070726.

20   *U.S. Metro Economies: Current and Potential Green Jobs in the US Economy* (*Global Insight*, October 2008), p. 3: http://www.usmayors.org/pressreleases/uploads/greenjobsreport.pdf.

21   Dorling, Danny, *10 Billion: The Coming Demographic Crisis and How to Survive it* (Constable, 2013), p. 3.

22   Data taken from the World Meteorological Organization, an agency of the United Nations: http://www.wmo.int/pages/mediacentre/press_releases/pr_983_en.html.

23   Although the WWF estimates that at least 10,000 species become extinct each year, the figure could be as high as *100,000* species every year. This de-speciation is estimated to be at between 1,000 and 10,000 times higher than the background extinction rate: the rate of extinction on the planet before humans: http://wwf.panda.org/about_our_earth/biodiversity/biodiversity/.

24   Over a billion people already live in water-scarce areas according to the Potsdam Institute for Climate Impact Research, a research agency funded by the German government: http://www.eurekalert.org/pub_releases/2013-10/pifc-mt5100713.php#. In addition, our consumption of water is today increasing at roughly double the rate of population growth: http://www.populationinstitute.org/external/files/Fact_Sheets/Water_and_population.pdf.

25   Four separate polls were taken between May and August 2014, with between 1% and 3% of respondents naming "Environment/Pollution" as the most important non-economic problem: http://www.gallup.com/poll/1675/most-important-problem.aspx.

26   *The People Who Share, The State of the Sharing Economy* (Opinium Research, May 2013): http://www.thepeoplewhoshare.com/tpws/assets/File/TheStateoftheSharingEconomy_May2013_FoodSharingintheUK.pdf.

chapter 2

We the People

Selfish Sharers

21st-century worker bee

It was supposed to be a leisurely brunch but Brittney Bedford was hard at work. By most people's standards, Bedford does not have a job. By most people's standards, she is also a workaholic. Bedford placed her iPhone between us on the diner's Formica table. Every other minute it vibrated with a new notification from the many apps that fill her working life. "My office is my phone," she told me, one eye on the screen of her scratched iPhone. Bedford makes her living solely through sharing economy platforms. The 27-year-old Oakland resident rents out a spare room on Airbnb. She sells second-hand clothes on Poshmark. She dogsits on DogVacay. She runs errands and does chores on TaskRabbit. Between mouthfuls of scrambled egg, Bedford flicked through new TaskRabbit postings and Airbnb enquiries. "This is my job so I try to be as professional as possible," Bedford told me. She explained how 80-hour working weeks are common and how she and her husband have been trying to take a day off for over a month.

When we met, Bedford's portfolio career meant project-managing a fit-out for a real estate company, cooking soups for a health-conscious entrepreneur, and managing an Airbnb listing in San Francisco's hippie fallout zone, Haight-Ashbury. But her favorite task as a sharing economy jack-of-all-trades was getting paid to drive a Rolls-Royce for a wedding. Her work ethic translates into meaningful financial rewards: since quitting her job as a chef, Bedford's salary has practically doubled to around $1,500 a week. But more than the cash, working in the sharing economy gives Bedford the freedom that she craves. "I feel totally in control of my life," she told me before excitedly talking me through her plans for an upcoming 3-week trip to Central America. Bedford chooses when she works and what she does, picking only the "gigs" that she fancies. Indeed, she outsources her own chores that she dislikes, paying a house cleaner and a part-time assistant to do her admin. When I asked Bedford what it would be like to get a regular job again, she gawped at me like I had just broken into Swahili. Finally, she shrugged and said, "I don't know what that would be like."

I asked Bedford whether she was concerned about the lack of employee benefits like health insurance. She told me that she did not have any before. *What about job security?* She said she feels more secure now that she has a variety of income streams. *Lack of career progression?* "One of the great things about TaskRabbit," Bedford told me, "is that you meet lots of people. It's networking." Bedford is an on-call assistant to a number of influential San Franciscans and told me about a recent gig at a multimillionaire's mansion. Just as I felt Bedford beginning to relax, she spotted a task that she wanted: picking up some someone's groceries from Whole Foods. The next moment, we were in her pick-up, her bulldog Otis clambering all over me. Bedford paced up and down the Whole Foods aisles with an efficiency that made the other shoppers look like amateurs. She double-checked that she had everything on the task, snapped a photo of the receipt, and was on her way.

Make money, you were born for it

Bedford is not alone. Somewhere between 20% and 33% of the US workforce are now independent workers according to a 2013 study by Accenture.[1] As Carole Cadwalladr writes in *The Guardian*, "[Airbnb] is succeeding in doing what Margaret Thatcher wanted to achieve but ultimately failed to do: it's creating entrepreneurs out of ordinary people." Many freelancer beneficiaries are online workers in developing countries where they can arbitrage low wages against lower living costs. Even artists are riding the trend. deviantART is the world's biggest art community of over 30 million artists and art lovers. We will see in this chapter how all kinds of people are applying this entrepreneurship to all kinds of assets: real estate, cars, fashion, food, and more.

"Microcapitalism"—what Rachel Botsman calls "lemonade stands on steroids"—has become a global phenomenon. Its ubiquity suggests that it taps into a desire for freedom and self-reliance that makes us innately human. "All human beings are entrepreneurs," says Muhammad Yunus, the Nobel Prize-winning microfinance pioneer. He continues:

> When we were in the caves, we were all self-employed ... finding our food, feeding ourselves. That's where human history began. As civilization came, we suppressed it. We became 'labor' because they stamped us, 'You are labor'. We forgot that we are entrepreneurs.[2]

This is something that every CEO of a sharing economy company has seen. Chad Dickerson, CEO of one of the largest—giant handmade goods marketplace Etsy—is no exception. "There is," says Dickerson, "a hunger to own your own destiny." Perhaps Bedford is returning to a more natural state of providing for herself, one that seems—for all the grueling and unpredictable hours—to be a state of happiness.

Empowerment

There is one word that gets used time and again in the rhetoric of the sharing economy: empowerment. Brian Chesky, co-founder of Airbnb: "The sharing economy is empowering people to create physical things, services, goods, experiences and activities for the very first time." Jeremiah Owyang, collaborative economy consultant: "People are empowered to get what they need from each other." Rachel Botsman of CollaborativeConsumption. com: "At its root, this is about empowerment." Exit the elevator in the San Francisco office of crowdfunding startup Indiegogo and you step into a gloomy lobby. Then motion sensors catch you and a word burns in neon: "EMPOWER." It is a reminder to every Indiegogo employee of why they do what they do. Indiegogo is a platform that has let people crowdfund everything from coral farming to the ChargeKey, a key-ring-sized iPhone charging cable that travels everywhere with me. By harnessing the collective resources of the crowd, Indiegogo empowers people to realize their dreams and themselves.

This is freedom, the seductive lure underpinning Lyft's driver-recruitment billboards: "NINE TO FIVE." For Bedford, freedom means not having to wipe down greasy kitchen surfaces at 1 in the morning. For others, it is the opportunity to pursue careers that were once out of bounds. Many women would not feel safe driving a taxi, especially at night. Lyft gives women drivers peace of mind: the car is tracked via GPS and they can see reviews of passengers given by other drivers. With the added advantage of flexible hours for working mothers, 30% of Lyft's drivers are women. Deaf drivers who could not work for regular taxi companies also work for Lyft. When a passenger gets in, they speak their destination into the driver's smartphone. The phone does the hearing for the drivers. Many of Lyft's deaf drivers were unemployed before being freed to earn a dignified wage. Sometimes, this is freedom from being judged. On Shareyourmeal. net, a girl with Down's syndrome cooks meals for locals. According to her mother, "Bente would like to become a cook when she grows up. Thanks to Shareyourmeal, the neighborhood can now get to know Bente and see her potential instead of her limitations."

"Prosumers": reciprocal motivations

New technologies require new words. A new class of "homepreneurs" is building businesses from their bedrooms. Others build products as part of a new "Maker Movement" of small-scale manufacturing and invention. In this economy, we get to play several parts. We are no longer passive consumers but "prosumers": producers *and* consumers who create value at the same time as getting what we want from those around us. "Energy prosumers," for example, now generate and consume their own electricity, notably in Germany, where more than a million of them contribute 8% to energy output.[3] Brittney Bedford embodies the hybrid spirit of the prosumer. She is a seller of dog-walking services and second-hand clothes. But she is a buyer of cleaning services and administrative support. For some services like room rentals, she is flexibly both a seller and a buyer depending on the context. She "Airbnbs" her spare room in Oakland but will stay in Airbnb apartments on her travels around Central America. Peer-to-peer marketplaces in the sharing economy let us be buyers or sellers and sometimes both at once.

Reciprocity is at the core of the most successful and scalable peer marketplaces. One side saves money; the other side earns money. One side receives a social experience; the other side curates one. What draws buyers and sellers to these new services varies from platform to platform. However, three main motives are typically at work. Firstly and most importantly, sharing economy businesses realize efficiencies that create economic opportunities on both sides of their marketplaces. According to research based on interviews with over 2,000 UK adults in 2013, 72% of people who share do so with the primary motivation of making or saving money.[4]

Secondly, as we will see, sharing platforms can offer rich social experiences, again on both sides of the marketplace. I was approached to write this book because my editor had just such an experience as a customer of JustPark. It was during the 2012 Olympics Games that she parked her car at someone's house on England's south coast to watch the sailing. Her family and the homeowner's family got chatting and both sets of children ended up playing together in the homeowner's garden. It was a simple but beautifully unexpected social interaction. For many users, sharing economy services are attractive because they come with a sense of humanness and belonging. Whether you spend your money with Airbnb or Marriott, you are a speck on their profit and loss. But with the Marriott, you are more likely to feel like one. Airbnb, on the other hand, has been successful because it has been able to scale meaningful social experiences.

In addition to money and experiences, there is a third reason that users are flocking to these startups. Very often, both of the parties involved—and indeed the startups themselves—enjoy a powerfully aligned vision. Users believe in the principles behind the platform and vote with their time and their wallets. Sometimes, the social or environmental ethos of the platform chimes with users ideologically. At other times, there is a shared sense of purpose in pursuit of a concrete goal. Over $1.5 billion has been raised through Kickstarter because people share a vision about the world being a better place if a product can be built or a project turned into reality. Successful share platforms—like all of the most successful consumer businesses—find a way of making their customers feel good about spending their money.

The appeal of most sharing economy businesses blends elements of all three factors. As Juanjo Rodriguez, the founder of home-swapping startup

Knok, writes, "Some services combine advantages: co-working spaces are cheaper and can offer a better ambience than a traditional office. A city visit with a local guide is more enjoyable and also better value than a typical, touristy tour." For some, the benefits of alternative share platforms are so all-encompassing that they have adopted them as a whole way of life: an extreme version of Botsman's "Collaborative Lifestyles." In Berkeley, California, eight people have embarked on a project called The Sandbox House, whose residents aim to earn a living and consume entirely via sharing economy platforms. In their world, job titles—and walls—are porous. When there was a fire on their street, their homeless neighbors gravitated to their home to stay the night.

New categories, unique products

The sharing economy is opening up new categories to the masses. Airbnb's luxurious residences are nothing like 5* hotels. Conversely, its cheap rooms are unlike B&Bs and their still-sharp hierarchy between host and guest. It is a radical change that an intimacy between host and guest is part of the attractiveness of the accommodation rather than something that a guest will pay to be insulated against. Pre-Internet, pre-Facebook, wanting to learn about your host would have marked you out as nosey at best and a predatory pervert at worst. But every day, thousands of Airbnb guests choose accommodation because they want to get the best out of their destination with the help of a brief but powerful bond with their host.

onefinestay has created another new category in accommodation. Sometimes called "the posh Airbnb", onefinestay lets you rent out multimillion-dollar private mansions in London, New York, Paris, and Los Angeles. Unlike Airbnb, onefinestay homes come with hotel-like luxuries such as linen and towels from The White Company as well as access to maids and personal chefs via an iPhone that is preloaded with personalized recommendations. The company has also patented a device called Sherlock that lets people unlock front doors with a phone. It adds up to an experience so distinct that onefinestay needed a new word to describe it. "There's this new thing," they write on their website, "the *unhotel*. And we're it." It is smart branding and market positioning. But onefinestay has also invented a genuinely new category.

Yet more than new product categories, this is about unique products. As Airbnb co-founder Brian Chesky puts it:

> What the industrial revolution created was a multi-hundred year world where everything was the same: mass production ... What [the sharing economy] is, is the thing after mass production. I actually think that if you go back in human history and you put the Internet before mass production, would mass production even have happened.

Products in the sharing economy do not emerge identikit on conveyor belts. Etsy is a collection of cottage industries like handmade paper-making and wood-carving that industrialization was supposed to have swept away forever. Now they can thrive via an online marketplace that links sellers' kitchen tables to a global demand for artisanal products. The best-renting properties on Airbnb are often unique. This is increasingly a consideration for buyers in the primary market. The apartment I bought is in a church, complete with stained glass windows and a room in the church tower. My rationale was that the property's appeal to tourists looking for a memorable vacation would translate into attractive yields.

Real estate: putting space to work

Property is the most valuable asset most of us will ever own. For tenants, rent is almost always their biggest outgoing. Here in London, rent averages an eye-watering 59% of income.[5] With such large sums at stake, even a small amount of idling capacity translates into substantial earning potential. Short-term rental startups like Berlin's 9Flats or Madrid's Alterkeys give owners and tenants the flexibility to make income from short voids, often allowing them to part-fund a vacation through a vacated apartment. Landlords normally earn a higher yield through offering frequent short lets than through long lets, but as one told me, "it's more work with all the messages and changeovers." Although they may not realize it, landlords are getting not only income, but capital appreciation too. By accruing good reviews on a site like Airbnb, they are adding digital value to their bricks and mortar. An apartment with high-quality reviews on a short-term rental site is worth more to a buy-to-let, or as we will see "buy-to-share," investor than an identical apartment with no online footprint.

How do these websites work? Property owners start by listing their property for free. Larger platforms like Airbnb arrange for professional photography at their expense via a roving global army of freelance photographers. Once properties are up on the site, owners control their property's availability through an online calendar and communicate with potential guests through their internal messaging systems. Usually, the platforms charge the guests but Airbnb also charges the property owner 3% of the booking value. The platforms also deal with payments, allowing hosts to be paid in their local currency. Ultimately, the platforms earn their commission for the distribution they give to a property. With Airbnb, this means getting the property on its well-trafficked website and mobile apps. With Singapore-headquartered Roomorama, properties appear on its website plus Craigslist, QXL, and around 200 other classified sites.

How much money can someone make by renting out their property? Like the primary property market itself, the range is vast and will depend on the property's size, luxuriousness, and, above all, location. On Airbnb, you can find François renting out his charming beachfront guesthouse in the poor West African country of Benin for $21 a night. It may be cheap by Western standards, but that is good money in a country where it was only in 2005 that the United Nations found that half the population was living below the international poverty line of US$1.25 per day.[6] Or if you happen to be the Earl of Sutherland, you can pull in a princely $8,360 a night by renting out Dunrobin, your 186-room Scottish castle. Between these two extremes are hundreds of thousands of ordinary people earning thousands of dollars a year.

Idling capacity in real estate is highest in second homes that sit vacant for most of the time. Derek Thompson lays out their punishing economics in *The Atlantic*:

> The average cost of owning a summer home is more than $100,000 a year in mortgage, upkeep, and insurance [but] the average use is only 17 days a year. That comes out to almost $6,000 per vacation day – equal to four rooms at the Four Seasons Hotel George V in Paris – and that's after you've bought the home.

The holiday home rental market leader is HomeAway. Together with its many sub-brands including VRBO and Owners Direct, it lists over a million second homes. Traded on NASDAQ with a value of over $4 billion,

HomeAway connects holiday homeowners with holidaymakers, typically families looking for a more relaxed environment and more space than a hotel. Unlike Airbnb and other short-term rental marketplaces, HomeAway works mostly on a subscription model. Property owners pay $349 a year to receive commission-free bookings.

Sites like Spain's Knok and the UK's Love Home Swap offer property owners a third model: swapping. Here, too, members pay an annual subscription to access, in the case of Love Home Swap, over 55,000 properties in 150 countries. A "classic swap" comprises a simple exchange of one member's property for another's. The exchange does not need to be simultaneous as often one property owner has a second home and flexibility around timing. Members can also access properties by redeeming "swap points" that are accrued by letting people use their home. As Love Home Swap's website suggests, "Have someone from Barcelona stay in your London apartment, and then use the points that you earn from that pledge to book time in a beach property in Sydney."

Less obvious real estate

Real estate does not only mean somewhere to sleep. It can also mean somewhere to store that glut of things we own. Peer-to-peer storage marketplaces like Washington's StorageMarket and the UK's Storemates let people rent out their attics, basements, and sheds. As with room rental sites, the platforms provide a suite of tools from messaging and secure payments to legal contracts. The website of another new entrant, Storenextdoor, features a tool that allows property owners to enter the dimensions and location of their space in order to estimate its rental value. Storenextdoor claims the average owner earns £90 a month through the site. During the listing process, property owners usually specify what items they will allow to be stored, from books to boats, and any security features and access restrictions.

JustPark lets property owners monetize another form of neglected real estate: their parking spaces and driveways. Revenue from over 150,000 parking spaces at homes, churches, offices, and schools flows through our platform to their owners. For most of our property owners, it feels like found money: they never expected to earn a cent from the previously dead space outside their doors until they discovered the service. JustPark provides pricing recommendations by crunching data on the performance of nearby listings. Property owners can also opt into automatic bank deposits by syncing their bank account to their profile. Once a driver has parked at their house, the money hits their bank account. Thousands of property owners are making over $1,000 a year simply by letting drivers come and go from their driveway. Those with spots near stations or airports, or in more built-up areas, are making over $5,000 every year.

Shared real estate can also mean somewhere to work. The co-working bug spread from a live–work unit in a converted hat factory in San Francisco where developers could turn up with their laptops. Today, there are over 700 co-working spaces in the US alone. In New York, they run the gamut from the boisterous AlleyNYC ("The Most Badass Space on the Planet") to the zen-like serenity of Grind, all polished concrete and white (the touches of orange, I was informed, increase productivity). Some co-working spaces even share space between themselves as members of "The League of Extraordinary Coworking Spaces." Outside the US, there is Betahaus in Berlin, CoWork Station in Moscow, and The Trampery in London to name but a few. Impact Hub is the nearest thing to a co-working giant, with 54 locations across six continents. With more freelancers than ever, aspiring digital Donald Trumps can smell opportunity. According to trade journal *DeskMag*, the number of co-working locations grew by 83% worldwide in the year to 2014.[7]

Finally, real estate can also mean somewhere to shop. When Eric Ho was walking through Manhattan's Lower East Side, he was astonished by the number of empty shop fronts. In fact, there were over 200 of them that together represented $20 million in rental values. miLES, short for Made In the Lower East Side, works with landlords and small businesses on New York's Lower East Side to open up unused storefronts to pop-up shops. Appear Here and We Are Pop Up do the same in the UK, with a greater focus on partnering with major brands looking to open attention-grabbing temporary retail space. They let landlords list units for free and aim to make renting them out as easy as booking a hotel room. This retail match-making is not only benefitting the two parties involved. Retail space that is frequently refreshed and creatively used is helping to rejuvenate flagging high streets, to the benefit of other tenants and local residents.

Real estate: saving money

Whether space is used for sleeping, storage, parking, or shopping, using existing, underused space is almost always a cheaper option. Peer-to-peer storage is about half the price of self-storage. JustPark spaces are around half the price of on-street parking. Peer-to-peer accommodation is usually far cheaper than a hotel, especially in cities like Brisbane or Tel Aviv where a shortage of hotel rooms has led to inflated nightly rates. Economics blog Priceonomics analyzed the costs of a one-night stay with Airbnb in 65 US cities. It found that renting an Airbnb apartment was on average 21.2% cheaper than a hotel. For travelers content to stay in a private room at a host's house, the average savings rocketed to 49.5%.[8]

Still too expensive? Couchsurfing offers accommodation ranging from a patch of carpet or spare bed to the eponymous couch in over 1,000 cities for free. Indeed, charging is strictly forbidden. "Couchsurfer" Josh Cahill recounts in his blog GoTravelYourWay.com how he traversed five continents without spending a dime on accommodation. For Cahill, who grew up in a "tiny little village in Germany ... somewhere in the mountains, a place people usually never leave," Couchsurfing has allowed him to visit the places he read about in storybooks as a child. Victor Eekhof is another Couchsurfer, a 30-year-old Dutchman with very itchy feet. Eekhof "couchsurfed" (like the names of many successful technology companies, it has become a verb) from the North to the South Pole for charity. Extraordinary tales of adventure and generosity have been par for the course since Couchsurfing was founded in 2004. One of the original we-conomy platforms, Couchsurfing is today 7 million members strong.

A word of warning: Couchsurfers should not overstay their welcome. When I was at law school, we put up a French Couchsurfer who decided to pay us in hand-drawn cartoons. It was fine for the first week. Then the cork board got full up and he started taping cartoons to the walls.

Beyond the bucks: experience

Most renters on real estate share platforms are not only in pursuit of savings. They also desire authentic travel experiences that are far removed from what they would get in a generic hotel. It was precisely experience that I was after on the next stop of my trip. I booked an Airbnb in a New York neighborhood that I had longed to get to know: DUMBO, an acronym for a pocket of Brooklyn that is "Down Under Manhattan Bridge Overpass." In DUMBO, restored warehouses squat beneath the floodlit steel hulk of the Manhattan Bridge. Gentrification has marched right through it, led by the Double Tree group of real estate mogul David Walentas. On the walk from the subway, the guys exiting the apartments looked like JP Morgan bankers. They probably were. But I wanted to experience the old DUMBO. Gentrification had not touched the one place where I was headed: 135 Plymouth Street.

Once the largest factory in the world, 135 Plymouth Street is home to a loose collective of artists and eccentrics including my Airbnb host, Adam Click. The buzzer, covered with soggy Post-its, was broken. The ancient elevator was wrapped in dusty chains. I heaved my suitcase up to Click's floor. His shaved head showed his 37 years but he greeted me with a teenager's rascally grin. Click led me down a corridor covered with lewd murals and over floorboards patched with metal plates to what he called his "dream studio." I could see why. A forest of flowers hung from the ceiling, light rippling through their fluorescent petals. A wrought iron spiral staircase ascended to a ramshackle mezzanine—my room—before disappearing like an M.C. Escher drawing into the ceiling. A circus trapeze swung back and forth. I took a seat gingerly on the red velvet sofa, outlandish in any other context but almost humdrum in the dream studio. Only then did I notice the human skeleton nailed to the wall. I hoped it wasn't a previous Airbnb guest.

I was a day early so in this fluid space I was relocated into the loft of Click's neighbor, Drew. When Click walked me there, we crossed an entire floor crowded with empty dumpsters of every shape and size. I totted up tens of millions of dollars of unused real estate. Drew was a Christian Bale lookalike with bleached hair. He shook my hand with an alarming firmness while Click took a half-moldy pancake out of Drew's fridge and divulged, perhaps in jest, that I should call him, "Shallow Throat." A skinny girl in black lingerie strolled through the room. I assumed she was Heidi because Drew informed me that, "Heidi barfed in my bed last night."

"*Dude!*" said Click. "What kind of customer service is that?"

I was considering making a run for it when a heavily built man emerged from a door that I hadn't noticed and eyed me up and down sinisterly.

I got the fear. *What was I doing there?* Maybe I was the dumbo.

That afternoon, over a coffee in a hipster Brooklyn café, Drew told me how the gifting culture at Burning Man made them more able to share their living spaces. Drew, it turned out, was a medical engineer. Heidi worked in asset management. It turned out that these people are wonderful and warm-hearted. 135 Plymouth Street was the sharing economy distilled. "It's like living in an adult dormitory," Drew told me, "walking into each other's apartments in your underwear, stealing each other's beers." While people drift through each other's lives and spaces, the building is a cohesive community. It has its own website and Facebook page. Airbnb has added an extra layer to the community. 135 Plymouth Street was fun but it is no theme park; it was a slice of New York more real and fascinating than the streets outside.

In the space of a few days, I became friends with Click, Heidi, and Drew. I partied with them and even had a disagreement—and only because they had been themselves from the moment I walked in. Never before had the accommodation itself added so much to the richness of a stay. Waking up on my first morning, I opened my eyes on the East River. It was glinting like a carpet of diamonds. As I stared through that old factory window, it felt like that loft was my home and DUMBO was my neighborhood. Airbnb does not rent rooms. It provides an exhaustive menu of experiences. Click's advert had warned me: "**EXPECT A GRITTY AND OCCASIONALLY NOISY BROOKLYN EXPERIENCE**." I was paying for that wonderful feeling as I stared at the East River, and I was paying for the broken buzzer—and even Heidi's barfing.

Car-sharing: cash plus convenience

After buying a property, the largest investment that many of us ever make is in a car. With even greater idling capacity in cars than property, the sharing economy is unlocking huge value in this asset class. Car-sharing companies like RelayRides and its archrival Getaround, and the two major European competitors, Drivy and SnappCar, follow many of the same paradigms as home rental marketplaces. Users list their property—in this case, a vehicle—for free, build up their profile to increase their trustworthiness, and accrue star ratings. These startups also make use of internal messaging systems that allow both parties to ask each other questions and arrange the handover of car keys. San Francisco-based Getaround claims that its renters are making up to $10,000 a year against average annual running costs of $8,000.

For the car-less, these startups are saving drivers money, especially those who only occasionally need a car. This has been the main appeal of the world's largest car-sharing company, Zipcar, since it was founded in 1999. Zipcar puts a "savings calculator" on its website to show drivers what they could save on fuel, insurance, maintenance, road tax, car financing, and parking. According to Zipcar, UK members save around £3,000 a year. Renters also avoid the cost of replacing their car when their needs change, for example on becoming a parent. But this is also about convenience: if the appeal of the real estate sector is savings plus experience, the appeal of car-sharing is savings plus convenience. With paperwork and maintenance, it is hassle as much as cost that is turning people off car ownership. Inspired by the success of Zipcar, car-sharing services now abound in countries big and small from GoGet in Australia to SigoCar in Costa Rica.

Bums on seats

What about drivers who do not want to share their cars? The sharing economy speaks to them too. Drivers with spare time can earn money driving around town using apps like Lyft and Sidecar. Lyft passes 80% of fares onto drivers and claims they can make around $35 an hour. Unlike Lyft, which controls the metering of rides, Sidecar lets drivers set their own rates. Ridesharing does not only mean e-hailing a ride across town: it also comes in a long-distance, inter-city form. Drivers can sell empty seats to passengers on longer journeys that they were making anyway on Germany's Carpooling.com and the biggest player in the space globally, France's BlaBlaCar. As per normal, users connect through Facebook and build up online reviews to increase the trust between the parties. Both companies also offer a "Ladies Only" service for women who prefer to travel in a female-only vehicle. For frequent or so-called "power users" of ridesharing services, picking up passengers is part of their weekly routine. With fuel costs split up to five ways, driving is no longer an expensive indulgence. BlaBlaCar claims to save drivers over $400 million a year.

The savings for passengers are even greater. Since drivers are not legally allowed to make a profit but only to offset the cost of gas—in the US, for example, the cost per mile is capped by the AAA at $0.25 per mile—passengers can travel long distances between cities at "cost price." Long-distance ridesharing is now outcompeting the rail companies, compared to which it can cost half the price—or less. In the UK, where the rail network has been franchised to train operating companies, or indeed on Amtrak in the US, last-minute tickets often cost more than flights. On Carpooling.com, a passenger can travel from Paris to Brussels for just $26. Or sit back and be driven the 470 miles from Moscow to Kiev for just $44. Long-distance ridesharing will in time achieve massive adoption in emerging markets. Tripid is a Philippino service that does not even charge passengers the low commission rates of its larger European competitors: it makes money by charging drivers $3 to have their license and ID validated.

FIGURES 2.1 Brussels to Amsterdam: with Taxistop in 1975 ...
Source: Taxistop vzw

FIGURES 2.2 ... and with BlaBlaCar's iPhone application in 2014
Source: Comuto SA

There has long been a latent demand for these services. Taxistop, one of the earliest carpooling initiatives, was founded in Belgium way back in 1975, and some countries have had carpool lanes—lanes reserved for vehicles with two or three passengers—for years. But for the most part, travel has ceased to be social. "Progress" has largely put an end to the days when it took ages to get anywhere and friendships were made along the way. I have caught just glimpses of the old ways. During my second year at university, I hitch-hiked from Oxford to Morocco to raise money for charity. It took 6 days and was the most exhilarating journey I have ever made. Bonding with a fascinating cast of strangers, all of them so unlike myself, was cathartic and inspiring.

Ridesharing is now bringing hitch-hiking into the 21st century: online, transparently safer, and powered by social media. With new technologies, the private car is now becoming a public and social form of transport. UK carpooling startup GoCarShare has the slogan, "Journeys are better together." Lyft's slogan is "Your Friend with a Car." Indeed, sometimes more than friendships form in the close confines of a car. On October 6th, 2009, Julia Kowalewski picked up her Carpooling.com passenger Dominic Mallek in a gas station. Both were German students of Polish descent who happened to be headed across Germany from Kiel to Regensburg. Over the course of the 800 km journey with another female passenger in the car vying for Dominic's attention, they began to fall in love. When I spoke to Kowalewski, she was pregnant with their second child.

Wings, wheels, and rudders

The success of car-sharing and ridesharing has spawned imitators in every mode of transport. The sharing economy now has offerings for bicycles, scooters, boats, and even planes. Spinlister lets people rent out their bicycles. Scoot Networks, for now just active in San Francisco, lets people borrow electric scooters that are clustered around the city for $3 a ride. Helmets are stowed in the scooter's seat and the scooters themselves work by plugging a smartphone into the dashboard.

Boats have perhaps the greatest idling capacity of all. On average, they sit bobbing up and down for over 95% of their lives, costing their owners dear with insurance premiums, maintenance costs, and harbor fees. In fact, the 17 million boats in the US cost their owners roughly $8 billion a year.[9] Boatbound in San Francisco and Cruzin in Florida are boat rental marketplaces that are unlocking the value in this downtime. Plane-sharing offers an alternative to the fractional ownership model of Warren Buffett's NetJets. Wheels Up is private jet by annual subscription. JumpSeat charges the rich to list their empty seats on its platform to other members of their community, a process they call "aerial matchmaking."

As with Zipcar, those renting the assets get a combination of savings and convenient access. Perhaps someone is testing out cycling to work. Perhaps they just want to cycle during the summer and not have to store a bike during the winter. Instead of owning a bike, millions can now access one using a bike-sharing scheme such as Bicing in Barcelona or Hubway in Boston. Unlike the standard inventory of a city-wide bike scheme, the varied inventory on a peer-to-peer marketplace allows consumers to choose the right bike for them and the occasion, whether that is a fixed-gear, a BMX, or a mountain bike. Boats are so expensive that few renters are thinking about buying them. For them, marketplaces like Boatbound democratize access to boats and the wind-in-your-hair, out-on-the-ocean experience that was once the preserve of the rich. Meanwhile, plane-sharing gives the already rich access to assets that were once the preserve of the unfathomably rich.

Opening our warbrobes

Owners that succumb to the economic logic of sharing their expensive assets can open up to sharing cheaper ones. Car-sharing schemes in particular are a gateway asset for sharing. "Automobile ownership is a linchpin of the consumer economy," says of Neil Gorenflo of *Shareable*. "Once we change our relationship to cars, we change our relationship to everything. When you try it and it works out for you, you're like, 'What else can I share?'" Often, this can mean lower value items like household goods and especially fashion. Here, the economic arguments are less compelling. It might be as much work to rent out a dress as a car but with comparatively tiny financial returns. However, clothes "recommerce" platforms like Poshmark and Tradesy now allow millions of women to monetize clothes in their wardrobes that they seldom or never wear.

Power sellers on these platforms are earning living wages. For some, this income has been nothing short of a lifeline. Poshmark told me about one user who has been fighting lupus for the past 4 years and uses Poshmark to cover her ongoing medical bills. Usually, the clothes move peer-to-peer, but not always. Some platforms like Threadflip receive all of the inventory direct from the sellers and take on the hassle of cleaning, photographing, and then selling it on their website, albeit for a hefty 40% of its sale price. French startup Rentez-vous uses dry-cleaners as drop-off points for clothes. Women wishing to rent the clothes turn up and browse them on the rails. The dry cleaners collect the cash on behalf of the clothes owners and, for their trouble, win the business of cleaning the clothes between rentals.

Clearly, second-hand clothes are dramatically cheaper for the buyers or renters of them. Second-hand branded children's clothes on thredUP come at discounts of 60–80%. Half a million Americans now use the site to save money on their clothes bills. A quick browse on Tradesy revealed some nearly new Christian Louboutin pumps for $328, an impressive discount on a retail price of $1,200. US-based Rent the Runway and the UK's Girl Meets Dress apply the business-to-consumer centrally owned Zipcar model to sharing. They mail out designer dresses (along with an extra size just in case) to women who may not have the means to buy them new. Women can wear designer dresses by the likes of Alexander McQueen at up to 90% off their retail price. TradeYa lets people swap fashion as well as electronics and tickets. Money still rules though: the friction of finding counter-parties with the same wants at the same time makes matching hard. While peer-to-peer fashion commerce is booming, none of the pure swapping sites have scaled—yet.

Household and student goods

If car-sharing opened the door to fashion-sharing, fashion-sharing may open the door to the sharing of even lower value items. The platforms in this space are a combination of eBay-like resale platforms and lending or gifting platforms that promise people the ability to get their hands on whatever they need from their neighbors. As the saying goes, one man's trash is another man's treasure. This is never truer than with goods like children's clothes that have a short useful life. reCrib lets parents sell their kiddy clutter, freeing up space in their homes and providing the "feel good" of knowing that their possessions will be reused rather than sent to landfill. Peerby lets people lend to their neighbors. yerdle lets people gift to them everything from a surfboard to a Magimix. The yerdle founders discovered that their early users actually preferred to give their items away in order to get new ones from their community.

Conversely, borrowers or recipients get what they need for a fraction of the item's first-hand cost or for free. OpenShed is an Australian goods rental marketplace. I found a projector on the site worth 2,000 AUD to rent for 20 AUD a day. An iPad was going for just 3.50 AUD a day, a fraction of the cost of leasing it from a specialist company. While yerdle is the sharing economy's most exciting gifting platform, Freecycle, originating in Arizona, is by far its largest. With 7 million members, Freecycle's local chapters list thousands of items going for free. Once, when my iPod broke, I picked up a free one on Freecycle from someone's house the next day. Aside from Freecycle, no item-sharing or gifting platform is yet international. Instead, they exist in local pockets: yerdle in San Francisco, Ecomodo in London, or Peerby in Amsterdam.

Often, sharing low-value goods is simply too much hassle: most people would not bother picking up a desk fan when they could get a brand new one the next day for $15 on Amazon. For students, however, even slender money-making and saving opportunities can be attractive. Chegg is the leading student textbook rental community. Rentals cost around half the price of a new book. Half.com, another textbook rental company, which was acquired by eBay for $350 million, rents out over 400,000 textbooks a year. Others like Australia's Zookal are pulling out all the stops to tap this tech-savvy segment and have even started delivering textbooks by drone. Some schools also have peer-to-peer goods exchanges. UC Berkeley has "ReUSE stations" where students and faculty members exchange clothes, school supplies, and furniture. Other programs include MIT's Furniture Exchange and the University of New Hampshire's Trash 2 Treasure, all of them helping to keep goods in circulation.

Breaking bread

There is perhaps nothing more naturally suited to sharing than food. As is often the case in the sharing economy, an online model is seeking to recover something that we have lost. By 2010, Americans were eating around half their meals outside the home, many of them alone while walking down a street or sat in front of a laptop. Back in 1900 America, however, just 2% of meals were eaten outside a communal home setting.[10] But sharing food is vastly more ancient still. "Bioarchaeologist" Martin Jones explores, in *Feast: Why Humans Share Food*, how sharing food at communal meals is so fundamental that we have been doing it for half a million years.[11] The original food sharing website, HomeFood, is a little newer, dating back to 2004. HomeFood is an Italian website that lets tourists book meals cooked by domestic "Empresses" in their homes at €50 apiece.

Today, numerous meal-sharing startups have sprung up in the wake of Airbnb proving that millions of people are prepared to open up their homes to strangers. Feastly and Bookalokal in the US, Cookening in France, and MealMeets in Spain among many others are building platforms that allow anyone to turn their home into a restaurant, selling covers at their kitchen table. These companies may be starting local but they are after a healthy slice of the $1.9 trillion global restaurant industry. The most established of them all is Israel's EatWith, operational in 18 cities in the Americas and Europe. After commission—EatWith takes 15% of the booking value— the platforms offer money-making opportunities for chefs ranging from enthusiastic amateurs to seasoned semi-professionals.

While the equivalent meal is cheaper than at a restaurant, diners come primarily in search of a social experience. Diners get social upside from not only the hodge-podge of guests, but also the chance to mingle with the chef. One user of Feastly discussed his experience on techy Q&A site Quora, "After dining out so many times, I had rarely met the chef behind the food I eat…Whenever I have the privilege to meet the chef, I find my dining experience more personal and memorable. For me, it feels like meeting the architect of your building or the designer of your favorite dress." Some of the chefs are experiences in their own right. Rasanath Dasa, a cook on travel experience site SideTour, quit his job on Wall Street and took a vow of celibacy to become a Buddhist monk.

A second food-sharing model involves home chefs providing an alternative to the unhealthy fast food and takeaway sectors. On Cookisto, chefs whip up home-cooked food that is either collected or delivered by arrangement. Cookisto also takes a 15% cut. I decided to try it out. Or more accurately, I decided to try out "Dan D.," a home cook who lives 5 minutes' walk from me in North London. I ordered two portions of lamb rogan josh from the Cookisto website at a reasonable £4.50 each. The next evening at the allotted time, I nervously pressed the buzzer of Dan's apartment. The door swung open on a disheveled 20-something. It looked like Dan had just woken up. I entered his apartment sheepishly and Dan handed me the foil containers in a tatty plastic bag. I could feel they were almost cold.

Back home and already feeling slightly exploited by the experience, I heated up the rogan josh in a pot. Suddenly, my nostrils filled with an incredible aroma. It turned out that Dan had made me one of the best curries I had ever eaten, intricately spiced and nothing like a greasy takeaway. It had cost me barely more than what I would have spent on ingredients. Similar cookery platforms to Cookisto may one day lower the cost of living by undercutting even the cheapest restaurants. Unsurprisingly, Cookisto has taken off in its home market, crisis-hit Greece, where it has attracted over 1,500 cooks. While EatWith is throwing open strangers' doors to enchanting dinner parties, Cookisto is providing a social safety net for cooks and those whom they feed.

For the truly penniless, there are freebies. LeftoverSwap is to EatWith what Couchsurfing is to Airbnb: it turns out that there is such a thing as a free lunch after all. "You're hungry. And cheap. We understand," says LeftoverSwap on its website. Open their iPhone app, and tempted by a photo of a neighbor's slice of congealed pizza, off you go for your second-hand snack. Yet reducing food waste is no trivial matter. Every day the US creates enough food waste to fill a 90,000-seat football stadium to the brim.[12] Meanwhile, over 16 million Americans regularly go hungry.[13] Redistributive peer-to-peer models can reduce these shocking inefficiencies. With the cost of smartphones falling, there may be a time when every homeless person can connect to a public wifi network to locate their nearest Samaritan chef, sparing them the indignity of rifling through trash cans.

The streets outside

The sharing economy is also letting people utilize intangible assets like time and expertise. Vayable is a San Franciscan startup that puts experiences on tap by connecting tourists with locals who provide tours of their neighborhoods. Vayable relies on over 5,000 "Insiders" who serve as a global network of local guides. All of a sudden, just knowing your local area and having the gift of the gab can get you a job. For travelers, Vayable's experiences range from a birdwatching tour in the Peruvian wetlands with a local birder to a visit to Istanbul's markets with a local Turkish belly dancer. Backed by one of the founders of Rough Guides, Tripbod is a UK competitor. Other companies are entering the fray, such as Houston-based CanaryHop, co-founded by Saturday Night Live star Andy Samberg, and Athens-based, Dopios, which means "local" in Greek.

During my stay at 135 Plymouth Street, I used Vayable to take Jeff Orlick's food tour of Queens. A self-proclaimed "Queens cultural ambassador,"

Orlick charges $59 per person which includes food. He is also the only person I've seen who gives their job title on LinkedIn as "American," although his primary line of work is as a cameraman. We met beneath the plastic fascia of Kebab King in Jackson Heights, at the noisy junction of Indian, Italian, Tibetan, Thai, and Philippino neighborhoods. Orlick set off, following his nose like a middle-class Navajo tracker. Within minutes, we had met Kamala, a Tibetan chef, in a local restaurant and were discussing her favorite dried beef dishes as a girl back in her home country. As she struggled to describe the taste in her broken English, she was palpably moved. So was I. Like Click and his dream studio, Orlick was in the experience business and I was a happy paying customer.

Cash: keeping it between us

Interest rates in the US are currently just 0.25%, their lowest since President Nixon decoupled the dollar from the price of gold in 1971. Here in the UK, they are just 0.5%. Suffice to say, holding onto cash is yielding miserable returns. Sharing economy businesses are also eyeing up the underutilized cash in people's bank accounts. Compared to the derisory interest rates offered by retail banks, peer-to-peer lending sites offer depositors some comparatively mouth-watering ones. Funding Circle boasts an average return of 6.1% after fees and bad debts. US peer-to-peer lender Prosper offers 8% interest. The main catch is that loans are unsecured but, for investors looking for less risk, Germany's Auxmoney lets investors make secured loans, sometimes with the borrower's car as collateral. Accounting for defaults, Auxmoney claims that, over 7 years, loaned monies have returned 6.7%. All the lenders slice up the loaned monies between multiple borrowers to reduce risk.

For those unable to finance their credit card debt or other spending, the same platforms provide fixed-rate loans, provided that the borrower passes their various credit checks. Peer-to-peer lenders usually offer no repayment fees and better interest rates by avoiding the huge overheads of running a bank: the thousands of employees and hundreds of branches. The UK's Zopa claims to have saved borrowers more than £369 million in interest payments since it was founded in 2005. The largest company in this space, however, is the US's Lending Club. Like most peer-to-peer lenders, Lending Club assigns borrowers a credit grade that determines the level of interest rates that lenders will receive. Lending Club is now lending over $350 million every month.[14] If you are in the US and looking to refinance credit card or other debt, it may be worth a look.

Skills and services

What if you don't have a pile of cash, a little-frequented Parisian pied-à-terre, or a yacht you rarely find time to sail? If you have spare time, you can earn money doing jobs on shared labor platforms. TaskRabbit is the most well-known and well-financed of the lot, but there are countless others. Australia's Airtasker is a peer-to-peer local marketplace that lets people make money by doing tasks from repairing computers and gardening to carrying out house removals. Many marketplaces focus on specific verticals. Gigwalk specializes in sourcing temporary workers for local retail stores. Zaarly focuses on household chores and gardening. Instacart is about same-day grocery deliveries. Postmates let users get on their bikes to peddle parcels around New York, Seattle, and Washington DC. But no leisurely cups of tea for the road—the site pledges to get deliveries across town in under an hour.

The aggregation of service providers has clear benefits for the buyers of these services on the other side of the marketplaces. The competition inherent in the marketplaces pushes down prices and raises standards. On TaskRabbit, I found a TaskRabbit who had completed the time-consuming task of tracking down locally made honey in NYC and delivering it to the requester,, who harbored the belief that local honey could relieve her allergies. The payment: just $8. Peer-to-peer marketplaces that are pitched to amateur service providers are often cheaper since they tend to comprise people looking only to top up their earnings rather than earn a living exclusively through the platform. On the platforms populated by more professional users, such as Elance for freelance web developers or Zirtual for college-educated personal assistants, prices can be higher.

Time is money

Walk into the British Museum in London's bookish Bloomsbury neighborhood and you can see a "10-hour bill." It dates from 1833 and the founding of the National Equitable Labour Exchange. At the Exchange, goods were priced according to how long they took to make. The Exchange did not last—there were too many labors of love that no one wanted. But the concept of time as a currency survived. Law professor Edgar Cahn is the inventor of modern-day timebanking. Now CEO of nonprofit TimeBanks USA, Cahn came up with the idea for timebanking when he was recovering from a heart attack and told that he could only work for 2 hours a day. Cahn began thinking about how he could remain useful at the same time as getting value for himself. He formulated the simple rules of time banking. An hour of time, however spent, has the same value: a "time dollar." Babysit for an hour and you earn a time dollar. Then spend your time dollar on getting your leaking tap fixed or whatever else you might need.

Time banking grew dramatically during the recession. There are now 276 time banks in the US and 292 in the UK. One time bank in a deprived inner-city area in Glasgow, Scotland has helped to maintain a community theatre and provides gardening, tuition, and even funeral services. The US's largest time bank is the Visiting Nurse Service of New York (VNSNY). Its 3,000 members teach, cook, and clean for each other without a cent exchanged. VNSNY has seven paid employees: a very lean structure given the value of goods and services being traded. It is up to the employees to guard against freeloaders getting into debt by not giving back. For some members, the time bank offers a partial alternative to a pension and even family. "I'm saving up my hours," says Cathy Sadowski, 61, a VNSNY timebanker who lives alone in Brooklyn, New York. "You hear stories about people who get old and have no one to take care of them. I don't have to worry. If I ever got sick all I'd have to do is call the time bank."

Time Republik is the sharing economy's best-known time bank. Its website proclaims itself: "The ultimate Sharing Economy: a global Timebank where you share your skills, your talent in exchange for time!" Co-founded by two Swiss childhood friends, Time Republik is working to create one global system for timebanking, uniting the small fragmented time banks around the world. But the slickest new player in the small world of timebanking is Echo, short for the "economy of hours." Based in trendy East London, Echo focuses on B2B timebanking, allowing businesses to trade skills via the currency of "Echos" (again, 1 hour equals 1 Echo). Estonia's Bank of Happiness goes yet further, not linking work to hours but evangelizing the altruism of gifting goods and services as an end in itself. Their website has many more offers of help than requests. "That's as it should be," says founder Airi Kivi. "The bigger reward comes from giving."

The nitty-gritty: insurance, contracts and tax

The potential of share platforms to exploit idling capacity makes compelling theoretical sense. However, turning that theory into hard cash takes time and work, as Brittney Bedford knows well. JustPark may require less work than any other share platform: drivers come and go from someone's driveway and their parking fees drop into the property owner's bank account. It is "Airbnb without washing sheets" as a co-founder of Yelp put it. Still, the most successful property owners make sure they collect good reviews by responding promptly to questions. Some go far in the pursuit of happy parkers, giving free car washes or ferrying families to their ultimate destination. When considering whether a share platform is for you, ask yourself whether you have the time to provide a good service. This includes the time to acquaint yourself with any relevant insurance policies and legal documents. Is the website's insurance policy adequate or do you need your own insurance? Would freelancing breach the terms of your employment contract? Will renting out your attic breach your lease? Would renting out your company car affect the tax status of your employment benefits?

Indeed, tax is often the knottiest issue. To quote Benjamin Franklin, "in this world nothing can be said to be certain, except death and taxes." Changing either is beyond the powers of the sharing economy. Fortunately, help is at hand. 1099.is is a website that assists those earning money in the sharing economy to comply with their tax obligations. Its name comes from the 1099 tax return that freelancers submit in the US. Since freelancers get audited more often than company employees, those earning a taxable income should take no chances. 1099.is answers questions like "Are Kickstarter and Indiegogo crowdfunding perks considered charitable donations?" (Answer: "Generally not."). Or "I haven't sold anything for money but have bartered goods using an online exchange. Should I report that?" (Answer: "Bartering is an exchange of property or services and the fair market value of the property or services received in bartering must be reported in income."). The questions were crowd-sourced from users of the platforms in true sharing economy style. In time, consolidated resources like 1099.is will doubtless appear in jurisdictions outside the US.

Risky business?

However much platforms increase their trustworthiness, things can still go very wrong. In June 2011, a blogger identifying herself only as "EJ" told the world a story that was Airbnb's nightmare waiting to happen. "Three difficult days ago," wrote EJ, "I returned home from an exhausting week of business travel to an apartment that I no longer recognized. To an apartment that had been ransacked." In painstaking detail, EJ describes how guests spent a week systematically destroying her home and her identity. They smashed through cupboards to steal valuables including her grandmother's jewelry. They used her credit cards. They destroyed a hard drive containing the only copies of personal photos. They poured bleach over furniture. It is fair to say they were never aiming for a five-star review. A week later, another Airbnb victim came forward. Troy Dayton, a host in Oakland, had returned home to find crystal meth pipes in his living room. Again, the guests had stolen valuables and identity documents. As a direct result, Airbnb introduced a half million dollar insurance policy, which they upped in 2012 to a $1 million of cover.

Then in March 2014, a yet more lurid scandal broke. Unsuspecting Airbnb host, Ari Teman, received a message from "David" who wanted to stay in his apartment while visiting New York for a wedding. There was no wedding. "David" turned Teman's apartment in exclusive Chelsea into a venue for an "XXX Freak Fest" sex party. Teman, a comedian, saw the black comedy, or at least career mileage, in the publicity. "Aside from the illegal orgy destroying my apartment," he tweeted, "it was a lovely weekend." He also got up a Tumblr blog. "Dear Brian and the AirBNB team," he wrote. "Usually I am a fan of your service. However, I have a minor bone to pick with you, in that it appears my apartment was reserved for some major boning." After wiring $20,000 to Teman's account and arranging (ironically) a hotel for him, Airbnb's CTO and co-founder Nathan Blecharczyk leapt to its defense. "What's noteworthy is not the sex party, but the fact that … stuff like that rarely happens at our scale. And when I say 'our scale' … we have 150,000 people staying in other people's homes every single night."

Blecharczyk is right about the tiny statistical risk of negative incidents. A further point he could not have made without reproach is that, unpleasant as those experiences are, they are hardly life and death. Consider, in that respect, the thousands of people this year who will die in car accidents. Motorists could take the bus: research from Northwestern University shows that you are 67 times more likely to die in a car than a bus.[15] But we all still get in cars. Why? Above all, it is because we have had 150 years to get comfortable with their lethal risks. When early road locomotives arrived on British streets, a society that knew only horse-drawn transport was terrified. The 1865 Locomotive Act required locomotives to obey a 4 mph speed limit. In town centers, the speed limit was slashed to a thoroughly British and sensible 2 mph. Like driving once was, Airbnb is a higher risk way of consuming. But we should not be frightened into thinking that new risks are more dangerous than they are.

Sector-specific risks

Generalizing is itself risky. When participating in share platforms as either a buyer or a seller, users should pay close attention to the risks of that particular activity and of the specific transaction with that specific stranger. Never be afraid to follow your instincts or ask for more information. Consider, for example, the risks in peer-to-peer storage. Storers will fear for the safety of their goods. Property owners will be concerned about the contents of those boxes. Or the risks in food. No government inspector had been to visit Dan D.'s kitchen to undertake hygiene checks before I ordered my rogan josh on Cookisto. Again, do not assume that more familiar patterns of consumption are necessarily safer. Journalist Emily Badger spent days interviewing the chefs behind Mealku, a home-cooking cooperative that delivers lunches by bike to homes and offices throughout New York. "Spend enough time talking about food with these people," writes Badger, "and it starts to seem like the true risk-takers are the diners who order takeout sweet-and-sour shrimp surprise from Bob's Chinese Buffet around the corner."

The stakes are highest for borrowers of third-party vehicles. How can you know that the boat you are renting off Boatbound is properly maintained? Will it take in water in the middle of the ocean? Are there flares? Liz Fong-Jones rented out her car on RelayRides. The driver, one Patrick Fortuna, tragically never made it back. The fatal crash report discovered that Fortuna died while traveling south in a northbound lane. As the owner of the car, Fong-Jones was caught up in litigation involving other injured parties and insurance companies who were unfamiliar with the new peer-to-peer model. In the end, RelayRides' $1 million insurance policy covered Fong-Jones and the crash's surviving victims. Interestingly, Fong-Jones put her next car back onto RelayRides. "The original reason I signed up is still very much true," she says. "I don't drive the car very often and am environmentally-minded and want other people to use the car rather than buying cars of their own."

Fong-Jones understands that the sharing economy is in some ways no different from the old economy. Those who want to play the game must accept the risk of injury. It may be some consolation that at least they are not the only risk-takers.

Notes

1   Gartside, David, Silverstone, Yaarit, Farley, Catherine, and Cantrell, Susan, *Trends Reshaping the Future of HR: The Rise of the Extended Workforce* (Accenture, 2013): http://www.accenture.com/SiteCollectionDocuments/PDF/Accenture-Future-of-HR-Rise-Extended-Workforce.pdf.

2   Muhammad Yunus in conversation with Paul Solman on PBS NewsHour, November 22nd, 2006: http://www.pbs.org/newshour/bb/business-july-dec06-yunus_11-22/.

3   An Accenture report in 2013 noted that more than a million consumers and small businesses in Germany generate their own electricity: http://nstore.accenture.com/acn_com/PDF/Accenture-New-Energy-Consumer-Handbook-2013.pdf. This is claimed to contribute approximately 8% to Germany's total energy output, as quoted by Mathilde Richter, Agence France Presse: http://www.businessinsider.com/homemade-electricity-is-catching-on-in-germany-2014-5.

4   Data taken from *The State of The Sharing Economy*, a research report compiled by Opinium on behalf of The People who Share in 2013: http://www.thepeoplewhoshare.com/tpws/assets/File/TheStateoftheSharingEconomy_May2013_FoodSharingintheUK.pdf.

5   Taken from a 2013 report by housing charity Shelter and quoted by BBC London, January 8th, 2013: http://www.bbc.co.uk/news/uk-england-london-20943576.

6   United Nations data in 2005 showed that 50.0% of Benin's population lived below the international poverty line of US$1.25 per day: http://www.un.org/esa/socdev/rwss/docs/2010/chapter2.pdf. More recent data in 2011 from the World Bank found that 36.2% of Benin's population was living below the national poverty line: http://data.worldbank.org/indicator/SI.POV.NAHC/countries/BJ?display=graph.

7   *Deskmag* is an online magazine about co-working that conducts annual surveys into the sector. http://www.deskmag.com/en/2500-coworking-spaces-4-5-per-day-741.

8   Airbnb vs Hotels: A Price Comparison, a 2013 study from economics blog Priceonomics: http://priceonomics.com/hotels/.

9   Data quoted by Jessica Reeder in Captain Up: Cruzin Launches P2P Boat Sharing (*Shareable*, February 5th, 2013): http://www.shareable.net/blog/captain-up-cruzin-launches-p2p-boat-sharing.

10 Data taken from Mark Hyman, MD, How Eating at Home Can Save Your Life, (*Huffington Post*, September 1st, 2011): http://www.huffingtonpost.com/dr-mark-hyman/family-dinner-how_b_806114.html.

11 Jones, Martin, *Feast: Why Humans Share Food* (Oxford University Press, 2008).

12 Quoted by Jonathan Bloom in Americans Waste Enough Food to Fill a 90,000-seat Football Stadium Every Day – What Can We Do About It? (*Alternet*, September 15th, 2011): http://www.alternet.org/story/152429/americans_waste_enough_food_to_fill_a_90,000-seat_football_stadium_every_day_--_what_can_we_do_about_it.

13 Over 16 million Americans are "very food-insecure" according the US Department of Agriculture, meaning they cannot afford enough to eat: http://www.marketplace.org/topics/business/maps-food-stamps/more-15-americans-go-hungry.

14 Data taken from the peer-to-peer lending data site, LendStats.com. http://www.lendstats.com/.

15 Savage, Ian, Comparing the fatality risks in United States transportation across modes and over time (*Research in Transportation Economics*, July 2013). Savage finds that, "Relative to mainline trains, buses and commercial aviation the risk was 17, 67, and 112 times greater, respectively": http://www.sciencedirect.com/science/article/pii/S0739885912002156.

3 Founders

Visionaries and Doers

Just a few years after the greatest downturn since the Great Depression, it felt like the economy was healthier than ever. At least in some places. I was perched on a stool in a sleek, candle-lit San Francisco bar surrounded by 30-somethings drinking wine at $15 a glass. I was there to meet Shelby Clark, the founder of RelayRides. The last time we had met, he had pulled up in a bright yellow convertible. This time, Clark went one better. He strolled into the bar in a flared orange suit, holding aloft a giant disco ball. With his handlebar moustache immaculately curled above his huge and infectious smile, Clark explained that he had just come from RelayRides' Halloween party.

Clark was at Harvard Business School from 2008 to 2010 when the world was being turned upside. He was one of the entrepreneurs who found history on his side—or rather put history on his side. Yet Clark's journey to founding what is now the world's largest peer-to-peer car rental business started much earlier. I wanted to probe not only Clark's journey, but also the journeys of the entrepreneurs who had founded and run the world's most successful sharing economy businesses. Part of my reasoning was selfish: as a CEO myself, I wanted to learn from their successes and spare myself the pain of their mistakes. Some of their lessons would apply to any person running any company. Others spoke more specifically to the challenges of building a sharing economy platform.

Shelby Clark, founder, RelayRides

Clark's career started in humdrum fashion as a management consultant. Keen to expand his horizons, he took advantage of a nonprofit fellowship run by his consultancy at Kiva.org, the peer-to-peer microfinance platform. Today, Kiva has made half a billion loans and lifted millions of people out of poverty. But Clark joined as Kiva's sixth employee during its "really, really early days" when Kiva had arranged just $200,000 of "microcredit" loans. Before he knew it, Clark was on a plane to Uganda, where he stumbled upon Kiva's first major case of fraud. A Ugandan pastor overseeing the loans was suspected of stealing a quarter of a million dollars. Clark unwittingly found himself caught up in a scandal of international proportions. As the truth unraveled, not everyone was happy. Clark later fled the country, fearing for his safety. "It was pretty wild," he told me with a grin.

Kiva's loans to micro-entrepreneurs across the developing world awakened Clark to the potential of entrepreneurship to improve lives. Kiva's small team seemed to prove anthropologist Margaret Mead's famous edict, "Never doubt that a small group of thoughtful, committed citizens can change the world; indeed, it's the only thing that ever has." Although Kiva is nonprofit, some of the most impactful organizations it partners with are for-profits. The experience of working with them taught Clark that "A properly directed business can have a huge social impact, possibly bigger and more sustained than a charity or a nonprofit." Kiva inspired him to start his own business but there was just one problem: *where to start?* As Clark put it, "I didn't have any ideas or money or partners or things that might be helpful. So I thought, maybe I'll go to business school." Clark enrolled at Harvard Business School: a man in search of a big idea.

"There was definitely a light bulb moment," Clark told me. "Thanksgiving Day, 2008." Clark was going to visit his cousins and he needed a car. The closest Zipcar was two and a half miles away. "It was a frickin' awful winter day in Boston," he recalled. "It was snowing and the freezing wind was coming from every direction and I'm biking through the snow and sleet to get to this damned car. Meanwhile, I'm passing all these cars that are covered in snow. They clearly hadn't been driven in weeks." *What if there was a platform,* he wondered, *where you could rent out normal people's cars?* Clark searched online. No one was doing peer-to-peer car rentals. He delved deeper and discovered that the barrier was insurance: no policy had ever been written to allow car rentals between neighbors. Undeterred, Clark began working on an entirely new kind of car insurance on which the future of his new business hinged.

It was an emotional rollercoaster. "On many days," Clark said, "I'd fly to the sky and drop to the floor in the course of an hour." Once, Clark was sat nervously in Harvard's auditorium awaiting the results of whether RelayRides had advanced to the finals of the university's prestigious "Business Plan Competition." Behind the scenes, Clark's new insurance policy was months behind schedule and the founding team—all of whom apart from Clark later quit—was in turmoil. While Clark sat there, he got "the most abrupt email of my life" from an investor. *"You must shut down RelayRides immediately,"* it read, *"due to your failure to keep a team together and your inability to keep investors informed."* The next second, the auditorium reverberated with the word: "RELAYRIDES!" They were through. Moments later, a journalist from *The Economist* phoned: he wanted to feature RelayRides in their next edition. In all, it took 18 months for the long-awaited insurance policy to come through. Clark launched RelayRides a month after graduating from Harvard.

Lesson #1: finding a startup idea

How did he do that? He had the resolve to keep fighting for his vision and the charisma to attract employees and investors. But before any of that would have been possible, he focused on what he knew was lacking: the big idea. Like many aspiring entrepreneurs, Clark sorely lacked one of those. However, unlike the vast majority of them, Clark did everything in his power to maximize his statistical chances of finding that elusive idea. How did he do that?

Firstly, Clark forsook safety—in his case, life as a management consultant— and embraced a riskier, less certain future. Indeed, almost all the world's top technology entrepreneurs are dropouts: from Zuckerberg, Gates, and Larry Ellison to Michael Dell and PayPal and Tesla founder, Elon Musk. Without a safety net, Clark was putting helpful pressure on himself to find an idea.

Secondly, Clark physically moved by relocating to Uganda with Kiva. Anecdotally, we have long known that travel "broadens the mind" and that a new perspective can help us come up with ideas. Now neuroscientists understand that exposing the brain to new environments can forge fresh neural pathways and connections that may increase our creativity.[1]

Thirdly, to quote Paul Graham, the founder of elite startup accelerator program Y Combinator, "Live in the future, then build what's missing." Clark was living in the future by using Zipcar as an early adopter. RelayRides' vision came from what Zipcar was missing: the convenience of rental cars on every street.

Fourthly, Clark surrounded himself by high achievers who could be helpful and inspiring, in his case by taking an MBA. It is often said that the best thing about an MBA is not the course content so much as the networking opportunities that it can provide. His new contacts gave him ready access to human and financial capital.

Finally, Clark stayed focused on finding that idea. Alertness made him stitch together his knowledge of car-sharing with his learning at Kiva, that online platforms can empower entrepreneurship. RelayRides has since turned any car owner into a potential entrepreneur. Had Clark not been actively looking to start a business, he might not have thought about renting a snow-covered car. The billion-dollar idea will not find you. You have to go hunting.

Manish Chandra, co-founder and CEO, Poshmark

Across a boardroom table in Menlo Park, Silicon Valley, a short walk from Facebook's sprawling campus at 1 Hacker Way, Manish Chandra looks me intensely in the eye. He has the measured confidence of a seasoned entrepreneur who knows what needs to be done. Chandra sold his last venture, Kaboodle, to media giant Hearst for $30 million. These days, he is in pursuit of a much bigger exit as CEO of Poshmark: a community of women who buy and sell used clothes from each other. "Shop the closets of women across America—and sell yours too!" promises its slick mobile app.

The business is built entirely around mobile. Chandra described to me how before 2010 there was no easy way for women to trade fashion with each other. But with the iPhone 4's retina display and high-quality camera, *"finally* you had a platform that could be used for quick merchandising, quick browsing and quick transactions." Buyers can shop anywhere and anytime. Sellers snap a photo of their second-hand threads and apply an Instagram-style filter that gives the app what Chandra calls a "magazine-like experience." Once their item has sold, Poshmark emails them a $4.99 "PoshPost" USPS shipping label to slap on their package.

The app aims to create a fun, social experience that is as addictive as Facebook, a place where women go to discuss clothes as much as buy them. Poshmark is an example of so-called "social commerce": a commerce experience built on social interactions. Its social nature reaches a crescendo at the virtual "Posh Parties," where up to 250,000 items from tens of thousands of users' closets are chucked into a vast virtual shop and women scramble over the best things in real time. Trading through the app is so easy that when Poshmark held real-world parties for its members, they stopped bringing clothes: physically browsing and transporting garments was more hassle than buying and selling online. The startup also runs "PoshFest," a 2-day Las Vegas extravaganza where members of their community can meet in person.

But Poshmark's early days were far humbler. While in the private beta phase, Poshmark hand-picked its first 100 users and then asked each woman to refer a friend. Its user base was tiny but encompassed deeply engaged browsers of each other's closets. Once it had seeded the platform with this initial community, Poshmark built out its constantly updating "newsfeed" of merchandise. Like the Facebook newsfeed, it uses machine learning to show more relevant content over time. Poshmark becomes like a digital personal shopper that is unique to every woman, understanding their tastes better than their friends do, better perhaps than they themselves consciously understand it. Chandra's job is to surface the right item at the right time for the right woman: no easy feat when over $1 million of clothes is uploaded onto Poshmark every day.

Lesson #2: target a big market

When I asked Chandra what the sharing economy meant to him, it was not surprising that he evoked it in terms of the mountain of inventory that he deals with at Poshmark. He is clearly fascinated by the mammoth dormant value in people's wardrobes. "We've all been buying and consuming—*not even consuming*—just buying resources at a high velocity," he told me. "People are now looking at those resources and realizing that there's a huge amount of value without producing more. The sharing economy is an attempt to re-vector distribution of an overproduced society. We've built more homes than we need, we've produced more fashion than we need, we have *way* more cars than we need."

Chandra's amiable smile straightens when he starts to talk numbers. "In the United States alone, we consume about $350 billion of fashion a year. Let's assume 75–80% of that is women's fashion. That means the women of America are putting over a trillion dollars' worth of fashion every three years into their closets. By any estimate, somewhere between 25–50% of it is never worn. That means several hundred billion dollars of fashion every three years is never or seldom worn." Chandra moved through the numbers with fluency and conviction, traits that have helped him to pull in $16 million of investment. Clearly, he is right: there is big money in fashion. Out of the world's 20 richest people, none made their fortunes in oil, real estate, metals or mining while two—the founders of H&M and Zara—made them in fashion.[2]

Chandra's route into this huge market goes deeper than iPhones and Posh Parties. "Poshmark is a platform powered by love," he told me. "And if you focus on love, the money comes in a virtuous cycle." For Chandra, love is the feeling when women wear their most cherished clothes and see their clothes cherished by other women. When they sell items that they love, he told me, women are left with "a hole in their heart that they need to refill. Because fashion, at its core, is about love." I catch Chandra's assistant looking reverently at him. It was the look of someone who understands that her employer is trying to do something as big as change the way women shop.

Andy Ruben, co-founder and CEO, yerdle

One day, Andy Ruben's friend moaned to him about needing to buy his son a new pair of shin pads. For the friend, it seemed like only yesterday that his kid had outgrown his last pair. Ruben realized that all of his friends must be buying new shin pads for their growing children. Meanwhile, countless shin pads in larger sizes had to be gathering dust in other families' homes. Shin pads were just the tip of the iceberg of the 251 million tons of garbage that the US Environmental Protection Agency estimates Americans create each year.[3] Ruben's hunger to end this pattern of buying and binning and to unite it with a cheap, convenient way of getting goods led to the founding of yerdle with fellow entrepreneur and environmentalist Adam Werbach.

A gifting platform, yerdle allows people to get anything from bread-making machines to kids' clothes. It is like a huge communal attic without the dust and spiders. "Why shop when you can share?" runs yerdle's tagline. yerdle works by giving users credits when they join that they can spend to get free goods from anyone else. Similar to eBay, users can either enter an auction for an item and bid a certain number of credits, or pay a "Get It Now" price in credits. When users list items or refer a friend, they earn more credits. yerdle focuses on two segments. The first is urban and tech-savvy, the type of person who might use Couchsurfing. The second is the thrifty, community-focused mum in Middle America who can always drive to pick up items in her car. Ruben spent 10 years living in Arkansas and thinks that, in the long run, yerdle will achieve greater adoption there than in California.

Lesson #3: know your market

If preparation is everything, few can better Ruben. He has spent an entire career working for the conglomerates that yerdle is now trying to disrupt. Ruben served 20 years in consumer products and retail at P&G and at Walmart, where he ran global strategy and oversaw the integration of stores and online services as the giant led its push into "omni-channel" retail. Ruben bubbled with sector knowledge as he described to me how retailing goes through a complete transformation every 30 or so years and how Amazon—still not yet a top 10 global retailer—will rise to become the top retailer within a decade. "The cards for the current game have already been dealt," Ruben told me. "They will play out and the winner will be Amazon who operate on information rather than distribution." With yerdle, he is looking much further ahead. "We're much more interested in *the hand after this hand* which is about social commerce."

Unlike Poshmark, yerdle's take on social commerce is about getting things from those in close proximity to you. Based on their prelaunch research,

Ruben believes that 25% of the $1 trillion spent each year on durable goods in the US could be met through items that are sat doing nothing in someone's closet or garage. Of course, listing undervalued or unused second-hand goods online is not new. But as Ruben notes, "Craigslist, eBay and Freecycle have scaled the supply and demand side but not the social side. They were pre-mobile and pre-social." Like most of the businesses in this chapter, yerdle is conceived for a mobile age and built with community in mind. Ruben told me about the turntable he himself got from yerdle. "Every time I look at it, I think about the phenomenal guy I got it from, an engineer at Change.org. We're still in touch."

Ruben imagines a world where getting goods from people who live around you is almost as normal as buying new ones. "At the moment, Amazon shows: 'New and used: 20 items'. In 2018, it will show: 'New, used and shared', shared being items that can be borrowed or got for free. Vastly more items will be moving laterally." Ruben also expects pervasive wearable technology to reduce the friction in peer-to-peer sharing. Hardware like Google Glass, Google's Internet-enabled glasses, could automatically value your table as $30 or 300 credits as you stare at it. Ruben predicts that shareable items will be forward-deployed in pick-up points alongside new items as the e-commerce giants and startups alike get more adept at using data to predict what people need—and when and where they will need it.

Doing his time in industry has given Ruben a deep insight into the sector that he is now playing in with his sharing business. Almost as importantly, it has given him the gravitas to raise money from a syndicate of well-respected angel investors who are backing him to realize that vision. I'm not suggesting you do 20 years. But if you want to shake up a sector, do some time in that sector. You'll be able to look someone in the eye when you tell them that it is broken. Moreover, startups, as we are about to see, are almost never overnight successes. A "just do it" attitude is great if you have the skills and expertise to execute at speed. If you don't, think about waiting until you know your market. Ironically, it might save you time.

Anthony Eskinazi, founder and CPO, JustPark

In 2006, Anthony Eskinazi was trying to park for a baseball game at the Giants stadium in San Francisco. When he drove past a tantalizingly empty driveway, he knew there was an opportunity for a website that would let property owners rent out their driveways. He did not park in that empty driveway that day. But he returned home to London, taught himself to code, and released a basic website called ParkatmyHouse.com. Anthony's plan: run the fledgling company alongside his day job at Deloitte, the top accountancy firm where he had just started his training. It was a tougher juggling act than Anthony anticipated. He found himself rushing out of accountancy exams to take calls from journalists. For before he knew it, the newly released ParkatmyHouse.com was appearing in national and international press. The normally sober British newspaper *The Guardian* proclaimed the "groundbreaking scheme" under the headline "Park for £10 and make me a millionaire."

Six weeks into his new job, Anthony quit, resigning himself to life at his parent's house for the foreseeable future. It was never going to be easy. Firstly, Anthony was a sole founder. "If I could go back," he says, "I wish I had a co-founder. It's very rare you have a business you can sell in a few years. Being able to share the ups and downs and excitement with someone else is so important." Secondly, Anthony was starting an online marketplace: a notoriously hard task as it involves building supply and demand at once and overcoming the "chicken and egg" problem. In Anthony's case, that meant how to attract driveway owners when there were barely any drivers to rent them, and drivers when there were barely any driveways on offer. Thirdly, Anthony had never founded a company before. In fact, he had barely even worked in one before. He was just 23. For 5 years, Anthony plugged away: writing every line of code, answering every customer support ticket, often while holding down a second job.

Lesson #4: keep going ...

"For the first two years," says Joe Gebbia, a co-founder of Airbnb, "we had dismal traction, no growth at all. The numbers would have told you to quit and go work on something else." Gebbia and his co-founders kept going and the rest is history. But persevering is far tougher for a sole founder without that companionship. I asked Anthony what kept him going. "In the early days, it was the PR." The press brought the first customers and messages of support from as far away as China and

Australia. When most entrepreneurs have the sneaking suspicion that they might be mad—they often are, after all, attempting something that has never been done before—the stories validated the concept in Anthony's own mind. Finally, the PR was morale-boosting and meant that, in the eyes of others, his new venture was a success. When the company was turning over almost nothing, it was something to cherish. "I'm not sure this company would exist if it wasn't for PR," says Anthony. "Each PR hit was a giant pat on the back. And you need those in the early days." But PR can only do so much to scale a business and its fortifying effects on morale wear off. *What then?*

"I always wanted to do my own thing. I didn't think I could have much impact working in a big company." Even from the early days, Anthony could see he was making a difference. One of ParkatmyHouse.com's early customers was not a house but a church. It was making thousands of pounds a year (the church is still on the platform and has made over £200,000) that was paying for communal meals for homeless people and substance abuse clinics in an area of London that suffers from major social deprivation. Something was taking shape and Anthony's entrepreneurial instinct kept him hungry. He had always been wired that way. After university, he started a website selling second-hand games consoles and an online gaming affiliate business that exploited loopholes in the referral programs of gambling websites. Anthony got his first taste for how easy it could be to make money online when he made $1,600 in 4 hours. The party ended when George Bush signed in antigambling legislation. However, Anthony's affiliate earnings funded the round-the-world trip on which he would have the idea for ParkatmyHouse.com.

But still it was not easy. In 2010, Anthony was at his lowest ebb. ParkatmyHouse.com was making just £1,000 a month and there was no money to recruit any help. As a junior and self-taught developer, he was bogged down trying to build a complex availability system to manage the bookings at people's driveways. Anthony estimates that he burned out on 10 separate occasions through working relentless 18-hour days. "I remember waking up one particular morning and I realized that I physically could not move my body. Eventually, I got myself in front of the computer and my fingers could not type. For about 2 weeks after that, I found myself in this weird, dream-like state, unable to concentrate. It was my body saying, 'don't do this to yourself.' I was working way harder than investment bankers and I wasn't even getting paid!" Little did he know, the business was about to turn a corner.

By 2011, Anthony had hustled his startup to over 100,000 users and put it on the radar of venture capitalists and major companies. One day, he got an email from BMW asking if he would like to discuss "an innovative project that may really get some traction." The email signed off, "It would be best to have a little chat about this." "It was ridiculously cool," says Anthony, "that BMW wanted to jump on a plane and meet me." Within weeks, Anthony was in BMW's headquarters negotiating a term sheet across a boardroom table with their new $100 million venture capital fund. Today, ParkatmyHouse, rebranded as JustPark, is the global market leader in booking parking online and one of the world's largest sharing economy businesses. In 2014, the company raised further investment from Index Ventures, the venture capital firm behind Skype, MySQL, and Dropbox, and more than a million drivers park via its mobile applications.

James Reinhart, co-founder and CEO, thredUP

It was 2010 and James Reinhart was standing in front of his wardrobe, staring in disbelief. It was a collection of clothes that had taken him years to assemble and cost thousands of dollars. Yet for all that time and money, there was not a single thing that Reinhart wanted to wear. It was a first-world problem: clothes in perfectly good condition had become junk. *Why had he not got rid of them?* Reinhart knew that he could sell his second-hand clothes at consignment stores or on eBay but that felt like a lot of hassle: photographing every last hoodie, answering questions about every old t-shirt, and mailing packages all around the country. Reinhart just didn't need the money badly enough for that rigmarole. All he wanted was a solution to his overcrowded wardrobe and a fair financial return for his labeled clothes. He reasoned that millions of other people might want the same. Reinhart's suspicions were confirmed when he asked his friends and found that about half of them did not wear about half the stuff in their closets either.

Reinhart launched thredUP, his new startup trading men's and women's shirts. It bombed. So Reinhart relaunched with a focus on children's clothes. His prediction: as kids grew out of their clothes, liberating space in their closets would be more of a priority. It turned out that mums also wanted to use the site to buy their clothes. So Reinhart moved back into womenswear. Next, Reinhart tested a "consignment model." Rather than asking sellers to organize their own dispatch, thredUP began posting them a plastic bag. Sellers stuff the bag with their clothes and leave it on their porch for collection. thredUP sorts the clothes in their warehouse, photographs them, and pays the sellers up front for any clothes they list on the website. In this way, Reinhart has lowered the barriers for his members—typically, rushed-off-their-feet mums—to free up their closets. Over 3,000 of thredUP's green polka dot bags now arrive on American doorsteps every day. Reinhart's vision is very large and very simple: a thredUP laundry bag for unwanted clothes in every single home in America.

Lesson #5: … but know when to pivot

Sitting in his boardroom above San Francisco's Market Street, the good-looking, spiky-haired Reinhart, who looks not unlike a retired 30-something member of a boy band, paraphrased a Larry Page mantra: "Being 2–3x better than an already existing alternative is not enough. You need to be *10x* better." In pursuit of that high bar, Reinhart restlessly tested new hypotheses and pluckily switched to a consignment model even when the startup had hundreds of thousands of members. Now with well over a million members and as the US's largest online consignment stores for kid's clothing, thredUP has continued to evolve. Obsessed with data, Reinhart analyzed the time it was taking for items on the website to sell. A pattern emerged: expensive, high-end clothes were going the quickest. The marketplace had spoken. In 2014, thredUP launched its "X Collection": their play for the second-hand women's designer clothes market.

Sometimes, it is wrong to just keep going. In one of the canonical texts of startup ideology, *The Lean Startup*, Eric Ries introduced a scientific methodology to founding and scaling startups. Some of Ries' concepts have become so widely adopted that they are now firmly startup clichés. Chief among them is his notion of "the pivot": "a structured course correction designed to test a new fundamental hypothesis about the product, strategy, and engine of growth."[4] Another graduate of Harvard Business School, Reinhart knew that many of the most successful companies—tech and non-tech) alike—had taken these radical corrections. YouTube was originally a video dating site. Samsung started life selling noodles and dried fish. Groupon was initially a platform called The Point that was about coordinating social protests before it set itself on a course that would make it, by many metrics, the fastest growing company in history. Reinhart has built his business with pivots. "If you want to build a super-high-growth business," he says, "don't be afraid to shake things up."

Robin Chase, founder, Zipcar

Zipcar is one sharing economy company that needs little introduction. After getting people into communal car-sharing at scale, the next task that Zipcar founder Robin Chase set herself was getting people into each other's cars through her new current startup, Buzzcar—a French competitor to RelayRides. Renting a car from a neighbor was a task she considered that the American consumer was unready for at the turn of the millennium when Zipcar was founded. Others did not agree. When she was working on Zipcar, one man emailed her every week pleading with her to apply the Zipcar model to the excess capacity that already existed. But back then Chase felt that "we were changing enough variables." Chase's endeavors in shared mobility go yet further: she has also founded social carpooling site GoLoco.

Chase was in London to speak on a panel on the future of mobility at The Royal Institution, the elegant neoclassical building that had been the talking shop for Britain's greatest scientists for more than 200 years. I met her that afternoon in the lobby of her hotel in London's exclusive Mayfair. Short-haired with a youthful complexion that belies her 50-something years, she speaks about ideas with the intense excitability of someone far younger. Though not quite Peter Pan, it is easy to imagine her as a young, strong-willed MIT student. Yet for all that, Chase has the world-weary look of someone who has battled hard for her success. When I ask her to describe the experience of founding a global brand, her response is, "I tell a story of disappointment," quickly countering that, "there is a lack of failure talk from successful entrepreneurs."

Chase took me back over 13 years to Zipcar's founding in Cambridge, Massachusetts. To the outside world, the new startup had the aura of an incredible success. It had extensive, glowing press not only in Boston but all around the world. "Pretty much from day one," Chase told me, "we had cars on the road and happy customers." On the surface, all appeared to be well. It was 2000 and by September of that year, Chase felt that there was enough "critical mass" to assess the unit economics underpinning their radical new business model. Back then, Zipcar's back-end systems were so rudimentary that Chase had to review all of the paper booking slips manually. It was the moment of truth and there was trouble brewing.

Lesson #6: be honest

Chase finished the analysis in mid-October, 2 weeks from closing their Series A fundraising. The results horrified her. Zipcar's revenue was 50% lower than she had projected in their business plan for the new investors. Still working out of her house, she described to me how she, "went into [her] bedroom, closed the door and wept." Not only did Chase feel she was letting down her customers, but with all the favorable press in Boston's renowned newspapers, it also felt like the city of Boston itself was expecting. After 2 hours alone in her bedroom, Chase's staff came nervously knocking. Zipcar had 400 members who had joined on the basis of a price pledge. Some of their members had already sold their cars. The team concluded that they needed to hike their daily price by 25% to survive. Chase sent the bad news email in the middle of the night to minimize the torrent of abuse. The next day, she arrived at work, "crushed and tortured, anticipating the worst."

"19 for you. 2 against!" shouted out one of her colleagues cheerfully. Her customers had been overwhelmingly supportive of her honesty. Some replied telling her they had thought that it had been too cheap to begin with. As for the "2 against"? Chase telephoned them. Neither left Zipcar and went on to become one of the company's greatest ambassadors, doing countless press interviews over the ensuing years. Three months later, Zipcar's insurance premium rose and Chase had to raise the prices yet again. "I tell entrepreneurs they have to be intellectually honest," Chase told me. "No one knew the price of a Zipcar because no one had ever priced it before." Chase learned that, deep down, people root for the underdog, all the more so if they share your vision. Respond to their respect with honesty. In any case, in a world that is more transparent by the hour, lies and half-truths will always catch up with you in the end.

Giles Andrews, co-founder and CEO, Zopa

Zopa was the world's first peer-to-peer lender. Borrowers can get a loan to buy a car, finance a wedding, or repay a credit card debt with no early repayment fees. Lenders, ranging from young people interested in the concept of peer-to-peer finance who might lend just £10, to retired people with large nest eggs lending hundreds of thousands of pounds, can earn higher returns than they would at a high street bank. Zopa finds the "ZOPA" between these two counter-parties: a term Andrews learnt in business school that is short for the "zone of possible agreement." If, for example, a lender is happy to receive an interest rate above 5% and a borrower is happy to pay up 7%, then their ZOPA is between 5% and 7%. To diversify the risk from defaulting borrowers to the lender's capital, Zopa carves it up between numerous borrowers.

Zopa makes money by charging lenders 1% of their loans and charging a fee to the borrower. Andrews claims that it has lower default rates than all the major UK high street banks. This is partly a function, he believes, of its curation of a community of responsible borrowers and the greater sense of obligation that is felt to repay a crowd of individuals compared to a faceless institutional lender. Andrews told me that some borrowers have made a point of repaying their Zopa loan in full before declaring themselves insolvent. For the same reason, he told me that they recover roughly twice as much bad debt as a bank. It all seemed to make sense. Just one problem: *who in their right mind would trust their hard-earned cash to some startup with a funny name?*

Lesson #7: compete where you can

Andrews needed to convince people that they could and should trust their money—potentially their life savings—to an unfamiliar business with an unfamiliar business model. He also had to persuade lenders to trust the borrowers whose responsibility it was to repay their money with interest. "Lack of trust was the biggest single obstacle we faced when we were a tiny little business operating from grotty little offices," Andrews told me from across a meeting room table in their now distinctly ungrotty office in the City of London. When Andrews co-founded the company in 2005, he realized that banks enjoyed what he calls "hard trust": they were "big buildings with a vault in basement" that people trusted to keep their money safe. Andrews knew that Zopa could never compete with that.

Yet the banks had an Achilles heel: Zopa's research told them that people did not believe that banks acted in their best interests. Banks were out for themselves. So, in the absence of a track record, Andrews focused on what he calls "soft trust." It meant talking to people in jargon-free language rather than corporate speak. It meant stripping out lengthy terms and conditions that require a law degree to understand. Zopa also worked diligently to build a community with early adopters by running uncensored forums (Andrews told me he has only kicked out "a couple" of users in 9 years for using offensive language). He recalled with a flush of delight when, early in his company's history, he read a forum comment from a woman that said she trusted Zopa more than her bank. Her comment began, "I've worked in the banking sector for over 20 years."

Then Zopa got its big break: part luck, part function of a system that was respectable on the outside but—as Andrews knew—dysfunctional within. Two years after Zopa was founded, exposure to US subprime debt led to the collapse of Northern Rock and the first run on a UK bank in 150 years. Suddenly, sane people were arguing that trusting your money to a bank might be no wiser than stashing it beneath a mattress. That "hard trust" began to evaporate. Andrews describes the crisis as a "fantastic own goal for the banks." Money started flowing to Zopa, and from those deposits it built a track record that attracted more capital. To date, people have lent over $1 billion to each other through Zopa and it has more than 2% of the UK unsecured personal loan market. I asked Andrews where he wants to take Zopa. "I want my children," he said, "to think that borrowing money from a P2P lender is as natural as going to an ATM."

Martin Varsavsky, founder and CEO, Fon

Even the most unlikely of assets can be shared. Fon is shared wifi. Fon members who share their bandwidth can roam the world for free using Fon's giant network of 13 million wifi hotspots. Their wifi signal is shared via a special router, the "Fonera," or via an increasing number of other routers that have the same functionality built in. These clever routers split a wireless signal in two. One slice is prioritized for home use, the second slice is shared with other Fon members, and between the two slices is a secure firewall. Newer Foneras even support Facebook login, allowing users to share their wifi with their Facebook friends. Fon initially called its shared wifi model "Linus" after Linus Torvalds, the architect of the open source Linux operating system. Nonsharing members buy wifi passes to access the shared network.

The man behind this audacious venture is seasoned Argentine entrepreneur, Martin Varsavsky. By the age of 26, Varsavsky had developed 50,000 square meters of industrial buildings in Manhattan. He next founded a biotechnology company that pioneered the development of HIV testing. He has also founded a slew of other companies in the telecoms sector, two of which he floated and another of which he sold to Deutsche Telekom for $800 million. I found a way into Varsavsky's carefully managed schedule for a Skype. I asked him about what attracted him to models of sharing. "My general thinking at the time was that we live in a world in which benefits are only accrued through economic growth and the endless consumption of resources, and that there had to be other ways that are of more benefit to people," he said. "Think of a marina full of boats. How frequently do those boats go out?" Indeed, Varsavsky uses a service called YachtPlus to share his own super yacht with other co-owners.

Lesson #8: close big strategic partnerships

When Varsavsky was starting Fon, he realized that there was a major obstacle to getting people to share wifi: it was not theirs to share. ISPs limited the use of that wifi to one user. Varsavsky knew his strategy had to be to "convince the people blocking you that sharing is good *for them."* *Why would a telecoms provider want to partner with a peer-to-peer player that could become a competitor?* Fon demonstrated that by giving wifi to the telcos' customers outside their homes, the telcos could reduce churn as well as the abandonment of fixed-line for purely mobile Internet usage. "We have stopped that trend," says Varsavsky. "We have made fixed more useful." Fon also lets mobile operators offload cellular capacity to its distributed network, saving them on costly infrastructure investments to keep up with their customers' growing data demands.

"It turns out," continues Varsavsky, "that sharing is accretive, that is actually creates value." Rather than working on the slower task of bringing about regulatory change, Varsavsky took the quicker route of proving to companies that it was in their best interests to collaborate. Instead of each company competing for the biggest slice of the pie, Varsavsky convinced them that together they could create a much bigger pie. Fon itself has had most of its success not through the Linus model of sharing wifi but by leasing it via its wifi passes. As a result, the entire business has changed. Originally a not-for-profit focused on sharing, Fon has become the world's largest wifi network through the short-term rental of bandwidth. "Purely sharing efforts are altruistic and sound beautiful," says Varsavsky, "but whether we like it or not, the profit motive is the main engine for a lot of activity on this planet."

Once it became clear that rental rather than pure sharing of wifi was the model that would scale, Fon ended up "sleeping with the enemy," as Varsavsky jokes with some of the world's largest telecommunications companies. Fon's largest partnership to date is with Britain's BT. As a result of taking strategic investment from BT, Fon's software is now incorporated into BT's routers and BT's broadband customers get access to Fon's network when they are out the house. Fon has pulled off similar deals with Deutsche Telekom, Japan's SoftBank, and Russia's MTC. "We succeeded," says Varsavsky, "because we found a way for everyone to benefit: the consumer, the telcos and Fon." Today, Fon is on its way to cloaking the planet in Internet.

Nathan Blecharczyk, co-founder and CTO, Airbnb

Joe Gebbia and Brian Chesky were two jobless friends living together when they received a terrifying letter from their landlord. "Your rent," read the letter, "is now 25% higher." For the broke Chesky, the maths did not look good: his next rent payment would be $1,150 and he had $1,000 in his account. He had days to find a solution when the two noticed all the unused space in their living room. *What if someone would pay to sleep there?* Gebbia had just been camping and had an airbed. They blew it up and squeezed in another two airbeds and came up with the concept of "airbed and breakfast": cheap accommodation on airbeds with a no-frills breakfast of Pop-Tarts. Two days later, www.airbedandbreakfast.com was live. But they realized they had another problem: how to get people to the site.

As luck would have it, there was an international design conference about to hit town and the recommended hotels on the conference website were booked up. Chesky and Gebbia emailed design bloggers who covered the story. The next day they had emails, even résumés, from people pleading to stay at their new concept of airbed and breakfast. Six days later, their first guests arrived: a young man from India, a 35-year-old woman from Boston, and a father of five Mormon from Utah. It was an "amazing social experiment," recalls Chesky. They took their guests to the Golden Gate Bridge and for burritos in the Mission. The three guests entered as strangers and left as friends. They formed such a bond that 2 years later, Chesky and Gebbia received another letter. Their Indian guest, Amol, had sent them invitations to his wedding.

With old roommate Nate Blecharczyk as their third and technical co-founder, they planned to launch the business with a bang at South by Southwest in Austin, Texas. A geeky tech conference and drunken playground rolled into one, it is where Twitter and Foursquare got their big breaks. South by Southwest's concentration of media and money has the potential to catapult a startup to the top of the hype tree. The idea was sound: visitors to the crammed city would choose a cheap Airbnb apartment over Austin's hotels and their jacked-up rates. In the event, Airbnb got two bookings. One of the two was Chesky's. The co-founders spotted another chance with the Democratic National Convention in Denver in August 2008. Barack Obama was the star attraction as 100,000 people headed to a city with 20,000 rooms. Again, they wrote to the national press and were widely covered. Again, they thought they had made it. Again they hadn't.

After a surge in online traffic and a spike in their website's analytics report so exciting that they even telephoned their mums, the team entered what Gebbia jokingly calls "the Mid-West of analytics": a stretch of desolate flatness. The problem was that almost no one was booking Airbnb rooms and apartments outside periods of freakishly high demand. They met investors who thought the idea was crazy. One, a well-known Silicon Valley angel investor, was so uninterested that he walked out of their meeting sucking on his smoothie while Chesky was mid-sentence. But all this time, the founders were building their community brick by brick. In that tiny community—one that would grow and grow more rapidly than anyone could ever anticipate—were the seeds of a massive global business.

FIGURE 3.1 Airbnb co-founder Nathan Blecharczyk at a 2013 Airbnb host meetup in Tokyo, Japan

Source: Dairo Koga/Airbnb.com

Lesson #9: build a community

In *Tribes,* marketing guru Seth Godin describes how the Internet creates self-identifying "silos of interest" that are waiting to be led. As an entrepreneur, you need to find and nurture the particular silo of interest that is excited about your innovation. It helps when both founders and customers are in the same silo. What the Airbnb team and its first hosts were most excited about in fact had nothing to do with making rent. "The surprise outcome of that first weekend," Blecharczyk told me, "was the friendships that were created and how magical it was for Joe and Brian to be a host for their city. That was the magic part that we discovered and hoped to recreate."

Airbnb built its community in the offline world. As an unknown startup, they would email their "few dozen" users and invite them to get-togethers. "Some of these meetups were literally a couple of people," Blecharczyk said. "But we heard some of the same magic in the stories of our early hosts about their hosting adventures. It reassured us that we were on a path to success as we had successfully replicated that magic." Blecharczyk also tells a good yarn of when the co-founders met Paul Graham on their first day of Y Combinator, the highly selective startup accelerator program in Silicon Valley. "It's really important to meet your users," said Graham. "Where are they?"

"New York," said the Airbnb guys.

"Well, what are you doing here!" said Graham.

"We're here on Y Combinator," said the Airbnb guys, confused.

"Go to New York!"

"We can't afford to," they replied, wanting to show a frugal attitude to the $20,000 that Y Combinator had given them.

"Use the money I've given you to go to New York!"

More intimately than through shared beers, their community was built in shared living rooms and kitchens. One of the founding myths of Airbnb concerns what happened when Brian Chesky was made homeless after the startup's home office expanded into his bedroom. Chesky spent a year roving from Airbnb to Airbnb, meeting his community and evangelizing their mission like some kind of cross between the Buddha and Richard Branson.

What about when it was no longer possible for a co-founder to stay with every host? How do you scale community to millions of users? When the Airbnb co-founders realized that Paris was picking up, they found a French friend to go and replicate that same person-to-person model. As Gebbia says, "You can't localize without a local." Today, they still run meet-ups for their hosts and guests, except that now around 200 people attend and spaces fill up in hours. Airbnb also uses online groups that are similar to forums to allow hosts to give advice to each other. Airbnb's 2014 rebrand was another attempt to scale the values that underpin its community. The company introduced the symbol of the "Bélo" to represent its aspiration that you can "Belong Anywhere" (by renting an Airbnb, naturally). In the future, Blecharczyk believes that the Airbnb community will resemble an "extended support network" for people in their city.

Sharing economy startups should cultivate their community for at least three reasons. Firstly, a vibrant community makes its members feel like they are part of something momentous and fun. It gets them excited about the brand and keeps them loyal. Secondly, a community provides invaluable product feedback. Each time Airbnb's growth slowed, user feedback led to breakthroughs. Thirdly, a healthy community lures in new members. "People would talk about their experience to their friends and colleagues when they returned from a vacation," explained Blecharczyk. "So there was quickly a global cross-pollination between cities." At JustPark, we measure community through the metric of "viral ratio": the number of new users that each user brings in, usually through word of mouth. A viral ratio above 1 leads to exponential growth. That's what Blecharczyk, Chesky, and Gebbia cracked. Today, Airbnb is valued at over $10 billion. It makes the three co-founders, each who retain a stake of around 15%, the sharing economy's first billionaires.

Frédéric Mazzella, Nicolas Brusson, and Francis Nappez, co-founders, BlaBlaCar

It was Christmas and Frédéric Mazzella wanted to spend it with his parents in their country house outside Paris. It shouldn't have been difficult to make the short trip from one of the largest, best-connected cities in Europe, but it was. All the trains were booked up and Mazzella did not own a car. Compounding the frustration, Mazzella realized that many of the cars in the mass Christmas exodus from Paris were half-empty. He would happily have paid for a seat in one of them. *Surely some of their drivers would happily have taken his money too, if only he could connect with them, if only enough trust existed for them to let him—a total stranger—into their car?*

When Mazzella discovered that no website existed to make that connection, his own journey as an entrepreneur began. After graduating from "techpreneur" factory Stanford with a Masters in Computer Science, he brought in a second co-founder, Francis Nappez, from French dating website Meetic—a "thousand times better developer than me," admitted Mazzella. Then, while at top European business school INSEAD, Mazzella added Nicolas Brusson, a former venture capitalist, as the third co-founder.

How does BlaBlaCar work? People making car journeys list their route and time of departure on the website or mobile apps. The website calculates a recommended price per seat based on the distance and cost of petrol. As long as the price of seats only offsets the shared cost of petrol, passengers are protected by the drivers' car insurance and any money that drivers make is tax-free. BlaBlaCar takes an 11% commission on the booked seats. Passengers in need of a lift simply browse the upcoming journeys and book themselves into a spare seat. If you're wondering about the name, it comes from how people designate their chattiness on their profiles: those wishing to meditatively watch the world go by are "Bla." Averagely chatty road trippers are "BlaBla." The real motor mouths call themselves "BlaBlaBla."

Mazzella had his Christmas epiphany in 2004. By June 2014, BlaBlaCar had 10 million members and was growing by half a million members a month. It has built a transport network on top of an existing one that moves over 2 million people a month: more people than travel by Eurostar. Paradoxically, many of the employees at this car-based startup have green credentials as the company is moving all these extra people with almost no incremental pollution. Again, this is about efficiency: the 65% efficiency increase BlaBlaCar creates by raising the occupancy of the average car from 1.7 people to 2.8 people. "If you think about the biggest excess capacity," says Nappez, "they're not in planes or trains but in cars. We're turning the car into practically public transport." BlaBlaCar has grown to become one of the world's largest sharing economy businesses. As *The Guardian* puts it, "If Airbnb is the American-born poster child of the new trust economy then BlaBlaCar is fast becoming Europe's riposte."

Lesson #10: scale internationally

"It's all about how you keep the startup mindset while growing," explained Mazzella when we grabbed lunch in their health-conscious canteen. New joiners are expected to contribute to their collaborative, bottom-up culture. At the company's most recent annual skiing retreat (where the entire team went down an Olympic bobsleigh run), BlaBlaCar crowd-sourced its company values. "Values replace process, showing our team the 'why' but making the 'how' up to them," said Mazzella. "It's about motivation. Humans who do things because they want to are ten times more powerful than those who are made to." The recruitment process is similarly collaborative. Each successful applicant is interviewed not only by a co-founder but even by their most junior future colleagues. Unanimity is required and CEO Mazzella has been overruled in the past. This is in stark contrast to most companies where junior employees feel like foot soldiers in their general's vision.

While Mazzella looks after culture, co-founder Nicolas Brusson works on scaling the company operationally. BlaBlaCar is active in 12 European countries from Portugal to Russia and employs 125 people. I asked Brusson how he managed the formidable challenge of growing so many marketplaces in a region as linguistically and culturally diverse as Europe. First, Brusson is single-minded about the need to raise substantial amounts of capital. BlaBlaCar's requirement for cash has been even larger since it waits until it has a critical mass of drivers and passengers in any new market before charging for its service. A penny saved is a penny earned, so Brusson also dispenses with a Head of Marketing and oversees the marketing budgets at the same time as fundraising so that he can have "One foot on the gas and the other on the brake." Given that BlaBlaCar closed a $100 million round in 2014, they can afford to go hard on the gas.

Once BlaBlaCar got traction in France and proved the model to investors, it quickly bought up foreign local competitors via "acqui-hires": low-value acquisitions made primarily in order to bring in the team of the target company. BlaBlaCar bought a total of four small competitors to help them launch in Germany, Italy, Poland, and Russia. At the same time as overcoming most startups' greatest challenge—how to hire the best talent—BlaBlaCar was neutralizing the local competition. Brusson advises early-stage companies not to think of mergers and acquisitions as a tool only for large companies. He carefully incentivizes his new local teams with long-term share options linked to the value of the BlaBlaCar as a whole rather than being tied to local metrics. That way, Brusson fosters the same culture of collaboration between Country Managers. He also candidly notes, "It's very hard to pick the best KPIs [key performance indicators]. I'm not going to incentivize people on metrics we are still trying to understand."

Brusson spends two-thirds of his time as "the co-founder living out of a suitcase," managing a network of regional offices. But BlaBlaCar HQ is in Paris: a big chic space with displays of vintage toy cars, a "wall of fame" with photos of its power users, and a huge roof terrace that boasts panoramic views of Paris from the Eiffel Tower to Sacré-Cœur. Every 6 weeks, BlaBlaCar's Country Managers converge there for knowledge sharing on different topics. The "Growth Team" is also based in Paris. It is their job to review the reams of data coming out of the different countries and help refine the playbook for launching new markets. BlaBlaCar's "New Business Team" appraises the next launch countries. Right now, Brusson told me that they are weighing up Turkey, India, and Brazil. The US is on hold. "Things have changed," he said. "You can raise plenty of money without a US growth story." If the BlaBlaCar team can continue their march across Europe, it may not be on hold forever.

A broad church, broad enough for you?

I recall being at a sharing economy drinks event at Google Campus, the hip co-working space in London's "Tech City" built by the search giant. To my left, a prominent member of the Occupy movement was explaining his utopian peer-to-peer currency startup while slamming the evils of unchecked capitalism and investment bankers. To my right, a guy shuffled nervously in his suit before introducing himself as someone very interested in the sharing economy though currently working in private equity. No drinks were thrown. The sharing economy is a broad church, a place where you will meet hippies, bankers, and everything in between. It is also—even in situations like that—a very friendly church. Many of the challenges that sharing economy startups face are identical. If you are interested in founding one, ask for help on social media and attend the many free events listed on Eventbrite and Meetup.com. You will be surprised by how much help people give you.

Many of the share platforms themselves can help founders by lowering the cost of starting a business. Co-working spaces allow startups to retain flexibility over their rent. "Maker spaces" provide shared tools. Specific marketplaces address other specific needs: a construction business, for example, can cost-effectively rent machinery through Getable. For design work, Melbourne-based 99Designs crowd-sources graphic design. For repetitive tasks, look at CrowdFlower, an offshored labor marketplace. What about the presumably pricey software that you will need? Finland's Sharetribe and San Francisco's Near Me offer white label marketplace software for founders without coding skills: WordPress for the sharing economy. As we will see in the next chapter, shared models are also dramatically lowering the cost of capital.

Do not neglect the money-making potential of sharing economy businesses either. Tracy DiNunzio founded peer-to-peer fashion platform Tradesy using $28,000 of Airbnb earnings from renting out her apartment. It is a common story. The co-founder of one startup I met in a New York co-working space also funded his own his startup through Airbnb. On top of the capital to start his company, Airbnb gave the New York entrepreneur a business network. When his guests returned home, they spread news of his startup and he would see far-flung countries on Google Analytics lighting up with overseas visits to his website.

What about the skills you need to start a business? Skillshare's online classes allow entrepreneurs to learn core skills at minimal cost. I took a class on how to double my productivity for $29. Its scientific analysis of a five-phase "GTD" ("Getting things done") theory has repaid its tiny cost many times over. Filter for "entrepreneurship" classes and you will see classes on launching a Kickstarter campaign, web design, and more. In the offline world too, peer-to-peer education is a growing trend. Trade School in New York is a self-organized learning school where students pay their teachers in barter. Knowledge Commons DC is "a free school for thinkers, doers, and tinkerers—taught anywhere, by anyone, for everyone." Like most education marketplaces, it is a platform where anyone can become a teacher or student or both.

If you aspire to the adrenaline rush of life as an entrepreneur, I hope that those 10 tales will inspire you to start a company. "Me?," you might be thinking, excuses at the ready. Do not worry about failing: it can be the best possible use of your time. Failure toughens and teaches, and many a successful entrepreneur carries his past failures like wounds from lost but glorious battles. "Fail fast," goes a Silicon Valley cliché. "Fail harder!" reads a t-shirt I got from a Facebook developer event. So happy failing. But succeed and you can change the world. Airbnb co-founder Brian Chesky was inspired to become an entrepreneur by his professor at the Rhode Island School of Design who told him, "You can live in a world of your own design." Now Chesky does.

And one final morsel of advice, this time from me: running a company and writing a book are two of the most fun and fulfilling things that anyone can ever do, but doing both at once is not recommended. Yet that is what running a startup is like: biting off more than you can possibly chew every working day (*that's to say every day*). Often, it gets easier. You can take solace in the knowledge that even those impressive entrepreneurs have not achieved all that they have on their own. They have large teams of developers, designers, sales people, online marketers, and others, working on shiny new computers in beautiful offices. In short, they have money— and plenty of it.

Notes

1   Neuroscientist Baroness Susan Greenfield's address to members of the ABTA association of travel agents, discussing the broadly accepted relationship between travel and creativity: http://www.marketingmagazine.co.uk/article/1217864/lessons-neuroscience-age-hyperconnectivity. This relationship has been noted in at least five academic studies: http://psycnet.apa.org/?&fa=main.doiLanding&doi=10.1037/a0014861.

2   Data taken from *Forbes* list of billionaires as of September 10th, 2014: http://www.forbes.com/billionaires/#tab:overall.

3   2012 data from the US Environmental Protection Agency: http://www.epa.gov/epawaste/nonhaz/municipal/.

4   Ries, Eric, *The Lean Startup* (Penguin, 2011), p. 149.

4

Investors

All Bets Are On (All $4 Billion of Them)

I was standing on hallowed ground. But I was determined not to wither in awe. I glanced quickly around the high-ceilinged lobby of Sequoia Capital, at the flat screen TVs and the framed logos of the once obscure companies that the venture capital fund has helped grow into giants: Apple, Cisco, Google, LinkedIn, Oracle, PayPal, WhatsApp, Yahoo, and—small by comparison but growing ever-faster—Airbnb. Those logos reminded me that Sequoia Capital is more than just Silicon Valley history, that its companies have shaped civilization as we know it. Every CEO in the world wants to meet with Sequoia Capital. I had an hour and I needed to give the pitch of my life.

I was dressed in a casual shirt and smart jeans. This was the Valley not Wall Street after all, a place where billionaires can wear t-shirts to work. Which is not to say I would recommend turning up late to pitch Sequoia Capital in pajamas. A young Mark Zuckerberg tried that. Instead of presenting on Facebook, he presented a spoof presentation about "Wirehog," one of his side projects. His PowerPoint presentation was called "The Top Ten Reasons You Should Not Invest." One of the reasons was, "We turned up late for your meeting." The prank was revenge on behalf of Facebook's then President Sean Parker, who had been ousted from his previous startup by Sequoia's powerful partner Michael Moritz, himself worth over $2 billion. The Sequoia partners sat in silence and took a pass on Zuckerberg. When you are Sequoia Capital, you can afford to miss a few extra billion.

Beside me was Mark Platshon, an advisor to one of our early investors, BMW. Mark is a big man with a kind smile whose words come out slow and deep, Solomon-like on discussion points in board meetings. I call him Big Wise Bear. He had picked me up from the Caltrain station in his vintage Porsche and driven me to the Sequoia offices on Sand Hill Road, a wide, nondescript highway running down one side of Stanford University's sprawling campus. But Sand Hill Road is no ordinary road. It has the greatest concentration of venture capital on the planet. Nowhere else even comes close. The firms headquartered behind the trees on this one road in Menlo Park, Silicon Valley manage over $100 billion of venture capital.

If Sand Hill Road is the center of venture capital, then one address is the center of the center: 3000 Sand Hill Road. Down an avenue fringed with immaculate shrubbery is a complex of understated low-rise buildings that looks more like a posh high school than the office of some of the world's most successful capitalists. No one here wants to be the center of attention. The firms and their partners are listed in discreet letters on noticeboards by the entrance to each building. The only show was in the parking lot: glistening Teslas lined up beneath maple trees turning red. And if 3000 Sand Hill Road is the center of the center, then the office of the legendary Sequoia Capital is the center of the center of the center.

"Good morning," said the receptionist.

"Morning," I said. "I'm here to see Alfred."

I had a 9:30 appointment with Alfred Lin, one of the most respected venture capitalists in the Valley. Before turning to what entrepreneurs jokingly call "the dark side" of venture capital, Lin was Chief Operating Officer of shoe e-tailer Zappos, which was acquired by Amazon for $1.2 billion. Lin is personally an angel investor in Uber, San Francisco's sexiest consumer startup. He sits on the Board of its second sexiest: Airbnb. The night before, I had lay on my bed in Cara's Airbnb, Googling him and watching YouTube videos. *TechCrunch*, the racy *Financial Times* of the tech world, noted that Lin's smallest personal success has been a $265 million exit. It seemed like everyone in tech wanted a bit of Alfred Lin. I fought back the nerves. Perhaps Lin would want a bit of JustPark.

"Will you be projecting?" asked the receptionist.

My stomach was doing somersaults; I couldn't rule it out.

"Yes," I said. "Do you have an adapter for a MacBook Air?"

"I believe so," replied the receptionist without a trace of irony as she slid open a drawer containing around 20 Apple adapters stacked in neat rows.

She led us down a corridor past countless rows of tombstones, not of entrepreneurs humiliated to death in past pitches, but the framed front pages of the prospectuses of Sequoia's big initial public offerings (IPOs). My eyes skated over the names of the investment banks underwriting them—JP Morgan, Goldman Sachs, Merrill Lynch—and dollar amounts with so many zeros that they stretched across half the page. We followed the receptionist into an enormous boardroom and she connected my laptop to the projector. The image covered an entire wall. I had paid to watch smaller screens in movie theatres.

"May I fetch you a drink?" she said.

I asked for a green tea. Big Wise Bear asked for a Coke. *God bless America.* I had already checked with him that I would be speaking American. Not "car park." *Parking lot.* Not "pavement." *Sidewalk.* Not "vicar." *Priest.*

Lin walked quickly into the room, a compact man of Taiwanese origin, his hair cropped to a military shortness. In a few seconds, he had shaken our hands and was seated opposite us, his hands hovering over his iPad, waiting for me to speak. I didn't want to waste his time by thanking him for it.

"Shall I dive straight into the deck?" I said.

"Sure."

I pressed the space bar and brought up the first slide: a picture of a smiling man in a black suit and dog collar, giant-sized on the wall. "This is Ted," I said. "Ted is a priest in London and JustPark lets anyone with a parking space—a home, a business, a parking lot owner, or even a church—make money from it. So how much has Ted made by renting out his parking on JustPark?" I paused for effect and looked across at Lin. His expressionless face suggested that he wouldn't be impressed by theatrics. "By renting out five spaces on JustPark, Ted has made over a *quarter of a million dollars.*"

We went through the slides and Lin grilled me on our metrics: *what's your LTV* (lifetime value of a user)? *What are your CPAs* (cost per acquisition, that is to say how much we spend acquiring a new driver or property owner)? *ARPU* (average revenue per user)? When companies are at an early stage, many venture capitalists will take a punt of several hundred thousand dollars on an interesting idea and a strong founding team. But when you walk into Sequoia Capital asking for $7 million dollars as I just did, your numbers don't need to work: they need to *fly*. A venture capitalist needs to have confidence that if you execute on your game plan, they will get back their investment at least 5-fold or "5×"— and often far more. They pursue huge wins. *Doubling their money? That's a distraction.*

Smart money—and lots of it

Of all the CEOs of all the companies in all the world, why was I able to get in front of Sequoia Capital? For investors like Lin, the sharing economy is hot for all the reasons that we looked at in Chapter 1, like the creation of trustworthy online identities through social media and ever-rising smartphone adoption. The sharing economy is as sexy as consumer web gets, as fashionable a category as big data but more PR-friendly. It is no surprise then that sharing economy businesses are lavishly financed. According to research by Altimeter Group in 2013, more than $2 billion of funding has been invested in the top 200 sharing economy businesses.[1] By the time you read this, that figure will be north of $4 billion. On top of BlaBlaCar's $100 million, Quirky, an e-tailer of crowd-sourced inventions, has raised $175 million. Taxi platforms Lyft and Uber have raised $333 million and $1.5 billion respectively: so much cash that in markets where they compete head on, they can afford to give passengers months of free taxis. Airbnb has raised $776 million. Its last round was a mammoth $500 million from private equity group TPG. Without adjusting for inflation, Airbnb's round is over 16 times the sums raised by Yahoo or AOL in their IPOs.

This is it not just quantity of capital: it is quality too. The sharing economy has attracted a roll call of Tier 1 venture capital firms. They often invest alongside each other in this incestuous world. Accel Partners is in BlaBlaCar and Etsy. Index Ventures is in Funding Circle, JustPark, and also in BlaBlaCar and Etsy. Union Square Ventures is in Kickstarter and also in Funding Circle and again Etsy. Andreessen Horowitz is in Lyft and Quirky. Kleiner Perkins is also in Quirky, Rent the Runway, and Lending Club—alongside Union Square Ventures yet again. Taking "smart money" from the elite funds helps companies to raise "follow-on capital," keeping any unprofitable noses above water for years to come. Having funded Amazon, the king of e-commerce, Kleiner Perkins is open to the possibilities of "*re*commerce" by monetizing the goods already in existence and sold on sites like Chegg and Tradesy. Having cleared more than $10 billion from Facebook's IPO, Accel is trying to cash out again by investing in companies like BlaBlaCar that are built on top of the social network. It is the job of venture capital firms to ride the biggest waves. They seem to agree that the sharing economy is one of them.

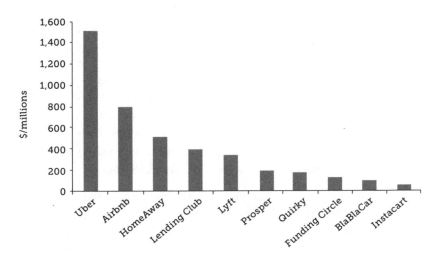

FIGURE 4.1 The 10 most financed sharing economy startups
Source: Crunchbase, November 15th, 2014

The balance sheet of life

There must be some correlation between how successful tech investors become and just how goddam nice they are. Being well liked gets a venture capitalist or "VC" a good "deal flow," giving them the chance to pick and choose their investments. With his breezy manner, Jeff Jordan makes you feel like pals catching up over a bottle of Bud even while you're sat in the immaculate offices of top venture fund Andreessen

Horowitz. That is the Silicon Valley way, uncorporate, genial, and modest. And Jordan (I can hear him saying, "Call me Jeff!") is one of the power players. He was GM of eBay, North America. He has served as President of PayPal. Jordan also floated OpenTable, now worth $2.6 billion, so knows all about business models that rely on increasing utilization, in the case of OpenTable the "open" unbooked tables themselves. These days, Jordan sits on the boards of Airbnb alongside Alfred Lin and crowdfunding startup Tilt.

Jordan approaches sharing economy investments by looking down what he calls "the balance sheet of people's lives." In other words, he is most interested in people's most valuable assets: real estate, cars, and designer fashion where idling capacity represents the largest unlockable value. For companies that target opportunities high up the balance sheets of our lives, the opportunities are staggering. Airbnb's 2014 investment round valued the 6-year-old business at several billion dollars more than the InterContinental Hotels Group whose origins stretch back to 1777. Up next: cars. As larger-than-life venture capitalist and investor in car-sharing company Getaround, Shervin Pishevar, notes, "Most cars are only used 8% of the time. This is incredible waste happening each and every day across the world." There may be a business opportunity renting out cheaper items, for example, lawnmowers, but probably not a huge one, not a venture capital-backed one.

All investors like big addressable markets. Three days after Steve Case resigned as Chairman of AOL-Time Warner having pushed through the catastrophic merger, he went for a pizza in Washington with an old AOL colleague, Donn Davis. Case wanted to discuss how they could disrupt industries in the same way that so many startups had disrupted AOL-Time Warner. The next day, Case summoned Davis to his offices. He said he had seen the potential in vacation homes. "It's a huge industry," Case told Davis. "It's an expensive hassle to maintain the houses. There's gotta be something there." This was 2003—before anyone had used the term sharing economy. By the end of the year, Case owned 80% of Exclusive Resorts, a vacation rental membership platform. Membership grew 100× over the following 3 years. Case and Davis looked down the balance sheet of people's lives and found cars. In 2005, Case took a majority stake in Flexcar and merged it—more successfully this time—with Zipcar. When Zipcar exited to Avis Budget, Case's fund pocketed $96 million.

Marketplace magic

There is a fundamental reason why many investors like sharing economy businesses: they are marketplaces. On the downside, marketplaces are notoriously hard to build as they require both supply and demand in the right ratio. On the plus side, when they work, they *really* work. Since buyers want to be where the sellers are and vice versa, marketplaces exhibit "network effects" where the value of the whole increases as it grows. JustPark acquires over 50,000 drivers a month and rising because the more parking spots we have, the more drivers join; and the more drivers join, the more property owners list their parking spots. Once a marketplace is established as the leader in its space, it tends to run away from the competition as the mass market of consumers gravitates towards it. "If it's not winner takes all," says David Hornik of August Capital, "it's winner takes *most*." For an investor who spots that future dominant marketplace, the rewards can be immense: they will end up with part of a potentially huge and high-margin business.

Peer-to-peer marketplaces also benefit from a cross-pollination of buyers and sellers. Just as sellers on eBay often start out making a purchase, so hosts on Airbnb often start out as guests. Airbnb's founding team noted how Parisians visiting New York would frequently become hosts themselves once they returned to Paris. Sometimes, a user would rent out their own apartment while they were on vacation in someone else's, allowing Airbnb to make double revenue from them. Finally, peer-to-peer marketplaces enjoy low marginal costs. A company selling tangible goods sees its cost base shrink only modestly with economies of scale: when Levi's sells thousands more jeans a day, each pair costs it less but only up to a point. But new users can be added to an online marketplace at almost zero marginal cost. Of course, becoming an Etsy or Airbnb is easier said than done. There are now, for example, over 30 peer-to-peer car-sharing companies globally. Only a few will emerge as global leaders, perhaps just one.

Venture funding is crucial to this process because a very large amount of capital is normally required to become a dominant player. "It is cheaper than ever to start a business," as Jeff Jordan told me. "The downside of that is that anyone else can start one too. As a result you have to get big fast and to get big fast you have to raise." After only 3 years as a venture capitalist, Jordan's companies have raised over a billion dollars of venture capital. This is the game: investors back the perceived market leader. Their money helps it to grow faster, allowing the company to raise more funding, which fuels more growth. As the company grows, so does the amount of money that it can raise at each funding round, putting it still further ahead of the pack. Meanwhile, other investors fear competing with a company with a large war chest. They start to think of a competitor as merely an acquisition target— not an exit that will get billion-dollar funds reaching for their checkbook.

Being located in the US can help a company to get on this virtuous cycle of growth. The quantity of available capital and high valuations in the US can allow a US-based company to raise more money than the equivalent European business. In 2008, the same year that Airbnb was founded, Stephen Rapoport and Dan Hill founded Crashpadder, a startup that was doing more or less the same as its more celebrated San Francisco counterpart. The London-headquartered company never raised venture capital and was a fraction of the size of Airbnb, which acquired it in 2012. Even had Crashpadder raised finance, it would, in all likelihood, have been an unfair fight: British knives against American guns. The gap is rapidly narrowing. But for credible founding teams, the US remains awash with cheap money by comparison with Europe.

Fred Wilson, Union Square Ventures

Career-VC Fred Wilson is the investor most associated with marketplaces. He is also arguably the most famous venture capitalist on the planet. Through Wilson's blog, AVC.com, and his 350,000 Twitter followers (he also put some of the first money into Twitter), he is known as the quintessential marketplace expert. I met Wilson in the offices of his firm Union Square Ventures, high above the Manhattan traffic. Low-key and cordial, Wilson let me in himself, appearing to be the first person in that morning. He had deep rings round his eyes. I liked that. Many a time, I'd gone to meetings at a venture capital firm looking frazzled and sat opposite an immaculate venture capitalist who clearly had far more time than me to get their beauty sleep and fix their wardrobe. 'How hard do they *actually* work for their companies?' I'd sometimes wonder. 'How much do they *really* care?' Sit opposite Fred Wilson and talk to him about startups and you don't have those concerns. He ended up hijacking the interview for this book and making me pitch JustPark for my life. Despite the rings, Wilson's eyes were alert. He knows that in tech you can miss things with a blink.

Thus he explained how Union Square Ventures ended up missing out on Airbnb:

> At that time, Airbnb was a marketplace for air mattresses on the floors of people's apartments … We couldn't wrap our heads around air mattresses on living room floors as the next hotel room and did not chase the deal. Others saw the amazing team that we saw, funded them, and the rest is history.

In a Union Square Ventures meeting room, Wilson keeps an Obama-themed cereal box on permanent display. It is one of the thousands that the Airbnb co-founders sold while bootstrapping Airbnb. Wilson put it there as a warning about "the classic mistake that all investors make." By that, Wilson means focusing on what a company is doing at any one time rather than seeing its potential to grow into something far greater.

Wilson understands better than anyone how to turn a well-funded marketplace into a large and profitable one. "Venture is a very good source of capital for these businesses," he told me in his measured, gravelly voice, "because if you keep your take rates low and invest in product and engineering you'll have negative cash flow for a number of years. But eventually, you will get to a scale which allows you to make money." Wilson recounted how Rob Kalin, the founder of Etsy, once told him, "In a perfect world, we would take no transaction fees and make all our money on advertising." Wilson explained that Kalin was pointing out that a marketplace should aim to take its transaction fees as low as possible to generate a total take that is higher without effectively taxing the marketplace. "That provides a pricing umbrella," said Wilson, "and makes it hard for anyone to come in underneath you and compete, and it also turns scale to advantage since value-added services [such as advertising fees] can turn into a lot of money whereas a new entrant can't possibly make money with them."

More marketplace mavens

The hottest sharing economy deals are so tough to get into that some investors try to carve out names for themselves as experts. Bill Gurley, superstar venture capitalist at Benchmark Capital and investor in dog boarding marketplace DogVacay and Uber, is one of them. The 6' 9" investor references his height and perspective on his blog entitled "Above the Crowd" and often features on Forbes' "Midas List" of top venture capitalists. Gurley's fund has always liked marketplaces. Benchmark invested $6.7 million in eBay in 1997 and got $5 billion back. Ironically, eBay never even cashed the check.

In 2013, another leading US fund, Greylock Partners, an investor in Airbnb, Facebook, and LinkedIn, allocated $100 million to marketplace investments. The initiative is fronted by Greylock partner Simon Rothman, who previously founded eBay Motors and grew it to a top 10 global e-commerce property. Greylock even hosts its own marketplace conference, "Greymarket." "In the next five years," says Rothman, "there will be more billion-dollar marketplaces built than in the last 20 combined ... Marketplaces are devouring whole industries, even the ones previously on the margins like healthcare and education, even they are now susceptible to the power of marketplaces to drive efficiencies."

Collaborative Fund is an entire fund that is focused on the collaborative economy and one of its major subsets, the sharing economy. The fund has backed some of the leading lights of the sharing economy including Lyft, Kickstarter, and Skillshare. Collaborative Fund's founder Craig Shapiro took an unorthodox route into venture capital. After part-financing the official documentary on Wikipedia, *Truth in Numbers*, Shapiro became fascinated by how "Wikipedia had built a more valuable asset than Encyclopedia Britannica in a fraction of the time at a fraction of the cost." Backed by the founder of YouTube and by superstar producer and recording artist Pharrell Williams, Collaborative Fund is guided by a belief in the environmental and social benefits of "progressive business models that take sharing, bartering, lending trading, renting, gifting and swapping into the digital age." Nonetheless, Shapiro is resolutely an absolute return investor. "The businesses with missions that align with ours," he says "are going to generate some of the best financial returns in the next decade."

In the UK, Piton Capital is a niche fund that invests only in businesses with network effects. Its two partners come from betting marketplace Betfair and auction site QXL. Piton has stakes in DaWanda, a German peer-to-peer handmade goods marketplace, and Videdressing, a French peer-to-peer luxury fashion marketplace. The larger UK funds cannot have niches: they have too much capital to deploy and do so across multiple sectors and in companies of varying maturity. They all invest in share platforms, but perhaps none is more bought in than JustPark's main investor, Index Ventures. Arguably Europe's top venture capital firm, Index Ventures is increasingly allocating serious cash to peer-to-peer startups. In July 2014, Index Ventures led a $100 million round in global long-distance ridesharing leader BlaBlaCar—the largest ever venture capital raise for a French startup. That same month, it led a $65 million round in debt crowdfunding site Funding Circle, having first invested in 2011 when Funding Circle was little more than an idea.

Robin Klein is a venture partner at Index Ventures and sits on the boards of JustPark and onefinestay among others. Alongside his investments at Index Ventures, he has built a reputation as one of Europe's most highly regarded angel investors through his own investment vehicle, The Accelerator Group (TAG), which he runs with son, Saul. They have a knack of picking winners, one of which, real estate listings site Zoopla, IPO'd for $1.5 billion while I was writing this chapter. "Marketplaces are as old as commerce itself," he told me in a bookshop café in his beloved Hampstead, a pretty village of cobbled lanes that sits high above the London bustle. "In their online form, marketplaces take time to build and can require large amounts of capital," Klein cautions. "But they can also lead to significant returns on investment. In the case of the sharing economy, the underutilized assets themselves can yield high returns."

Klein was an entrepreneur in the web's earliest days. As CEO of catalogue business Innovations, he conducted the UK's first e-commerce transaction in May 1995. Back then, the dial-up web was a painful experience—for the smattering of people that were actually connected. He recalls fondly how, "When I suggested we could sell things on the Internet, most people in the company thought: 'another of Robin's nutty ideas!'" But in the nascent Internet, Klein saw the potential to take massive cost out of business. In the case of Innovations, it was the cost of printing and posting over 20 million catalogues a year. "We could see that, one day, paper was going to be bits and bytes." Today, the web does far more than cut costs. "The role of the web is to make things cheaper, faster, easier and more fun," says Klein. "On all of those metrics, the sharing economy can create value."

With equity stakes in all of its fastest-growing startups, the venture capitalists hope that the sharing economy will create huge value for them too. Yet they don't have it all their own way.

The new kid in town: equity crowdfunding

Today, the swish venture capitalists themselves are at risk being disrupted by some of the very trends behind many of their bets. Parties who, at one time, were strangers can now connect directly, putting the venture capitalists themselves at risk of being cut out of the value cycle, or "disintermediated." *What if the venture capitalists' own investors or "limited partners" were able to source and invest in companies without them and their hefty management fees? What if a startup could raise the capital it needed by selling shares directly to individual investors, bypassing the venture capitalists and their onerous terms?* Equity crowdfunding is a major new financing model that may in time put plenty of venture capital firms out of business.

As we will shortly see, crowdfunding comes in two other flavors: "debt crowdfunding" and "rewards-based crowdfunding." All three of them fall within the definition of the sharing economy for several reasons. By allowing capital to flow straight from private individuals to entrepreneurs, they rely on a decentralized peer-driven model that circumvents traditional institutions. Investors are also using their resources more efficiently: crowdfunding platforms get "slack to the pack," that slack being spare cash. Finally, crowdfunding platforms are built around transparent communities. Users of crowdfunding platforms often log in via Facebook and LinkedIn and build public profiles where they showcase their portfolios. It is a far cry from the opaque relationships that exist between a venture capital firm's limited partners and the companies that ultimately receive their money.

Wesley Chan, the founder of Google Analytics and now an advisor at Google Ventures, describes venture capital pre-crowdfunding as "a smoke-filled-room thing." Some of the most exciting companies in the sharing economy are those now trying to clear the air.

Equity crowdfunding: how and why

How does equity crowdfunding work? A company wishing to raise money creates an online profile covering all the main bases such as its product, business model, management, and target market. Individual investors can browse the companies, ask the teams questions, and invest online using standardized contracts. Typically, the investment round only closes if a predefined amount of money is raised by a fixed date. If the amount raised falls short of that target, all pledged monies are returned. In the US, equity crowdfunding does not yet exist. There, as with any perceived high-risk private offering, investments are restricted to accredited investors: people with $200,000 a year in earnings or a net worth of over $1 million excluding their property. We will see that times are a-changin' with some forthcoming regulation, but for now startup investing in the US is, broadly speaking, a sport for millionaires only.

The center of equity crowdfunding in its true open and democratic form is Britain, where it first emerged. In the UK, investors are not subject to minimum income or net worth thresholds. Through Seedrs, a well-polished outfit run by a team of former corporate lawyers and techies, an investor based anywhere in the EU can today invest as little as £10 in a startup. Investment opportunities on Seedrs span the conventional, such as a new restaurant run by celebrity fund manager Nicola Horlick, to the downright wacky: IncuBus is a startup incubator for other startups housed on a converted London bus. One of Seedrs' largest fundraisings to date has been its own investment round of £2.6 million. But as its name suggests, its typical fundraising is far smaller, such as £60,000 for inter-city ridesharing startup, GoCarShare.

Crowdcube is Seedrs' maverick archrival. Based in the cathedral city of Exeter in England's rural south-west, it has been around longer and boasts the larger investor base of the two. There is one major difference between the platforms: Crowdcube allows investors to hold shares directly in the companies in which they invest. Seedrs, on the other hand, remains the legal owner of all the shares bought through its platform, holding them on trust for the crowd. Seedrs takes this approach to prevent a company's shareholders' table from exploding to hundreds of rows while aiming to give the crowd all the necessary contractual protections as minority shareholders.

With regulation still the biggest stumbling block, equity crowdfunding is struggling outside the UK, with a few immature examples like Ghana-based SliceBiz crowdfunding seed capital for startups across Africa. Startups in other countries like Germany try and sneak around restrictive regulation with smart "hacks." A platform like Seedmatch simulates crowdfunding by using subordinated debt where the terms of the loan track equity performance.

Why would a company equity crowdfund? Equity crowdfunding can allow founders to raise money at higher valuations than they could often get from a venture capital firm, causing less dilution of their own percentage shareholdings. It can also mean raising money without issuing preference shares with "liquidation preferences" that give venture capitalists powerful rights to get repaid in full before a founder gets a cent. Sometimes, the venture capital firm also gets "participating preference shares" that give it rights over and above its percentage shareholding to take further bites out of what's left on the table. Then there is the need for speed. Crowdfunding can be faster than what Jeff Jordan calls the "relatively analogue process" of the face-to-face pitching and negotiation of a traditional venture fundraising. As I—or any CEO of a venture-backed company could tell you—the amount of time it takes to close a venture capital deal can be a major distraction from the real job of running a high-growth company.

But perhaps the most exciting reason for a company to equity crowdfund is the chance to build an investor base that will serve as an army of passionate evangelists. Sometimes, investors will be customers who, having liked the company before investing, have an extra reason to support it. Others will be brand new to the business. But everyone is incentivized to pull in the same direction: to grow the company and, in the process, the value of their own stake. More than ever in our social media-infused world, businesses grow through word of mouth recommendations—and can do so through the mouths of thousands of shareholder evangelists. They can help in numerous other ways too, from product testing and recruiting to originating business deals through their networks.

Can you measure the impact of this evangelism? Crowdfund Capital Advisors, a consultancy that has advised the White House on equity and debt crowdfunding regulation, certainly thinks so. When in 2014 it researched companies that had equity crowdfunded, it found that the companies reported a staggering 351% jump in revenue from the year before.[2] We are right to be questioning of such bold claims. For a start, there is a self-selection bias when it comes to the people who chose to provide data, and the small sample size of just a few hundred companies. In the famous words attributed to British Prime Minister Benjamin Disraeli, "There are lies, damned lies and statistics." But while it may be hard to quantify the exact impact of evangelism, it is hard to deny its value too. As Paul Buchheit, founder of Gmail, puts it, "It is better to have a 100 people who love you than a 1,000 people who like you." Crowdfunding can be a shortcut to that 100 people. In fact, it can sometimes be a shortcut to thousands of people who love you.

Individuals risk investing, funds risk not investing

Sometimes, the companies raising money through equity crowdfunding are doing so because they have failed to cut a deal in the competitive world of venture capital: going out to the less fussy crowd can be a useful last resort. However, raising crowdfunded capital rather than venture capital need not reflect badly on a startup. Often, the companies utilizing equity crowdfunding are simply those that are not suited to raise venture capital as their business models do not offer the scalability and level of potential returns that venture capitalists typically seek. By democratizing investments in startups, equity crowdfunding is helping to fund companies that would otherwise be stillborn.

But the risk in democratizing access to capital is that many companies *should* fail to raise capital: they are simply not good enough to survive in the Darwinian business world. Crowdfunded capital that finds its way into those companies is wasted. In the coming years, the dangers could increase. If vast quantities of fresh capital from individuals become available, too much money could chase too few worthy investment opportunities. That would drive up valuations and depress returns, a trend reminiscent of the late 1990s when $100 billion of venture capital was invested annually compared to $25 billion today. That flood of capital led in part to the dot-com bubble. Conversely, by democratizing startup investing, equity crowdfunding leads to diversification: the money is split between more startups in more sectors. "The startup ecosystem back then was just too narrow to support that amount of capital," says Alex Mittal, founder of online venture capital fund FundersClub. "With more companies surfacing through equity crowdfunding, the risk of a recurrence of dot-com bubble 'group-think' is materially reduced."

While investors should (as ever) tread carefully, this new source of capital is unquestionably good for today's new businesses and entrepreneurs.

Increased competition to get into deals is also making investors raise their game. Through websites like AngelList where accredited investors record their investments, the investment world, like the rest of the world, is becoming more transparently competitive. It is ever harder to get into deals as "undifferentiated capital": just by providing cash as a commodity without any additional value-add. Investors increasingly need to demonstrate that they can help the startup far above and beyond writing a check. They will have to make good on their promises and add significant, measurable value to startups in order to build their reputations if they want to enjoy continued deal flow.

How will equity crowdfunding impact the venture capital firms themselves? "We benefit from early-stage seed capital being more broadly available," Fred Wilson told me. "More capital for entrepreneurs will be good for people who invest in entrepreneurs." Many venture capital firms are also throwing their lot in with the platforms. "We have to invest in the things that are eating us rather than run away from them," according to Craig Shapiro of Collaborative Fund. For the venture capital firms, time will tell, but many of the leading ones have no intention of waiting to be outmaneuvered: the risks for them are in *not* investing in the platforms. The leading US-based online investment platform, AngelList, is backed by dozens of investors including two of the most revered firms in venture capital: Kleiner Perkins and Draper Fisher Jurvetson. Arguably the number two player in the US, FundersClub, is backed by Andreessen Horowitz, Spark Capital, Intel Capital, and Draper Fisher Jurvetson yet again—doubly hedging its bets. One of the UK's major platforms, Crowdcube, is backed by top firm Balderton Capital.

As startups exploit these new sources of capital, it is creating a rebalancing of power between themselves and the venture capitalists. The commercial reality is that venture capitalists by definition need entrepreneurs, but entrepreneurs do not necessarily need venture capitalists. Nonetheless, Fred Wilson and venture capitalists at other leading firms are right to be confident. There is no shortage of high-quality companies queuing up to tap into their expertise, and the crowd may not be able to fund later, larger rounds in the tens of millions. Wilson's fund has also written big checks for crowdfunding platforms, especially debt crowdfunding ones: the most established type of crowdfunding, as we are about to see. But the crowd could crush lesser brands in venture capital, in particular those fighting to get into the same early-stage deals.

Debt crowdfunding

Debt crowdfunding lets a crowd lend money to individuals or businesses on the promise of repayment of the loan at an agreed rate of interest. Thus, consumers and businesses are able to raise finance directly from depositors. By cutting out an expensive and in efficient middleman—otherwise known as a bank—companies and individual borrowers can usually pay lower interest rates and depositors can receive higher interest rates. As with equity crowdfunding, debt crowdfunding is also providing a source of finance for people and companies that would not otherwise have had access to it. Debt crowdfunding, often called peer-to-peer lending, splits down into consumer and business debt. The challenge for the industry and investors is not casting the net *too* widely: if the challenge for investors in equity crowdfunding is to find companies that will succeed against the odds, the challenge for those in debt crowdfunding is to find companies and people who will not default.

The undisputed king of debt crowdfunding is Lending Club. By November 2014, Lending Club had originated over $6 billion of loans. Backed by $125 million of Google's cash, Lending Club IPO'd on the New York Stock Exchange in December 2014 at a price tag of $9 billion. Lending Club was also the first peer-to-peer lender to register its offerings as securities with the US Securities and Exchange Commission for trading on a secondary market. Prosper is Lending Club's archrival and the US's number two debt crowdfunding site, with over $2 billion lent. While Lending Club was the first to be regulated—a smart move in retrospect that has given it unrivalled credibility—Prosper was the first peer-to-peer lender to get to market. On Prosper's site, I can browse requests for individual loans and their varying interest rates or use their "Quick Invest" feature to automatically match up my money with loans that fit my risk criteria. As with Lending Club, Prosper's loans are 3 or 5 years, unsecured, and spread across multiple borrowers.

The UK also punches above its weight in debt crowdfunding. London's Zopa was the world's very first peer-to-peer lender and is today one of the largest. The world's leading debt crowdfunding website for business lending is also the UK's Funding Circle. Flush on the back of its own $65 million fundraising in 2014, Funding Circle has lent over £400 million to small businesses in sums ranging from £5,000 to £1,000,000.

Borrowers must have at least £100,000 of turnover and 2 years of filed accounts. They aim to lend to traditional businesses such as Kaizen Furniture, which borrowed £100,000 from 612 individuals to upgrade its workshop. The individual investors can pick the businesses they lend to, the amount to lend, and the interest rates as part of an online auction process. Alternatively, investors can use Funding Circle's "Autobid" function to automatically allocate loans according to predefined criteria. In 2013, Funding Circle marched into the US with its acquisition of Endurance Lending Network.

Rewards-based crowdfunding

Danae Ringelmann is a woman who hates money getting in the way. When her friends in San Francisco wanted to produce an Arthur Miller play, she helped organize a fundraising performance. Her fundraising strategy appeared sound: ensure the attendance of wealthy potential benefactors, the type who might open their wallets to their arts. But what she learnt would change her life and the lives of thousands of others. The wealthy playgoers, the ones she was counting on to produce the play, kept their checkbooks firmly inside their jacket pockets. Instead, the people that contributed financially were the audience and the actors. Between them, that group had enough money and vastly greater passion. It taught Ringelmann that fundraising did not need to rely on the top-down patronage of a handful of benefactors. The larger audience could bring in the dough. So Ringelmann decided to focus her attentions on the largest audience of them all: the Internet.

"When I think of the sharing economy," Ringelmann told me via Skype from her Los Angeles home, "I think of us returning to our roots as human beings with relationships based on personal interactions." Ringelmann's company, Indiegogo, is a pioneer in "rewards-based crowdfunding": the funding of goods or projects by offering each backer a reward for investing. Rewards usually relate to the project. Pay for a musician to record their album and they'll send you a copy. Pay for the R&D of a new gizmo and they'll mail you one. Generally, campaigns have a range of tiered rewards so the more you contribute, the better the reward. For the smallest investments, sometimes only the backer's name is recorded—just as Joseph

Pulitzer once did in his newspaper *The World* for every contributor to the Statue of Liberty's pedestal, no matter how small their donation. These days, less newsworthy missions can tap the crowd. Ringelmann told me about the founder of a bakery, Emmy's Organics. Rejected by every bank for a $15,000 loan, it raised the sum in 3 weeks by selling macaroons on Indiegogo. Afterwards, its new investors continued to eat away and evangelize the brand. Six months later, Emmy's Organics had distribution across America.

Indiegogo is not only about enterprise. Ringelmann points to the couple that used Indiegogo to raise $10,000 for a successful course of IVF. One widely covered Indiegogo campaign sought to raise $5,000 to pay for a "holiday of a lifetime" for bullied bus monitor Karen Klein. The campaign video used footage taken on the school bus by one of Klein's tormentors and shone a light on the vile abuse that the 68-year-old widow was being subjected to by a swarm of 7th-grade brats. The Indiegogo campaign was launched by a complete stranger, Max Sidorov, who happened to see the video on YouTube. Having been bullied as a child, Sidorov was moved to act. A crowd of 32,000 people responded to Sidorov's campaign, coming forward with a ludicrous $703,000 for Mrs Klein. Other Indiegogo projects are philanthropic. GravityLight is an LED lantern that is powered by the weight of a bag of rocks. Designed for the 1.5 billion people in the world without access to electricity, GravityLight raised $399,590 on Indiegogo, obliterating its $55,000 target. The lamps are now being tested by families in Guatemala and Bangladesh.

Crowdfund without giving away equity

Robotics designer Peter Dilworth was using his 3D printer one day when it skipped a line in the print. Normally, it would be an annoyance requiring the entire print to be started from scratch. But it occurred to Dilworth that he could finish the job manually by disassembling the 3D printer and holding the printer head as it extruded a string of plastic. It was then that Dilworth had the brainwave. *Why could you not have a 3D printer that you could hold in your hand and worked just like a pen?* Along with inventor Max Bogue, Dilworth cobbled together a prototype of a pen that let you draw in three dimensions. As the hot plastic left the pen's nib, it solidified at room temperature, letting you draw physical raised lines not only on paper but in the very air itself.

Looking for feedback on their new invention, Bogue met up with an old friend, software entrepreneur and former lawyer Daniel Cowen.

"What do you think?" asked Bogue with a mixture of eagerness and trepidation.

"What do I *think*?" replied Cowen. "I think this is one of the coolest products I've ever seen. You *have* to run with this!"

The inventors iterated the pen at Artisan's Asylum, a "maker space" in Boston. Meanwhile, Cowen looked into the pros and cons of licensing the invention versus going it alone. The decision made to go it alone, the trio knew there was one place their invention belonged: Kickstarter, the hip rewards-based crowdfunding platform where they could sell their creation to an audience of passionate geeks already familiar with the concept of 3D printing. This was uncharted territory for them all. They agonized over whether to cap the campaign at $30,000 or $40,000. Finally, they agreed that $40,000 was greedy—after all, they did not want to miss their target and leave with nothing. After 3 months of meticulous planning, three co-founder bags of nerves sat in Bogue's fiancée's Manhattan apartment and turned the campaign live for the "3Doodler": the world's first 3D pen.

It went off like a bomb. Every time they pressed refresh, hundreds of dollars more had been pledged. They hit their $30,000 target in under an hour. "It was crazy," Cowen told me from his office in Hong Kong where he now oversees production in nearby Shenzhen. "We were up for 50 straight hours answering emails and tweets while the funding kept rolling in." By the time that their exhausted heads hit the pillows, the 3Doodler had banked $1.2 million.

In the days that followed, money poured in at the rate of half a million dollars a day. The final tally: $2.34 million from over 26,000 backers. "Had we not purposely choked demand to ensure that we could deliver," says Cowen, "we could have raised twice what we did." The 3Doodler team now had a profitable order book, thousands of social media-savvy evangelists, and millions of dollars in the bank—and all without giving away a single share (Cowen steered them through a patent application too). All they gave up was a percentage of their funding: 5% to Kickstarter and 5% to Amazon, which handles payments. Cowen credits Kickstarter with letting them "leapfrog that terrible period where you have to go scrounging for money." Today, the 3Doodler is used around the world by teachers, architects, and artists. It has found a use for "instant braille" and to help visually impaired people understand 3D graphs with raised lines that they can feel.

3Doodler raised the fourth highest sum for a hardware startup in Kickstarter's short but dramatic history (it was founded in 2009). It is not surprising that Cowen tells me, "We're insanely grateful to our backers." Of course, the 3Doodler backers had their own interests at heart too. They were getting their hands on a fun product in time for Christmas, and for $75 versus the post-campaign price of $99. But above all, like many equity investors, they shared the co-founders' vision. Kickstarter backers see themselves as more than customers taking part in a polished pre-sell. Indeed, more often than is the case with venture capital-backed companies, rewards-based crowdfunded projects will owe their entire existence to their backers. These backers are in it to change the world. One of Indiegogo's films, *Curfew*, has even won an Oscar (Best Live Action Short, if you're wondering). *Now who would begrudge a few bucks to help make movie history?*

Kickstarter and the chasing pack

There is one big difference between Indiegogo and its main competitor, Kickstarter: Indiegogo lets companies elect to keep the cash if they miss their funding target. In that event, Indiegogo charges 9% commission rather than the standard 4%. People seem to like the "all or nothing" Kickstarter approach, one reason why it has cemented itself as the leading rewards-based crowdfunding platform. In 2013, $480 million was raised through the platform from 3 million people.[3] Some of the funded projects are truly mind-boggling. Think of a bicycle-powered helicopter that lifts the cyclist clean into the air as he peddles. That's Atlas. Think of a paper airplane with a tiny engine that is flown using a smartphone. That's PowerUp. Kickstarter also gave the world the highest profile crowdfunded project to date. Eric Migicovsky struggled to raise finance for his "smartwatch," an Internet-enabled watch. On Kickstarter, his "Pebble" raised over $10 million from 69,000 backers. Kickstarter also kickstarted the largest crowdfunded project ever: computer game Star Citizen that has raised $61 million and counting as of November 2014.

Success had bred fierce competition. RocketHub is a crowdfunding platform taking on the mighty Kickstarter from its backyard of New York City. The platform partnered in 2014 with Hearst and Disney, for Project Startup, taking some of its crowdfunded projects to a nationwide TV audience. RocketHub projects are as varied as on any platform. When I visited its website, I could back a company trying to reinvent ski poles with ones featuring built-in camera mounts and screwdrivers for on-slope ski adjustments. Or I could contribute to the sequencing of the genome of the blue beetle, an inhabitant of Death Valley that can live for a year without water and fake its own death. Rewards-based crowdfunding has gone international, not only through a global community of backers, but also at platform level. Melbourne-based Pozible is trying to tap into the comparatively neglected markets of Singapore and Malaysia. Lebanese startup Zoomaal is focused on the Arab world.

Countless other crowdfunding sites are busy evolving into the niches of this fast-growing ecosystem. UK-based Spacehive is the world's first crowdfunding platform for civic projects. Individuals can take to the platform to restore a statue or spruce up a local park. Wefund focuses on crowdfunding the creative arts. Teespring is a crowdfunding platform for the design and sale of t-shirts. MoolaHoop is a rewards-based crowdfunding platform for female entrepreneurs. Nap Time Startups addresses one of MoolaHoop's segments: "mompreneurs." Both are working to right the dire statistic that only 13% of venture capital goes to women-led companies.[4] Meanwhile, Tilt is crowdfunding group purchases. WeDid.it crowdfunds nonprofit businesses. Ulule crowdfunds independent, artistic projects. Petridish crowdfunds science experiments. MyEvent.com crowdfunds events. Pubslush crowdfunds new books. The list goes on.

Venture capital: following the crowd

Venture capital has also rushed into rewards-based crowdfunding. Kickstarter is backed by Union Square Ventures and Collaborative Fund. Indiegogo hauled in $40 million 2014 and is backed by a clutch of leading venture capital firms as well as eccentric British billionaire Richard Branson. But the venture capitalists are not only backing the platforms: they are backing some of the most promising companies on the platforms. Savvy investors and venture capitalists now prowl platforms like AngelList and FundersClub to find the pick of the early-stage companies. They will then track down the CEOs on LinkedIn, set up a call, and try and work out if they should position themselves as an investor for their next round. As Sherwood Neiss of Crowdfund Capital Advisors writes, "Investors (be it crowdfunders, private money, or public markets) want to invest in companies that have a great story, a great product, a great business model, and a great team—all characteristics that successful crowdfunding campaigns seem to demonstrate."

Investors love not only these platforms' treasure troves of glittering ideas, but also the fact that they can measure each idea's traction from right there on the campaign page. Rewards-based crowdfunding typically involves far larger crowds than equity crowdfunding. RocketHub's Brian Meece believes that "crowdfunded projects will be 10× more successful because they have community and social capital which ultimately gets converted into real capital." Indiegogo's Danae Ringelmann goes even further. "There will be a world where venture capitalists won't even look at potential deals unless those businesses have validated their product through crowdfunding." When Forest Whitaker funds movies with Indiegogo, it is not because he cannot raise film finance. It is to test demand for ticket sales. "We're becoming the world's incubation platform," says Ringelmann, "because we're creating an ecosystem and a mechanism where social projects, businesses, and creative ideas rise to the top algorithmically."

With the risks tolerably lowered for those projects with the most traction, in march the venture capitalists. After raising over $10 million on Kickstarter, Pebble raised $15 million from venerable Cambridge, Massachusetts venture capital firm Charles River Ventures, which was founded to commercialize research coming out of MIT across the street. Coinbase, the leading Bitcoin wallet, raised $165,000 on FundersClub before raising over $31 million from the trendy duo of Union Square Ventures and Andreessen Horowitz, among others. Kickstarter, once again ahead of the pack, has even had its first billion-dollar exit. Oculus Rift, the maker of a virtual reality headset for 3D gaming, raised $2.4

million on Kickstarter before raising a far heftier $91 million from venture capitalists and luring one of the giants of the industry, Marc Andreessen, founder of Internet browser Netscape, onto its board. It is fair to say the venture capitalists' big bet paid off. Four months later, Oculus Rift exited to Facebook for a very real $2 billion.

Invest in the crowd

Take investing in a startup or platform company one step further. *What if you could buy a stake in a human being?* Pave lets investors do just that. Investors browse "Talent Groups" like "Columbia graduates" or "Healthcare professionals" and then pick the individuals they wish to back to get a share of their future earnings. "Through Pave's proprietary Income-linked Payment Agreement, you receive monthly payments that target a 7% annual return." Each month, the Talent has to pay an installment to their backers—and if they don't? "In the event of continued nonpayment we follow standard collection procedures," says Pave's website. The "Talent" can also break free of their contracts by paying back five times the amount of the original loan. Less sinister than it sounds, promising students get an alternative to bank or credit card debt and the finance to pursue the career of their choice with an up-front loan. The Talents get not only money, but also mentorship. Pave is a form of 21st century patronage for a tech-savvy middle class. Pave's advisors include those modern Medicis—hedge fund managers—from GLG Partners, a $26 billion London fund.

Upstart is another startup letting investors cut out the banks who might otherwise take their pound of flesh from indebted millennials. The Silicon Valley startup crowdfunds student loans, taking a very different approach from Pave by ensuring borrowers' anonymity. Investors browse loans or invest automatically by setting their risk and return criteria. Founded by ex-Googlers, Upstart claims to use sophisticated underwriting models to protect investor capital. It analyses traditional data like FICO scores and credit reports as well as academic variables such as areas of study and grade point average to take a view on the borrower's likelihood of defaulting. A friend of mine, Brandon Chicotsky, used the lower rates on Upstart to refinance his student loans and build BaldLogo.com, a startup that lets brands buy advertising space on bald heads. No stooge of the company, he told me, "I'm going to be debt-free two years after leaving NYU. I don't know many of my peers who can say that! Frankly, I'd love my backers to earn well off me to honor that trust they had in me."

The big stuff

The crowd is speaking with its credit cards and PayPal accounts to fund gadgets, gigs, and games. It is even backing startups to the tune of millions of dollars. But in the scheme of things, that's petty cash. Peer-to-peer models may in time disrupt how people invest in two of the very largest asset classes: public market equities and real estate. Cyprus and New York-based eToro is the world's largest "social investing platform." By logging in through Facebook, users can see the stocks that their friends are buying on a social investment feed. It is Twitter-like too: users can "follow" their favorite traders to watch their investments. eToro's "CopyTrader" feature goes a step further and lets an investor automatically copy another's investments with one click. Inexperienced investors get guidance. Experienced investors earn commission based on their number of copiers, in effect a kickback to them for their hand in growing eToro's trading volume.

Through eToro's "OpenBook" platform, 1.75 million traders share trading information and investment strategies. All of the investments made through eToro are executed in the form of CFDs ("contracts for difference"), a type of derivative based on the share price of the underlying stock. Investors can also save on commission by buying financial instruments through a cooperative structure. From eToro's perspective, this is investment on the basis of James Surowiecki's notion of "the wisdom of crowds." But it is easy to imagine what a traditional contrarian investor like Warren Buffett would make of this sheepishness: he would fear that its herd-like mentality is a recipe for a bubble. Certainly, the dynamics of social media can stoke volatility. Consider the 2013 hoax tweet about an attack on the White House that knocked 0.9% off the Dow Jones.

Fundrise is a Washington DC-based platform that lets people invest directly in local real estate projects. Investors get a cut of the rent as well as a say on the buildings that go up in their area. "As your neighborhood grows, so does your investment," is Fundrise's call to action for those with the cash and desire to shape their area rather than have it shaped remotely by decision-makers on Wall Street or in the headquarters of real estate companies. "Real estate property is not some generic 'asset-class' that can be summed up as numbers on paper," continues the Fundrise website. "Each neighborhood, town, and city is unique … Institutional fund managers are disconnected from the places they are investing in and typically don't care if the projects being built are the right fit or not." As with equity crowdfunding, a new model in the we-conomy is bringing transparency to established sectors. "Very blackbox," is how Fundrise's co-founder, Dan Miller, described the real estate industry's current model to me.

How does Fundrise work? Investors buy shares in the buildings themselves and receive rent as dividends. Investors can also view analytics on the performance of their portfolio of local investments and join "Investor Networks," similar to AngelList's syndicates that allow them to club together to access larger deals. Fundrise is dramatically lowering the barrier to entry for those wishing to make investments in specific developments. For a minimum investment of $100, an investor could buy shares in the Transfer Station, a converted power station in Philadelphia. Indeed, the Transfer Station is itself the sharing economy in microcosm: a mix of co-working and co-retail space where retailers can rent shelves from $45 a month. Further benefits accrue to the Fundrise tenants: a group of well-connected, affluent locals have chosen them and may become some of their best customers and advocates.

Shared real estate investments are not restricted to cities. As Fundrise democratizes investment in prize downtown developments, so Fquare does for expensive tracts of farmland. Founded in 2012, Fquare applies the same fractional ownership model to investments in farmland. It works through sale and leasebacks: farmers sell land to accredited investors and the new "owner-farmers" see a return of 3–6% per annum. The lease expires at a time convenient to the farmer—typically retirement—at which point the land is sold, returning capital to investors. The odd name relates to the notion of each share representing a square foot of farmland. Fquare's founder Charles Polanco is bullish on farmland as an investment. He points out that the value of Iowa farmland has increased almost 600% since 1990 compared with a 270% increase for the S&P 500 index. Like Fundrise, Fquare hopes to unite economic with social good. It runs an initiative that aspires to feed the hungry by buying farms and donating their crops to food banks.

Health warnings

The risks of some sharing economy investments are stark. For example, almost all peer-to-peer loans are unsecured. In addition to the risks of losing the capital and illiquidity, the US peer-to-peer lenders are not covered by the FDIC, the federal agency for insuring bank deposits, or guaranteed. In the UK, investments in peer-to-peer finance platforms are not protected by the UK Financial Services Compensation Scheme, a similar government insurance policy that covers depositors in bank and building societies for up to £85,000 of loss. I have some savings in Funding Circle—money I will lose in full if my borrowers default. One cautionary tale from the sharing economy is Quakle, a tiny peer-to-peer lender that went bust in 2011. Credit-worthiness was assessed largely through a review system with lenders encouraged to engage with the personal (sob) stories of its heavily indebted borrowers. Default rates were close to 100%.

Thankfully, today's major players are far larger and less naïve, employing underwriters, credit agencies, and statisticians to carve up investments across potentially hundreds of borrowers. Lending Club's default rate is 3.0%, meaning not the percentage of nonpaying borrowers but the average amount of each investment portfolio that is lost each year to nonpaying borrowers. Prosper's default rate of 8.6% is much higher, mostly because their loans have historically had higher interest rates and risk than Lending Club's. In the UK, RateSetter operates a "Provision Fund" that at the time of writing has successfully protected over 17,000 lenders from losing a penny to defaulting borrowers. Nevertheless, higher than market returns will correlate to higher than market risk, particularly if the number of credible borrowers in the coming years does not increase with the inflow of capital.

When it comes to investing in the startups themselves, the risks are much greater. According to research from Harvard Business School, even the professionals usually get it wrong: 75% of the companies deemed sufficiently promising to raise venture capital fail.[5] The risks for amateurs of investing through platforms like Seedrs speak for themselves. After 4 years, half of all new businesses have folded. For technology startups, the risks are higher. Tech startup incubators pick the top few percent of applicants onto their programs: a distillation of some of the world's most ambitious and talented entrepreneurs. Approximately, 90% of these startups fail.[6] If failure rates are sky high, so too are prices. Spicy valuations are the norm, not only in sharing economy startups, but also in other "hot" areas like software as a service, or "SaaS," making startup investing more often than not a string of expensive mistakes. Good luck finding the next Google.

The sums at stake on rewards-based crowdfunding may be smaller but investments here too are fraught with risk. Kickstarter is assured of its fee but gives no guarantee that projects will ever see the light of day. Many run months behind schedule. "Vaporware" is the term for hardware projects that never ship, often because they are physically impossible. To reduce this risk, new Kickstarter rules ban whizzy product videos and simulations of "future capabilities." When projects do abort, Kickstarter offers no refund because it never holds the money: once a project is funded, the cash moves from a backer's credit card straight to the project creator's Amazon Payments account. Backers are thus wholly reliant on the project creators to refund their cash. Horror stories are rare but not unknown. In 2013, Erik Chevalier raised $122,000 on Kickstarter to launch a new board game. It never shipped and many backers lost their pledges. As Shapiro from Collaborative Fund puts it, "Crowdfunding is the wild, wild west." He too has been burned: one of his fund's write-offs was ProFounder, a failed crowdfunding platform.

The "buy-to-share" model

We have seen how venture capitalists and individuals are investing in share platforms and their most promising startups. But the largest asset class of all is the inventory that will ultimately be listed on the major platforms. "Investing in the networks that light up the sharing economy, like Airbnb, Lyft, Sidecar, and many others certainly looks like a good idea," writes Fred Wilson on his blog AVC.com. "They may just be opening up a massive new investment market in physical assets that produce income … that may turn into a very large capital asset class." Uber is at the forefront of what I call "buy-to-share": the purchase of assets specifically for the purpose of renting them out for the shortest of time increments on online platforms. In 2014, Uber lined up $2.5 billion of finance to allow its drivers to buy new GM and Toyota cars for the Uber platform. If the cars are not driven on Uber, the interest rates spike. But if they are, taxi drivers get cheap car finance and Uber gets a secure supply of drivers.

Amateur peer-to-peer investors are disrupting professional investors through crowdfunding. Now professional investors are disrupting the amateurs by operating a "buy-to-share" model. Peer-to-peer car-sharing is ostensibly about ordinary people renting out their cars when they are not being used. However, according to RelayRides' Shelby Clark, power users are buying cars just to rent out on the platform. Some owners, it is claimed, make more money in the first year of rentals than their new car cost, providing them with a free car plus an ongoing revenue stream. This trend reaches its zenith on room rental sites like Airbnb and HouseTrip. Professional, yield-hungry investors—a far cry from ordinary folk trying to get by—now play in these lucrative marketplaces. This is not a story that Airbnb is fond of telling: hence a *PandoDaily* exposé of "The Man Who Does Not Exist"—an Airbnb "host" backed by investors of his own who has bought a string of Manhattan apartments that rent out for $500 a night.

What are the implications if this "buy-to-share" model picks up steam? As we will see, trouble is brewing between the platforms and cities that are generally less inclined to provide special dispensations to professional investors. Down the line, internecine strife beckons within the communities themselves, between those that may have embraced the platform for social or environmental reasons and the brazen economic opportunists. Further down the line, the increased demand for high-yielding assets from buy-to-share landlords and owners may even move asset prices northwards. This is arguably already happening in certain city centers where short-term rentals have soared in popularity. Such price inflation could rip a rung off the bottom of the property ladder for millions. As sharing economy lawyer Janelle Orsi puts it, "The people who could get the most benefit from this cannot harness the capital needed."

Indeed, "buy-to-share" could ironically lead to a *drop* in asset utilization. *Slate* journalist Rachel Monroe puts it succinctly:

> One of the touted benefits of the sharing economy is that it enables people to make more efficient use of their resources. But increasingly, the effect is the opposite – property owners have a financial incentive to keep their houses empty more of the time.

Apartments that at one time were full for 52 weeks a year now empty out during low season and switchovers between the fleeting visits of tourists. Monroe noted the impact on her hometown of Marfa in Texas. "Properties are owned by people who don't live here, creating a slightly absurd situation in which a visitor from Portland pays Airbnb fees to a property owner who may well live in Portland herself." To an unknown extent, the market can be trusted to resolve these problems: if utilization falls too much, "buyers to share" will exit the market.

However, today at least, sharing economy businesses are overwhelmingly utilizing existing capacity. For every tenant served notice by a landlord looking for a higher yield, Airbnb and its competitors are helping vastly more of them to pay their rent, as well as helping owner-occupiers to pay off their mortgages. At the same time, new ways of accessing assets are leading to fewer purchases of houses and cars—our largest and most highly financed investments. In turn, that will mean less debt for bankers to collateralize and less systemic risk for the global economy. Sharing existing capacity can also slow our resource consumption and cut waste. But if we can break our addiction to buying and use what we already have instead, it might not be such good news for everyone. *What then for the great companies of the world?*

Notes

1 Research by Jeremiah Owyang, founder of Crowd Companies, July 11th, 2013 and updated in 2014: http://www.web-strategist.com/blog/2013/07/11/meet-the-investors-of-the-collaborative-economy/.

2 *How Does Crowdfunding Impact Job Creation, Company Revenue and Professional Investor Interest?* (Crowdfund Capital Advisors, January 15th, 2014): http://crowdfundcapitaladvisors.com/images/CF-Post%20Funding%20Research%20FINAL%20Jan%202014.pdf.

3 Data quoted by Nick Summers (*The Next Web*, January 8th, 2014): http://thenextweb.com/insider/2014/01/08/3-million-people-pledged-480-million-total-kickstarter-campaigns-2013/.

4 Data relating to venture capital raised by companies with at least one female founder was collected by PitchBook during the first half of 2013. The amount raised was up from a shocking low of 4% in 2004: http://blog.pitchbook.com/women-taking-a-growing-share-of-venture-capital/.

5 Ghosh, Shikar, *Why Companies Fail* (Harvard, 2012). Ghosh's statistic on the failure rate of companies is derived from his analysis of over 10,000 startups during the last 20 years: http://hbswk.hbs.edu/item/6591.html.

6 Data quoted by Peter Relan in *90% Of Incubators And Accelerators Will Fail And That's Just Fine For America And The World* (*TechCrunch*, October 14th, 2012): http://techcrunch.com/2012/10/14/90-of-incubators-and-accelerators-will-fail-and-why-thats-just-fine-for-america-and-the-world/.

5
chapter

Corporates
Angry, Afraid—and In

A severe grey-suited man stared long and hard at our passports. Then he locked them away and phoned ahead for clearance. At the BMW research labs in Munich, Germany, they take no chances. In 2011, BMW had invested in JustPark, then a tiny startup known as ParkatmyHouse.com. It was the beginning of an unusual collaboration between a startup that then had just a single employee and a corporate titan. But that was half the point.

Inside the gated compound, unreleased BMW models were disguised in swirling paintwork to hide their bodylines from the roving lenses of photographers. Anthony and I headed through a maze of buildings and down echoing long corridors. Finally, we found the room, its name a string of numbers and Zs like some kind of wartime code. We were there to discuss a top-secret collaboration between our companies: a parking app that would run on the sat nav of the MINI, a BMW-owned brand since the 1990s. For the first time in history, drivers would be able to book and pay for parking—and, of course, be taken there—using the sat nav in their vehicles. For the first time too, we would be taking e-commerce into the car itself.

Why did BMW need us? For all its resources, BMW knew that an organization of its size with process baked into its structure could not innovate at the speed of a startup. A lean upstart like Tesla can move faster. And an even smaller team can move even faster. Startups also hire the right kind of entrepreneurial people to make innovation happen: everyone in JustPark is an entrepreneur, right down to Julie, our chef, who manages her budget and owns share options. Finally, innovation requires an appetite for risk. A large company's brand is both its greatest strength and its Achilles' heel. While it can provide the company with its high profit margin, the need to protect a treasured brand can be paralyzing. By investing in startups, BMW was letting smaller companies—ones that are not statistically supposed do anything other than fail—take risks on its behalf.

FIGURE 5.1 JustPark's in-car app developed in partnership with BMW: the world's first in-car application allowing a driver to book parking through their car

BMW is right: large companies cannot easily become startups. When Ron Johnson left Apple to take the reins at JC Penney, he tried to turn it into one, rapidly iterating its offerings. JC Penney lost $4 billion in 18 months and Johnson lost his job. BMW knew that it could not make that transition either, but it could buy into it. BMW also knew that, with changing paradigms of ownership, it needed to look beyond selling cars. So in 2011, BMW set up its "i Ventures" fund, a $100 million fund run out of a stylish incubator space in Manhattan's West Village. The fund's remit: to invest in startups that would transform the way people get around cities—and not only in cars. The plan was simple. The startups would get the credibility of a trusted global brand and BMW would get access to emerging technologies. JustPark is discussed at BMW Board level because we are part of its plan to thrive in a digital rather than mechanical world, a world of apps rather than alternators. In our own small way, we are part of a blueprint not only for BMW's future, but for the future of the automotive sector as a whole.

Every corporate's worst fear: irrelevance

Most of the world's largest corporates now understand that new technologies can unleash more powerful shifts in consumer behavior than all the billboards and TV adverts ever could. A developed we-conomy would see many such shifts. Instead of HSBC standing between depositors and borrowers, they would be earning interest and getting credit from each other through a platform like Lending Club. Instead of Hilton providing a hotel room in a foreign city, homeowners and tourists would be renting directly through a platform like Airbnb. Instead of a professional services company like Accenture providing offshored labor, employer and worker would be meeting online through a platform like oDesk.

"If you don't build a value cycle," says economist Umair Haque, "one will be self-organized. And it will commoditize you ... Certain industries have to rewire themselves, or prepare to sink into the quicksand of the past." Countless public companies capitalized at hundreds of billions dollars are now at risk of disintermediation. "Corporate America will need to pay very close attention to this new paradigm," writes Arun Sundararajan of New York University. "The terms 'collaborative consumption' and 'sharing economy' might seem more reminiscent of flower power than of Gordon Gekko, but the business threats they embody are very real ... If your business relies on a model of consumption that is inefficient for your consumers, chances are that there's already a new sharing economy marketplace that is looking to streamline it for them."

This existential threat comes not from a company's conventional competitors—the ones it has been monitoring so diligently—but from its own customers, who may one day get along fine without it. That is a scary idea for companies who saw themselves as indispensable. Scarier still, these new entrants are competing with entirely different business models. It would require the corporates to make a change to their existing activities too complex and terrifying to contemplate, like asking the driver of a truck that is headed straight for a cliff to re-engineer his truck into a plane before it reaches the edge. Worst of all, once a company's customers find a better way of getting their product or service, they will abandon old forms of behavior for good. That might mean e-hailing a SideCar rather than phoning the local taxi company or hiring a dress from Rent the Runway rather than buying one at Bloomingdale's. Once markets are disintermediated, they stay disintermediated.

It is not surprising therefore that many large corporates are watching the tiny startups that threaten to unleash these shifts in behavior like hawks. Many are paying consultancies to keep an eye out for them. Trendwatching is one such consultancy, providing an analysis of future trends including the sharing economy to some 4,000 brands. Corporates differ greatly on how best to respond to these threats. Some, like BMW, are trying to rewire themselves to profit from the upheavals ahead. As we will explore, the sharing economy is replete with examples of large corporates partnering with small insurgents in the spirit of "If you can't beat them, join them." But others are gearing up to fight these structural changes. It is a fight that most will lose. In the next decade, some huge public companies will experience the corporate equivalent of the Kübler-Ross model of grief first observed in the terminally ill: denial, anger, bargaining, depression, and, ultimately, acceptance.

The music industry: a lesson for incumbents

For the last 30 years, the music industry has fought a bloody, losing battle with technology. In the early 1980s, the music industry mobilized against analogue tapes. I am just old enough to remember the British Phonographic Industry's well-financed campaign: "Home Taping is Killing Music." The chilling ads showed an analogue tape fashioned as a skull, its spools for eye sockets. When digital audiotapes arrived in the late 1980s, the industry mobilized again. This time, it did so even more aggressively since music could now be copied with no loss of quality. In the US, millions of dollars of lobbying led to Congress passing the Audio Home Recording Act in 1992. It mandated copy protection on digital audiotaping devices that prevented people from making copies of copies. It also slapped a big levy on digital audio or "DAT" tapes.

But by the early 1990s, the music industry had a new enemy: MP3s. This new format allowed songs to be stored in about a tenth the amount of computer memory as DAT tapes, a breakthrough that made them downloadable. The RIAA—the Recording Industry Association of America—was back in court suing Diamond, the makers of the Rio, the first commercially successful MP3 player. Back then, MP3s players were pricey devices bought in tiny numbers. However, the music industry's problems mushroomed once music files became easily transferable online. The RIAA moved to shut down Napster, Sean Parker's free file-sharing service. Hit-machine songwriter Mike Stoller, who penned Hound Dog and Jailhouse Rock among countless others, said at the time, "Today, I fear for the 17 year-old songwriter looking forward to a career in the music business … If Napster gets away with its thievery, it will turn that teenager's future livelihood into a mere hobby and in doing so, it will ensure that fewer and fewer talented individuals can afford to devote their efforts to expanding America's musical heritage."

Today, music is alive and well in America, unlike the record industry. If its fate tells us anything, it is evolve or die. Consumers get their way in the end. Rather than leading the change, the industry resisted only to see its market taken by technology businesses: Apple's iTunes, Google's YouTube, and, more recently, Spotify and Pandora. Indeed, music streaming revenues are on the up because "Convenience has trumped pirating," to quote *Forbes*, and not only in music but in streamed TV and film too. These spoils will now be divided between the tech giants. I cannot help but think of my school holidays in 1996 when I did an internship at Sony Music Entertainment in London, now a shrinking giant of the music industry. Every Friday afternoon, a trolley full of champagne was wheeled around the office. I was told that my boss bought a new Porsche every year. Rather than innovating, the titans of the music industry became decadent and self-serving. They fell from power and have only themselves to blame.

The auto industry: showing the way

According to the co-founder of *Shareable*, Neal Gorenflo, "The car industry is having a Napster moment but responding positively." JustPark is not the only sharing economy endeavor that BMW is involved in. In a joint venture with German car rental giant Sixt, BMW runs DriveNow, a premium car-sharing business in San Francisco and five German cities. The service has put over 2,000 BMWs and MINIs on the streets of those cities, rentable from 31 cents per minute in Germany including road tax, insurance, and fuel. If the car is parked during a booking, its GPS knows to drop the tariff. For the foreseeable half-century, there will be significant economic value in producing and selling high-quality personal vehicles, particularly in emerging markets. But in addition to ownership, BMW wants to benefit from the trend of on-demand access. DriveNow is the start of what may become a major shift in business model for the carmaker. DriveNow's website even goes so far as to announce the service is "*Besser als das eigene Auto*": better than owning a car.

BMW's great German rival, Daimler, is if anything even more invested in shared models. Its Car2Go service has been running longer than DriveNow and is operational in 16 North American and European cities. Both DriveNow and Car2Go have a big advantage over Zipcar: cars do not have to be returned to their bays at the end of a booking. The owner of Mercedes-Benz has also developed an all-purpose mobility app called Moovel. Currently only available in Germany, Moovel combines Car2Go, long-distance ridesharing in any make of car through Carpooling.com, bike-sharing services like nextbike, and public transit data. "It's all about access trumping ownership," says Michael Kuhn, Moovel's project manager, rolling out the hip sharing economy mantra on behalf of his grand old employer. In 2014, Daimler also acquired a similar US business, RideScout, a smartphone app that aggregates all mobility options including bicycle- and car-sharing.

BMW is also not the only automotive company to have its own venture capital fund. General Motors has GM Ventures, a fund that took a minority stake in peer-to-peer car-sharing startup RelayRides. "It was really inspiring to see that this little thing we were doing had caught the attention of the world's largest carmarker," RelayRides' Shelby Clark told me, "and that General Motors, a company that could have felt threatened by the rise of shared cars, wanted to support us." The partnership was designed to take advantage of GM's OnStar system to allow RelayRides users to securely unlock over 15 million GM cars with the RelayRides' mobile app. If we can borrow our neighbors' cars, it could indeed lead to lower new car sales. Yet the deal aimed to ensure that the ones being purchased would be made by GM. Through OnStar, GM bought the ability to get millions of potential buyers into its cars, opening up a new model for self-arranged test drives at far lower cost than through mass media and a network of dealerships.

The French car industry made similar moves into mobility services at the turn of the decade. Peugeot's Mu sub-brand plays to the breadth of its product range. Membership provides access to customizable Peugeot cars, electric scooters, bicycles, and vans in over 100 cities across Europe. "In the biggest cities in Europe, we see people giving up ownership of the car to switch to sheer usage," says Peugeot's Nadège Faul from its mobility strategy team. "Either we take care of it and recognize this new market or we might just as well lose these consumers for good." Citroën's Multicity is built around car and EV rental. Focused on France, Multicity also offers peer-to-peer car rentals and carpooling through partnerships with French startups OuiCar and BlaBlaCar. Not to be outdone, Japan's Toyota has i-Road. The Blade Runner-esque "personal mobility vehicle" runs on three wheels with its balance handled by computer chips and gyroscopes. Toyota plans to deploy i-Roads in fleets around cities: a safer, speedier alternative to shared bicycles for those who also don't like getting their hair wet.

Carmakers are wise to react: the economic implications of car-sharing are enormous. A study from UC Berkeley found that the average shared car removes between 9 and 13 other cars from the road.[1] The carmakers now embracing shared services are moving to a model that collaborative economy consultant Jeremiah Owyang calls "company-as-a-service," whereby the company rents its assets on a pay-as-you-go or subscription basis. Although car rental is not new, its flexibility and significance is. BMW and Toyota now allow car rentals straight off the forecourts of a growing number of their dealerships, as does Ford through Ford2Go, which launched in Daimler's backyard of Germany with provocatively similar branding to Daimler's Car2Go. Chrysler's Dodge has even experimented with crowdfunding cars. Hopeful owners invited friends and family to pay for sections of the car. The process was similar to a wedding list but instead of plates and sheets, invitees were suckered into a buying a tire or gearbox.

Of course, no one would expect the car rental giants to sit idly by while the carmakers move onto their patch. In 2013, Avis Budget Group shelled out half a billion dollars for Zipcar. While there are clear synergies between both companies, the price Avis Budget paid for a business that had struggled to scratch a profit illustrates the combination of fear and greed with which incumbents view the shared mobility space. Avis Budget CEO Ron Nelson said he'd been "dismissive of car sharing in the past" but had a change of heart when he realized the potential profit in providing hourly rentals to "younger, more wired consumers." Enterprise, the US's largest car rental company, is after the same segment. It has gobbled up Chicago's IGO CarSharing, Mint Cars in New York and Boston, and PhillyCarShare. Enterprise also covered its shared services bases by acquiring long-distance ridesharing app Zimride: think BlaBlaCar without the traction. Meanwhile, in the UK, in the absence of a suitable acquisition target, easyCar spun out its own peer-to-peer car-sharing service, easyCar Club. easyCar is backed by flamboyant entrepreneur Stelios Haji-Ioannou, the founder of budget airline easyJet.

But if there is any entrepreneur who personifies the progressive leadership shown by the automotive sector it is Bill Ford, the Executive Chairman of Ford and great-grandson of Henry Ford. Bill Ford is not your average Motor City executive: a taekwondo black belt, a vegan, and a lover of electric cars and startups. In 2009, he said, "The future of transportation will be a blend of things like Zipcar, public transportation, and private car ownership. Not only do I not fear that, but I think it's a great opportunity for us to participate in the changing nature of car ownership." In the same year, Ford founded and personally backed Fontinalis Partners, a Detroit-headquartered venture capital fund, to invest in "Next-Generation Mobility." Fontinalis' holdings include RelayRides and Zagster, a bike-sharing platform for universities, businesses, and hotels. Back in the late 1990s, the Ford Motor Company made billions, in part by selling gas-guzzling, high-margin SUVs. The world has moved on and Bill Ford is moving with it.

Taking on the hotels

The progressiveness of large corporates in the automotive sector is not mirrored by those in the hospitality sector. Hotel groups have been slow to adapt their business models to changing consumer habits for three reasons. Firstly, as we will see in the following chapter, short-term rentals operate in a less certain regulatory environment than car-sharing, increasing the risk for hotels of expanding into this market. Secondly, hotel companies have fewer technical staff and developers compared to carmakers, creating a skills gap when it comes to bringing new online products to market. Thirdly, it is more expensive and complex for hotel groups to adapt to a business model that is being disrupted not by a new way of accessing their inventory but by entirely new goods, that is to say private homes rather than hotel rooms.

But neither is it impossible. Hilton, for example, could launch "Hilton Homes": an offering of luxury properties a short walk from the amenities of its hotels. Instead of executives booking just a single room, they could make a family holiday of a business trip and book an entire luxury home at far greater expense. In order to minimize capital expenditure and risk, Hilton Homes would neither lease nor own the homes, but put its trusted brand to a curated marketplace, managing and servicing the properties with its nearby hotel teams. Today, the short-term rental luxury apartment market is being taken by onefinestay, a sharing economy company that a hotel giant may one day acquire. Hotel groups could also invest in peer-to-peer accommodation platforms. Or they could club together to start their own marketplace, as the leading UK realtors did when they founded Rightmove, now valued at £2.2 billion. As we saw in the music industry, if incumbents dally, technology companies will eat their lunch—as TripAdvisor is attempting to do via its 2008 acquisition of Airbnb clone, FlipKey.

For now, shared services innovation in the hotel sector is focused on co-working. According to research firm IDC, the number of global "mobile workers"—those without a fixed office space—will reach 1.3 billion by the end of 2015.[2] "The way people work is changing," notes Paul Cahill, Brand Vice President at Marriott Hotels. "And we're right there with them." In collaboration with LiquidSpace, a marketplace that lets mobile workers rent workspace by the hour or day, "Workspace On Demand by Marriott" lets people book workspaces at over 430 of its hotels. Marriott also offers many workspaces for free, knowing they would otherwise be empty and in the hope of attracting a well-heeled business segment into the hotel that will spend on food and drink. W Hotels, part of the Starwood Group, has made a similar partnership with LiquidSpace competitor Desks Near Me. Hotel chains like InterContinental and Kimpton are also increasing access to shared amenities. The "Hyatt Has it" program has seen lockers fitted in Hyatt hotels containing shareable items for guests, from phone chargers to yoga mats.

Matters have not reached crisis point for the hotel industry. In 2014, academics at Boston University conducted the first detailed study into the impact of Airbnb on the hotel industry. Looking at a local market in Texas, they calculated that a 1% increase in Airbnb listings led to a mere 0.05% drop in quarterly hotel revenues.[3] Airbnb was barely cannibalizing hotel revenues, but rather bringing new visitors to the area. The small drop that they did discover was concentrated among budget hotels and family-run guesthouses rather than listed hotel companies—it is an irony that the large hoteliers lobbying against Airbnb are far less threatened by shared models than the more progressive carmakers. Indeed, compared to Airbnb and its competitors, the hotel giants are still huge by comparison. In 2012, Airbnb celebrated booking over 14 million guest nights globally. Large as that figure sounds, according to research firm STR, the hotel industry sells over 1 billion nights a year in the US alone.[4] There will always be a need for hotels, especially luxury ones, and to meet the needs of business travelers.

But while the impact to date may have been slight, the tide is beginning to turn against the hotel groups. In 2014, Airbnb surpassed Hilton to become the world's biggest "hotelier" by beds with over 600,000 listings around the world, even though Airbnb does not own so much as a pillowcase. For hotels, the worry is not where Airbnb is today but where it may be in several years' time. It took Airbnb almost 4 years to get its first million guests. Today, more than a million guests stay on Airbnb each month. In some cities, hotels will see a drop in their key metric of "RevPAR"—revenue per available room—if Airbnb can continue its trajectory into mainstream tourist segment. The West Coast startup is even going after the business traveler market by integrating into expense management software and providing curated lists of business-suitable properties.

Meanwhile, more and more booking channels are opening up for peer-to-peer accommodation. Already, hotel and flight search engine Hipmunk shows apartments in its hotel search, and Expedia has partnered with HomeAway to show the latter's residential inventory in its search results. In time, hotels could also face far more competing private rooms if the asset class of rooms and apartments for short-term lets becomes properly regulated, giving the necessary comfort to investors to snap up properties on a buy-to-share model. Such residential inventory could ultimately outcompete many hotel rooms on price and space. They will also outcompete them when it comes to providing a memorable and "talkable" experience. Here as ever, sharing is viral. No one would write on Facebook that their Marriott hotel room was clean. *But posting a beautiful, albeit smug, photo of their yurt/castle/ houseboat/lighthouse/treehouse?* Now that's a different story. In fact, it is millions of stories, to be told time and time again.

Taking on the banks

The difference in size between sharing economy startups and the incumbents is even larger in finance than accommodation. But here, the Goliaths are if anything more afraid of their Davids. *The Financial Times* broke the story that Wells Fargo had gone so far as to ban its staff from using Lending Club and Prosper. "Peer-to-peer lending," read the leaked Wells Fargo memo, "is a competitive activity that poses a conflict of interest." *The Financial Times* explained the ban thus: "Tensions between banks and peer-to-peer platforms have arisen because the P2P model cuts traditional lenders out by matching capital directly with borrowers." To put the ban in perspective, Wells Fargo had third-quarter 2013 revenues of $22.3 billion. Lending Club, the leading peer-to-peer lender, recorded a mere $10.8 million over the same period. Peer-to-peer banking expert Simon Cunningham of *LendingMemo* notes that "Comparing GDP, this is akin to the United States of America issuing a trade embargo against the island nation of Mauritius."

However, the founder of Lending Club, Renaud Laplanche, has spelt out three reasons why the banks are right to be afraid. Firstly, he points to the efficiency of peer-to-peer lending: Lending Club's operational expense ratio is below 2% and trending lower. The banks' is typically 5–7%. "We have this 5% cost advantage that we can pass on to our customers," says Laplanche, "so it is really hard to see how banks could compete." Secondly, the new peer-to-peer lenders use modern, custom-built technology. The banks, on the other hand, run creaking legacy systems that came with years of mergers. Finally, the startups have a cultural advantage. "The kinds of people who come to work at Lending Club," says Laplanche, "are those who say, 'I want to transform the banking industry'." These same three rules—lower operating costs, the advantages of starting from a clean slate with regard to technology, and culture—extend to every sector touched by the sharing economy.

One could add a fourth reason to Laplanche's three: the lingering distrust of big banks left over from the credit crunch. And indeed a fifth: focus. The most successful apps generally focus on doing one thing very, very well. The most successful peer-to-peer finance companies are no exception. Andy Weissman is a partner at Union Square Ventures, an investor in Lending Club, Germany's Auxmoney, and the UK's Funding Circle. Weissman notes that:

> Banks and financial institutions often centralize things, capital, capabilities, credit, underwriting, risk assessment … and the last 20 years have seen the rise of integrated financial institutions and so-called 'financial supermarkets' that in theory gain from being able to provide every financial service available under one organization. But what if those capabilities were better performed separately and unbundled from the core institution; would the services be provided better (faster and cheaper)?

Weissman goes on to list high-growth niche players like payday loans company Wonga and money remittance service Dwolla. For now, these new entrants have a clear focus—Lending Club's is refinancing consumer credit card debt. But most aspire to build a suite of disruptive products one by one. Lending Club is soon to offer small business loans, opening up a second front with the retail banks.

For all these reasons, growth rates in peer-to-peer finance have been dramatic. The two big Americans, Prosper and Lending Club, have lent over $10 billion between them, while in the UK over $2 billion of peer-to-peer debt has been lent. It is no surprise that growth is robust given the attractiveness of interest rates. With UK market leaders Funding Circle and Zopa offering investors average returns of 6.1% and 5.1% respectively after fees and bad debts, they are unlikely to run short of capital. Unless hampered by regulation or discredited by scandals, peer-to-peer lenders all over the world will begin to lure in big checks from pension funds and insurance companies looking to take advantage of the same attractive rates as the crowd. No question, the risks of depositing cash with Prosper are greater than with HSBC. But trace these trends forward a few decades and it is not farcical for *LendingMemo* to speculate that "The greatest economic force in our nation today, arguably in world history, is *en route* to be humbled by a couple of hundred people and a server farm."

If any sector will not take well to being humbled, it is finance. *How are the banks fighting back?* In finance, as in most areas impacted by the sharing economy, not every incumbent views the upstarts as foes. Titan Bank and Congressional Bank, two US community banks, buy loans from Lending Club that are too small to profitably originate themselves without the economies of scale of a major retail bank. The larger banks are also partnering up. Santander and Funding Circle have started to refer business to one another. BlackRock—the world's largest asset manager following its acquisition of Barclays Global Investors—has hedged its bets by investing in Prosper. Some of Wall Street's most powerful and well-connected bankers are getting in on the action too. Former CEO of Morgan Stanley John Mack sits on the board of Lending Club and former Citigroup CEO Vikram Pandit has backed Orchard, a startup building a secondary market in peer-to-peer debt. Here too, technology companies smell opportunity. In 2013, Google Ventures ploughed $125 million into Lending Club.

Coping strategies

So what's a corporate giant to do in the face of these seismic shifts? Some of the strategies that the banks employ are not unique to the financial sector. There are four main coping strategies that can be used in tandem by those with most to lose.

1 Investing

These days, every self-respecting corporate titan has its own venture capital fund. Pharmaceuticals companies like Eli Lilly, GlaxoSmithKline, and Roche have funds. Citigroup has Citi Ventures for financial services investments. Siemens has one for engineering and healthcare investments. Total, Orange, and SNCF, France's state-owned train operator, have teamed up as investors in Paris-based Ecomobilité Ventures to invest in sustainable mobility. Above all, funds are *de rigeur* for any technology giant, whether its business is online advertising or hardware, software, or silicon. Witness Google Ventures, AOL Ventures, Microsoft Ventures, Intel Capital, Qualcomm Ventures, and Dell Ventures, to name but a few. Unlike the institutional money of a Sequoia Capital or an Accel Partners, these corporate funds invest for strategic reasons as much—and often more so—as they do in the hope of an outsize financial return.

Starting a fund is more than just something to do with a spare $100 million sitting in cash on a balance sheet: it gives a company a seat at the tables of the startups who may become its competitors. Often, as in the case of BMW's investment in JustPark, this means a literal board seat. From this vantage point, a large corporate gets a view on the shifting sands of its industry, letting it track the progress of sharing models from the inside and influence their trajectory. That is worth having, for what amounts to small change for a company of BMW's size. JustPark is not alone in the sharing economy in having powerful corporate friends. Microsoft and CBRE, the commercial real estate group, back desk rental startup LiquidSpace. Pet retailer Petco backs peer-to-peer dog-sitting startup Rover.com. On top of Lending Club, Google dropped $258 million into Uber.

Sometimes, a large company will buy up the whole business. In 2013, Groupon bought SideTour, a marketplace for travel experiences provided by locals. The year later, TripAdvisor bought a similar experiences startup, Tripbod. I used to share an office with Tripbod's founder, Sally Davey. "At Tripbod," she told me, "we had a built a community of engaged locals who can improve a trip by giving the right advice to the right person at the right time. It turned out that everything we were doing on a tiny scale at Tripbod matched up uncannily well with TripAdvisor's longer-term goals." Still, aside from the acquisitions by the major US car rental players, sharing economy acquisitions have been few and far between. This is largely because marketplaces tend to be binary. Very few will ever become worth buying. But those that are on their way to making it want to go all the way to the public markets.

2 Partnering

As with BMW's investment in JustPark, a corporate investment often goes hand in glove with a strategic partnership. GE is an investor in Quirky, a platform that crowd-sources and develops inventions. Quirky lets people submit ideas for inventions that many of us have every so often and do nothing with. If enough people in Quirky's million-strong community want to see a submitted idea become reality, Quirky does so via its team of designers, engineers, patent attorneys, and branding experts. Each week culminates in a live-streamed "Eval" at www.quirky. com/live, a theatrical brainstorm of the week's top ideas. One time, I tuned in along with 94,000 other viewers and voted for my favorite idea: a bowl that could inductively charge smartphones. Quirky's inventors plus anyone else who materially contributes get kickbacks from sales. Its best-selling product is the "Pivot Power": an adjustable snake-like power strip that has sold 700,000 units and made Jake Zien, its 24-year-old inventor, a millionaire.

How does this involve GE? GE has opened up a library of 1,000 of its patents to Quirky inventors. Sales of any products that use the patents generate revenue for Quirky, the inventor, and GE. With the help of aspiring inventors on a platform founded in 2009, the 19th-century conglomerate can monetize patents that were otherwise gathering dust. Quirky also works with other large corporates downstream. Once Quirky has developed and manufactured its products in its Chinese factories, they are distributed to e-tailers like Fab and Amazon as well as brick and mortar stores like Target and Best Buy. Quirky helps them to stock innovative and exciting inventory. When Scott Weiss, the venture capitalist who led Quirky's Series C investment round, interviewed its wholesale customers, he found them in awe of the products coming to market through Quirky's wildly collaborative model. Target's buyer told Weiss, "Nobody is innovating at the pace that Quirky is."

Other offline retailers are seeing the wisdom in partnering with their potential sharing economy competitors. One of the fastest growing of these online players is Brooklyn-headquartered handmade goods marketplace Etsy. Through the "Etsy Wholesale" program, home-furnishing chains West Elm and Nordstrom sell Etsy goods in purpose-designed concessions in their stores. By showcasing novel and frequently changing local producers, both brands are luring in new shoppers. Meanwhile, Etsy is able to make offline sales in the West Elm and Nordstrom stores without the enormous capital expenditure and distraction of leasing, fitting-out, staffing, and operating its own retail units. At one time, West Elm and Nordstrom would have viewed the more tech-savvy Etsy as something to be feared. Now they are partnering for mutual benefit.

Large companies are slotting the crowd into their business models. This can be through community-based customer support. Swiss telecoms provider Swisscom partnered with Mila, the Zurich-headquartered task marketplace, to launch "Swisscom Neighborhood." Swisscom uses Mila to undertake peer-to-peer customer service. Instead of summoning a highly paid engineer, Swisscom's customers can summon a Mila task provider. GiffGaff, a low-cost UK mobile network, lets its own customers answer other customer support queries, rewarding the most effective ones with freebies. Sometimes, incumbents are looking to complement their own offerings. Kelly Services, the global employment agency, uses oDesk's network of 4.5 million freelancers to meet its clients' needs for short-term project work. Microsoft has built LiquidSpace into its Office 2013 software, making the startup's flexible desks bookable straight from the Outlook email client.

JustPark takes bookings at the parking lots of Europe's four biggest parking companies and the world's largest hotel groups. As with our own partnerships, many of those between sharing economy startups and corporates exist in the mobility sector. Zipcar partners with Regus, the London-listed serviced office provider, to promote the idea of small businesses only paying for what they use—cars or offices—when they need them. Zipcar for Business members get annual Regus membership while Regus customers get money off Zipcar. Ridesharing is a common area of collaboration. IKEA has encouraged ridesharing to its shops in France via a partnership with BlaBlaCar. UK-based Liftshare provides white-labelled car-sharing platforms to many large corporates such as Cable & Wireless and Sky. Liftshare's scheme at Tesco involves about 20% of Tesco's 10,000 UK staff across 15 sites. Liftshare's schemes provides extra incentives to car-share, including reserved parking bays for shared cars.

Perhaps the most impactful sharing economy corporate partnership, however, is the one that will flow from Google's investment in Uber. Today, users can summon Uber cars from the Google Maps app. And one day, these cars will be the self-driving ones developed by Google. In fact, since Google will know where you need to be and when from your calendar, it may summon the vehicle on your behalf. The pick-up and drop-off times will be exact as Google knows how much traffic is on the roads, in part by acquiring the crowd-sourced traffic app Waze. Google won't only deliver people either. Uber aspires to be an urban logistics giant, moving everything around cities. It has tested distributing red roses on Valentine's Day and Christmas trees in partnership with The Home Depot. If all goes to plan, Google will outmaneuver Amazon and, in partnership with Uber, bring people and companies anything they will ever need at the tap of an app.

3 Expanding

Why partner and share the upside? Very often, the attitude of big company management is that if an opportunity is sufficiently interesting, they should be in that business themselves. After all, they have the brand awareness. They have the reach to their customers. They—despite the billions that have been invested in sharing economy businesses—can outgun these wannabees. Expansion sees a corporate move into an adjacent space in order to acquire customers that it will own outright. Without question, these are customers worth owning. Research from consultancy Crowd Companies involving over 90,000 respondents highlighted the affluence of users of shared services. Around 35% of Americans with earnings over $100,000 are so-called "neo-sharers": users of new sharing services like Zopa or Kickstarter rather than old ones like eBay.[5] This is not surprising. The middle classes are historically more receptive to new ideas, especially those that get greater coverage in the quality rather than tabloid press.

The Home Depot is one company that has much to lose in a world where people share items like power drills and ladders for the odd time that they need them rather than buy them new. Taking a leaf out of a peer-to-peer tool rental marketplace like 1000tools, The Home Depot now has a tool and truck rental unit that operates in half of its 2,000 stores. Michael Jones, The Home Depot's director of tool rental, emphasizes that the maintenance of its rental stock in top condition is a key advantage over its peer-to-peer competitors. Some corporates are stepping much further out of their comfort zones. Eni, the Italian oil and gas conglomerate, runs a car-sharing scheme in Milan, Enjoy Eni, with a fleet of over 400 Fiats. German enterprise software giant SAP has a carpooling platform, TwoGo. Built originally as an app for SAP's employees by two of its engineers, TwoGo is an enterprise carpooling app that helps companies get their staff to work sustainably and cheaply. It creates safety by only allowing users to register with their corporate email account.

Next up is distribution. Adopting the strategy of a peer-to-peer delivery network like New York's Zipments, Walmart is to start testing a radical strategy of getting in-store customers to deliver the goods bought by online customers in return for a discount. With tens of millions of Americans visiting its stores each week and driving home with partly empty trunks, the distribution opportunity is compelling. "I see a path to where [delivery] is crowd-sourced," says Joel Anderson, CEO of Walmart.com. Google is also working on distribution, knowing that if it does not offer it, the crowd could step into that market. Active in only seven US metropolitan areas for now, Google Shopping Express offers same-day delivery from local retailers. Above all, Google knows that by not offering distribution, it will be losing even more ground in e-commerce to its undisputed king: Amazon.

Indeed, when it comes to leveraging the crowd and access over ownership, Amazon is ahead of the game. On its "Marketplace," individuals can open up their own eBay-like online shop. Amazon's crowd-sourced labor marketplace, Mechanical Turk, has been running since 2005. With its witty tagline "Artificial artificial Intelligence," Mechanical Turk offers hundreds of thousands of tiny tasks, often worth only a few cents each, that anyone with an Internet connection can complete. Half a million so-called "clickworkers," usually those in the developing world, earn through the platform. Then there is Kindle. Since its launch in 2007, Kindle has almost single-handedly transformed the old paradigm of book ownership into one of book access. By 2010, Amazon was selling more e-books than paperbacks. Just as Kindle is about access over ownership, so too are its music and movie streaming offerings. Finally, Amazon plays in the recommerce space with "Amazon Trade-in." Send Amazon your old electronics and books to receive payment in Amazon Gift Cards.

Fashion retailers run their own versions of trade-ins. Stalwart of the UK high street, Marks & Spencer, has "Shwopping." Customers drop off old clothes of any brand in a "Shwop Drop": a large box near the stores' cash tills. The program has collected 5,500 tons of clothing for Oxfam. Swedish clothes retailer H&M provides recycling facilities at its stores, again for any brand of clothes. In return, it provides a £5 voucher towards a new purchase. ASOS, the listed British fashion e-tailer, has ASOS Marketplace, a place for individuals and boutiques to trade second-hand clothes. ASOS takes a 5% commission on all the clothes sold, a portion of which is donated to charity. Patagonia, the high-end adventure apparel brand, has its own eBay page for customers to sell or donate old Patagonia clothes. These are just some of the companies making it easier for people to clear out space in their wardrobes for more new items, and more guilt-free for them to replenish that space, knowing that a secondary market exists for their purchases.

Outside of fashion, mobile operators like T-Mobile and AT&T run trade-in programs for handsets. British catalogue retailer, Argos, does it for toys. Parents cart their kids' old toys to their local store in return for a £5 voucher to spend on new ones. Trade-ins have long been popular with DVD and video game merchants like Target and Best Buy. In March 2014, the world's largest retailer, Walmart, joined them. Gamers who return games earn credits that can be used on anything. Walmart label second-hand games in its stores as "Certified Pre-Owned." Recommerce is hardly a Western-only phenomenon: secondary markets are usually more developed in less developed countries. The major brands will do well to play to these cultural norms. Adidas branches in the Philippines, for example, operate trade-ins for worn-out running shoes. Like all of these companies, it recognizes that if too many objects stay put, they will silt up the great river of capitalism.

However, the most consequential expansion of all remains in the balance. In June 2013, news leaked that Google was planning to facilitate the sharing of goods. "Google Mine" was tested internally among Google's product team as an add-on to its social network, Google+. According to the leaked copy for employees, "Google Mine lets you share your belongings with your friends and keep up to date with what your friends are sharing." Many Google projects go dark. But if implemented, it would let the search giant inside people's homes to index people's belongings in line with its mission, "to organize the world's information and make it universally accessible and useful." *Own a juicer? Some stackable chairs?* Google wants that information in a structured form. Perhaps Google fears how companies buying its online advertising would react if options from the crowd were presented alongside the new products it was selling. We shall see. One thing's for sure: if Google—or Facebook—decides to act, it would change the course of the sharing economy overnight.

4 Brand-buffing

As well as expanding to generate new revenue, corporates are adopting sharing services to improve the perception of their brands. Sharing services can make a company look less grasping since they often positively impact what social enterprises call the "triple bottom line" of people, planet, and profit. Consider, for example, Virgin Atlantic's free service called Taxi[2]. Everyone has witnessed the absurdity of airport taxis driving into town half-filled and often with only a single passenger onboard. Taxi[2] matches up airline passengers to share onward taxis from their destination airport. The service is not proprietary so passengers from any airline can use it to save money and reduce pollution. "Digital hippies who support new artists on Kickstarter or make wine with Crushpad feel that they are smarter and lighter, at the forefront of a new wave. They feel cool," writes Lisa Gansky. "It's not cool to own," says Loïc Le Meur, co-founder of the LeWeb conference. "It's cooler to borrow a car." Corporates can tap into this same cool.

Sponsoring sharing services is one way that corporates can anchor their brands to this cool simply by writing a check—admittedly, a potentially large one. Barclays is paying up to £50 million to sponsor London's bike-share scheme. Citibank paid $41 million to sponsor New York's bike-share scheme, Citi Bike. The company's logo is now ubiquitous across New York on thousands of moving two-wheel adverts and 98,000 New York residents are members of the scheme, enjoying an intimate relationship with the brand. For Citi, the investment appears to have paid off. According to its data, the number of people saying they had a "favorable impression" of the bank climbed 17% after the bike-sharing program started. Vodafone paid just €4 million to sponsor Barcelona's bike-sharing scheme for 3 years, small change for a company with group revenues of over $65 billion.

B&Q, the UK equivalent of The Home Depot, sponsors its own sharing services: Streetclub. For now a UK-only initiative, Streetclub provides the tools to set up and run "streetclubs": local social networks in cities that get neighbors helping each other out by sharing their tools, time, and expertise. A 21st-century attempt to restore "the good old days" of close-knit communities, there are over 1,700 streetclubs across the UK. From the perspective of B&Q's owner, Kingfisher, the program could lead to increased spend on DIY since many streetclubs are motivated first and foremost by civic pride. Streetclub's boss described to me a typical project on the platform, how a community in a Welsh town had turned some scrap land into a paved garden that now serves as a physical hub for their community. Like the bike-share sponsorships, Streetclub is improving the perception of the mother brand by simply improving people's lives.

Major brands are running glossy cross-promotions with sharing economy companies, again ones that have far more to do with brand than driving revenue. For example, Pepsi teamed up with TaskRabbit to promote its new drink, Pepsi Next. Throughout "The Extra Hour Project," Pepsi drinkers could win a free hour from a "TaskRabbit" to run their errands or do a chore. Pepsi got to rub shoulders with a sexy startup. TaskRabbit got credibility and marketing reach: the promotion supposedly resulted in over 93 million impressions on Facebook. Another example saw NBCUniversal linking brands with gifting platform yerdle. As part of NBC's "Earth Week" of environmentally themed programming, NBC's "Share and Tell" initiative educated householders to lend and borrow underused goods with their neighbors. In one week, 2,400 Americans gifted their belongings to strangers on yerdle.

Sell-outs? When sharing economy startups expand

Back when JustPark was known as ParkatmyHouse.com, it was a purely peer-to-peer platform offering parking at private homes. The business model had only one small problem: you don't have driveways in city centers, where demand for parking is often highest. Today, JustPark takes parking bookings on behalf of the largest parking companies and international hotel chains like Hilton, Sheraton and Holiday Inn. Drivers book space at driveways in suburban areas and at parking lots in town centers. *Does working with multinationals make a sharing economy company a traitor to its peer origins?* The answer depends on the impact of that expansion on its community. JustPark's expansion has not alienated our homeowners because it is rare for driveways and parking lots to be in direct competition. Rather, by offering parking all over cities, we have attracted far more drivers, to the benefit of families renting out their driveways.

It may have suited JustPark's community to expand from a "P2P" to a "B2C" model but other sharing economy startups need to tread more carefully. Etsy, for example, has only ever let "handmade" goods be sold on its website. In 2013, it broadened the highly fraught definition of this key term. Now, once Etsy has manually approved a seller, it can employ workers and mass-produce its goods at external workshops. For some Etsy sellers, the change meant a welcome liberalization of pedantic rules that were impeding the growth of their startups. But for another segment of its sellers—the proudly small-scale artisans—it was the ultimate betrayal. These sellers felt that Etsy was opening the floodgates to unfair competition from cheap, factory-made produce. Startups needing to scale inevitably look to work with those who can scale alongside them. In this case, Etsy got it largely right: it kept tight controls in place while allowing its micro-entrepreneurs to grow their businesses from their kitchen tables.

There are lots of mammas and papas out there. But some sharing economy startups end up brazenly switching tack to focus their efforts on the conventional businesses and institutions that are already at massive scale. Lending Club now originates most of its funds through institutions like hedge funds rather than the crowd. I hope that it will not expand to the detriment of ordinary people investing money through its platform. Zaarly started out as a task marketplace that allowed users to request things from those around them. It has since pivoted to providing home services like gardening and cleaning that are largely undertaken by small businesses. If these startups transition to being platforms for businesses while continuing to exploit the sharing economy as PR-friendly window dressing, they will undermine the integrity of an authentic, peer-driven service like Lyft.

When individuals get corporate

We can all recognize a big company with its network of offices and hundreds of employees. But as we saw with Brittney Bedford, it is not always easy to tell the difference between a small business and an individual seller or "prosumer." Even that faint dividing line is blurring as individuals on the platforms continue to professionalize. Sellers are highly incentivized to raise their games: those who earn five-star reviews see their earnings potential climb far above the low-ranked hoi polloi. In fact, sellers on sharing economy marketplaces are often better incentivized to do a great job than most people working in conventional full-time jobs since their efforts more directly translate into cash. Gradually, these slick sharing economy sellers are beginning to morph into pseudo-businesses. Those who take it most seriously are emerging into a new class of "professionals" who rely on one or more sharing economy platforms for the bulk of their income.

This new professional class is breaking down the false dichotomy between businesses, with their supposed well-oiled operations that we can rely on, and people who, by contrast, must be a group of floundering nincompoops. Airbnb hosts Allison and Dave Shuttleworth are anything but. They give guests 45-minute introductions to the house and city, and cook them hot breakfasts every morning. "Airbnb is pretty much a full-time job right now," Allison told *The Financial Times*. "Dave and I are housekeeping, security, concierge, cook, tour guide. We are a five-star establishment." Professionalization is a process that the startups actively support: if the sharing economy is turning assets into services, the startups want those services to be as slick as possible. Some offer what amounts to professional training. Vayable even has its own MOOC or "massive open online course" about how to be the perfect tour guide or "Insider."

Often, service providers need all the help they can get, not least because most people parting with their hard-earned cash will cut them little slack.

"People expect the same customer service they'll get from Samsung," Daniel Cowen, co-founder of the Kickstarter-backed 3Doodler project, told me. "In fact, they almost expect more." Some sellers find these expectations overwhelming. Others thrive on them. As *The Economist* notes, "[ebay] is now dominated by professional 'power sellers' (many of whom started out as ordinary eBay users). The same may happen with the sharing economy." Indeed, the impact of professionals is already enormous. According to travel site Skift, 12% of Airbnb hosts have more than one apartment, but those multiple units add up to a staggering 30% of total units.[6] Ever more revenue goes through a professional segment. As with eBay, the increasing polarization of these marketplaces into professional and amateur sellers will fuel their continued growth.

According to former Kayak executive, Drew Patterson, the best way to understand these professionalizing platforms is that they allow "mass-franchising," with each entrepreneur performing the role of an individual franchisee. As with a franchise like McDonald's, individuals sign up to make their living from a brand that generates the demand centrally. The sharing economy startup also follows the capital-efficient model of franchising since each entrepreneur brings his or her own assets to the platform, whether it is a car to rent to a neighbor on an apartment to a tourist. Also in common with a traditional franchise, the platform denies its entrepreneurs most of the data, only passing them control of the customer on a transaction-by-transaction basis. Patterson predicts that, in order to protect their own brand, sharing economy platforms will exert tighter control over their micro-entrepreneurs in the coming years.

Time will tell whether sharing economy brands can go as mainstream as McDonald's without losing their humanity in standardization. Like BMW, their brands may one day be so valuable that they too will outsource their risk-taking. But before then, they have battles to fight.

Notes

1   Martin, Elliot and Shaheen, Susan, *The Impact of Carsharing on Household Vehicle Ownership* (ACCESS, Spring 2011): http://www.uctc.net/access/38/access38_carsharing_ownership.pdf.

2   Data taken from *The Rise of Mobility*, a report by technology research consultancy IDC: http://cdn.idc.asia/files/5a8911ab-4c6d-47b3-8a04-01147c3ce06d.pdf.

3   Zervas, Georgios, Proserpio, Davide and Byers, John, *The Rise of the Sharing Economy: Estimating the Impact of Airbnb on the Hotel Industry* (Boston University School of

Management Research Paper No. 2013–16, February 12th, 2014): http://papers.ssrn.com/sol3/papers.cfm?abstract_id=2366898.

4   According to STR, a leading provider of hospitality industry data, 1.11 billion hotel nights were booked in the US in 2013, with annual US hotel nights having been above the billion mark since 2009: http://skift.com/2014/04/08/blackstone-brings-la-quinta-to-ipo-and-raises-650-million/.

5   Owyang, Jeremiah, *Sharing is the New Buying* (Crowd Companies and Vision Critical, 2014), slide 16: http://www.slideshare.net/jeremiah_owyang/sharingnewbuying.

6   Data published by Jason Clampet in *Skift* on February 13th, 2014: *Airbnb in NYC: The Real Numbers Behind the Sharing Story:* http://skift.com/2014/02/13/airbnb-in-nyc-the-real-numbers-behind-the-sharing-story/.

Governments

Fits and Starts

10 Downing Street. I was in a grand and gilded reception room overlooking the Prime Minister's garden as Daniel Korski, David Cameron's suave special advisor, leaned over to me and said, "Write this. Write that in Paris they tried to ban sharing economy businesses and that in London, we invited you to Downing Street."

I had often walked past the turning to Downing Street, blocked off by high wrought iron gates and armed police, wondering if I would ever walk down the famous street on the other side. When I finally did, it felt strangely anticlimactic. Perhaps it was the familiarity of being in a place that I had seen so many times on the TV. Perhaps it was Downing Street's homely informality. It felt almost normal to stop outside its shiny black front door and stroke the Downing Street tabby cat. And so it was that, a few minutes after some security checks from jolly policemen, I found myself walking up Number 10's wide stone staircase. Lining the canary yellow walls were pictures of British Prime Ministers from centuries ago to the present day.

I was there for a Round Table on the sharing economy. Soon, I recognized some familiar faces from our small world, like Mark Walker, General Manager of Zipcar UK, and Benita Matofska from The People Who Share. After a breakfast of tea and pastries, the Chancellor of the Exchequer, the second most powerful man in the land, took the floor of the Pillared Room. "The sharing economy has the potential to totally transform industries," he boomed. "Tell us what we can do to help you break down barriers." I peered across at a 400-year-old painting of Queen Elizabeth I above a marble fireplace and wondered if the Chancellor said the same thing to the CEOs of Unilever and BP. "Good ideas," promised the Chancellor, "brought forward at this seminar will turn into Government laws." *Time will tell,* I thought.

We divided into discussion groups. I was in the "Accommodation and Space" group with the CEOs of residential rental businesses Love Home Swap, onefinestay, and HouseTrip. NearDesk was representing shared office space. Appear Here, a startup that places pop-up shops in vacant high street units, was representing retail space. We traded anecdotes about the regulatory issues affecting our businesses. Greg Marsh from onefinestay explored an issue affecting all of the home rental companies in their key London market. According to the Greater London Council (General Powers) Act 1973, renting a home to someone for less than 90 days is a "change of use" requiring planning permission. "With a stress on the nineteen *seventy-three,*" chimed in Patrick Robinson, Head of European Public Policy for Airbnb. On this issue, the government is now acting. Five months later, as I write, the new "Deregulation Bill" is making its way through Parliament. Once given Royal Assent, it will allow Londoners to rent out their homes for less than 90 days without breaching planning laws.

However, the main point of agreement that day was the need to revise another piece of outdated legislation. Dating from 1992, the "Rent a Room" relief provides UK homeowners with £4,250 of tax-free income from room rentals. Now that the Internet has created marketplaces in other kinds of space rental such as driveways and attics, it makes sense to extend the relief to reflect these new forms of behavior. By encouraging people to rent out their driveways, the government would also increase the supply of cheap parking around high streets, helping to lure back the shoppers who have abandoned them in large part because of expensive and hard to find parking. Finally, we were united on the need for the government to take a lead on encouraging sharing behavior not only privately within the walls of Downing Street, but also publicly and vocally. "This is not about the entrepreneurship of the people in this room," I said, inspired by the seat of power to find my glib inner politician. "This is about fostering the entrepreneurship of the tens of millions of people out there."

In a pickle … and out of one

JustPark's regulatory strife also stemmed from outdated planning laws. Over the years, some municipal authorities in the UK, or "councils," had taken the view that if a family rented out their driveway, their home became a parking lot, a change of use that required planning permission. The families on our platform were not paving over front gardens—that is building work that rightly requires planning permission and is not something we have ever seen running JustPark. Rather, councils were objecting to existing parking space being used for parking, precisely so we can make do with as little of it as possible. Many of our property owners had received letters threatening them with fines of up to £20,000 were they to continue renting out their driveways. The story made some national newspapers and London's *Evening Standard*. But nothing would prepare us for what happened next.

It was a Friday night when I received a phone call from the BBC. Eric Pickles, the Communities Secretary and a UK Cabinet Minister, had joined the debate, attacking councils for trying to introduce a backdoor tax through their threatened £20,000 fines. *The Times* was running with Pickles' push for driveway rentals on its front page and the BBC wanted me on its flagship *Today* program. The next morning, I was interviewed by Evan Davis before racing across London for a live interview on Sky TV. Meanwhile, JustPark's founder, Anthony, hurried between other studios for more live TV appearances. That Saturday, the team transformed a corner of a restaurant opposite the BBC offices into a temporary media center. It was all hands to the deck as we raced to keep up with incoming media requests and tweets between nipping into the quiet of the toilets for radio interviews.

It was the beginning of the end. After countless meetings telling MPs and councilors some of the stories of the 30,000 families using JustPark to let strangers park on their property, we got what we wanted. In March 2014, favorable guidance was issued allowing homeowners to rent out their own parking spaces without planning permission.[1] I can remember reading one email from a council enforcement officer the year before that read, "We regularly monitor your website for incidences of suspected parking." At the time, I had wondered what else they spent their taxpayer-funded time on. *Monitoring the Tesco website for incidences of suspected baked beans?*

Pragmatic guidance now allows families to earn some extra income from the property that they have worked so hard to afford. JustPark is getting there. Few other sharing economy startups have it so good.

Disruption

The world of startups, like any subculture, has its own clichés. Chief among them is "disruption": the process of reshaping an existing industry with an offering that is radically better. Investors wax lyrical about "disruptive innovation." Entrepreneurs strut about the stage on "demo days" showing off their new startup while proclaiming, "we're disrupting the $[insert large number] billion [insert relevant sector] industry." Leading tech news website *TechCrunch* even hosts conferences called "Disrupt." For us techies, disrupting sectors that have failed to innovate is our calling. JustPark disrupts the parking sector by giving people allocated spaces for a VIP-like experience that is also cheaper than on-street parking. Not content to disrupt only incumbents, startups also disrupt each other. Couchsurfing disrupted the youth hostel market by telling guests, *Why pay? Stay with a local for free.* Airbnb disrupted Couchsurfing by telling hosts, *Why not charge! There's cash to be made.* One day, someone will do the same to Airbnb with an idea that will seem obvious in retrospect.

There is a widespread perception among entrepreneurs that if you're not disrupting and frankly irritating someone, you're not doing something with the potential to be huge. In the last chapter, we saw how peer-to-peer models are disrupting major industries with highly paid powerful executives and thousands of employees. We looked at the strategies that these incumbents are adopting in response to these new threats. Here, we look at what happens when some of the incumbents fight back with their weapons of choice: the lawyer and the lobbyist. For ammunition, they have arguments that the lean models of the startups are illegal or unsafe. At the same time, the startups are annoying even more dangerous categories of opponents with business models that push at the seams of existing regulation and legislation. Disruptive innovation draws into the debate those who make the rules and must ultimately either enforce or update them: regulators and governments.

Theirs is not an easy task. Yanked back and forth by incumbents and startups, these powers must regulate and legislate for a present that is in flux and an uncertain future. *What is the right level of regulation for sharing economy companies?* Sharing economy lawyer Janelle Orsi uses a sneeze-guard as an example of the difficulties of striking the right balance. A US restaurant is required by law to install a sneeze-guard over a buffet. An EatWith host cooking meals for strangers in their home is not. If the EatWith model scales, restaurants will lobby for home-cooking regulation, as they have in cities where they have lost customers to the leaner business model of roving food trucks. Equally, if cities burden startups like EatWith with regulation, they will be accused of stifling entrepreneurship, not only of the startups, but also of the individuals making money through their platforms. And if someone gets severely ill by eating food from a home establishment that the city has failed to regulate, the victim may come for that city with lawyers. For politicians, the stakes are high: these online companies have the potential to transform the offline world. But to quote JFK in the face of a different clash of ideologies, "the greatest danger of all would be to do nothing."

Give the people what they want

In Ancient Rome, Pliny the Elder recorded a tale about an inventor granted an audience with the Emperor Tiberius to show him a wondrous invention: a glass that was unbreakable. Once before the Emperor, the inventor deliberately dropped the glass. It bounced. The inventor then took a small hammer and carefully tapped the dented glass back into shape.

"Does anyone else know of this invention?" asked the Emperor.

"No one," replied the inventor.

Worried that this new material might undermine the value of his hoards of gold and silver, Tiberius commanded that the man was to be beheaded. As a result, "vitrum flexile" or "flexible glass" may have been lost for 2,000 years until its rediscovery by NYSE-listed glass-maker Corning. Already the most powerful and wealthy man in the known world, Tiberius speculated that he had more to lose than gain through an invention of such unpredictable value. Thus, power suppressed innovation for millennia. Often, it is in the interests of the powerful to preserve the status quo; it has, after all, served them well.

Innovation cannot always be nipped in the bud. More than 1,500 years later, in 17th-century France, merchants had begun to import calico, a cheap printed fabric from Calicut in India. Far cheaper than the dyed, domestically produced fabrics, it proved an immediate hit with consumers. But calico had French artisans up in arms. Instead of changing to produce printed cloths, they lobbied the government to ban the imported calico. In 1683, the French government banned the import, manufacture, and use of printed cotton fabrics. New, thriving businesses using new technology— the startups of their day—were outlawed and millions of consumers denied cheap clothing. During the 70-year calico ban, an estimated 16,000 people died in armed uprisings and government executions for breaching anti-calico laws. France did itself no favors. Giorgio Riello, a researcher from the London School of Economics, posits that without the calico ban, France would have become the European leader in cotton textiles.[2]

These days, it is harder for the wealthy and politically powerful to run roughshod over innovation and deny people what they want. If unbreakable glass were invented by a lone genius today, the inventor would have raised millions of dollars on Kickstarter and videos of the glass bouncing off floors and walls would be going viral on YouTube. Or imagine how the calico printers and the millions who wanted their goods would be fighting for their cause through Facebook and Twitter with hashtags like #lovecalico and #caliconotmurder. Today, shutting down innovation that benefits society gets harder with every passing month. Policy makers must ensure, that unlike Tiberius and the 17th-century French political elite, they go down on the right side of history. These days, it is they who risk losing their heads.

A tale of disruption: when taxis suck

When it comes to taxis, we're spoiled in the UK. Minicab companies are generally cheap and reliable. Addison Lee, now owned by private equity giant Carlyle, is a model of efficiency with its "Auto Allocator" placing 20,000 jobs a day. Then there are the world-famous black cabs. Black cabbies must pass an exam called "The Knowledge": a test of London geography that requires the memorization of 25,000 streets and is so extreme that neuroscientists have tracked the structural changes it causes to drivers' brains.[3] As a result, cabbies know every road and traffic-dodging backstreet. Black cabbies in London and other UK cities are an honest bunch too and have perfected a mild grumpiness that is bizarrely invigorating. As for the cabs themselves, they may not win any land speed records, but by contrast to New York's yellow cabs are clean and spacious. Compared to most places, we have it good.

Across the US, however—ironically, a country more obsessed with customer service than any—it is a different story. I think of the grisly Russian cab driver in Boston who practically beat me up just for making conversation. I think of the booked and confirmed taxi to San Francisco airport that simply never showed up, almost causing me to miss a flight to London. I think of the Manhattan taxi driver who had seemingly never heard of Brooklyn. "I love San Francisco, I *love* it," RelayRides founder Shelby Clark told me. "No winter—*who wants winter?* Great people and it's the mecca of the world for startups. My number one complaint about San Francisco was the taxis. Taxis sucked. They were not a transportation option." Rob Pegoraro, tech journalist and former *Washington Post* stalwart, also complained to me about Washington DC taxis. "Zoning" meant Pegoraro would jump out of taxis away from his destination to avoid a fare spike by crossing into another zone. If any sector needed disrupting, it was this one.

In 2008, Garrett Camp and Travis Kalanick were at the LeWeb technology conference in Paris. Canadian Garrett Camp was a 30-year-old entrepreneur who had founded website recommendation service StumbleUpon and sold it to eBay for $75 million. Kalanick had also successfully exited a business, a peer-to-peer file sharing service called Red Swoosh, and was "still recharging from a 10 year nonstop startup." Like every entrepreneur, they obsess over making things better and sometimes that means whinging about things. "Jamming on ideas, rapping on what's next is what entrepreneurs do," says Kalanick. "Garrett and I got some good music, good drinks and jammed until 5am. Garrett's big idea was cracking the horrible taxi problem in San Francisco." As fast-living men about town, why should they have to put up with taxis that suck? Surely, there had to be a better way. It turned out that there was.

By January 2010, the duo had shipped a prototype "UberCab" app and had three luxury black cars cruising each night through the streets of New York's Soho and Chelsea districts. At first, just a handful of early adopters were using the app to summon a black car and get taken wherever they wanted. Garrett and Kalanick launched their hometown of San Francisco next. Like many successful startups, it had a tiny well-defined user group in the early days that helped the founding team to iterate the product. "When it first got going," says Kalanick, "it was really a lifestyle company. It was about us and our hundred friends being able to push a button and get around San Francisco like ballers." Trouble was brewing though: the new business model of e-hailing a taxi from a smartphone was just too good. Those it was trying to disrupt—the members of outdated cartels of licensed taxi fleets the world over—were in for a shock.

Uber: global skirmishing

Today, Uber is in 150 cities around the world. It is an expansion that has felt more like war between the startup—if you can still call an $40 billion company a startup—and the authorities in the cities where Uber operates. Uber also expanded from the on-demand hire of luxury black cars with a low-cost "UberX" offering that has fueled the majority of its growth. The more sharing economy part of its business, UberX lets individuals turn their car into a taxi by watching some videos, uploading insurance and license documents, and passing a vehicle inspection. City authorities are often acting in the face of the fear and anger of old-fashioned taxi drivers who stand to lose fares to Uber's slick smartphone app. It is exceedingly unlikely that they will offer consumers a better product to put the newcomers out of business. Their only hope is that the authorities will do it for them.

As VP of public policy for the Consumer Electronics Association, Michael Petricone represents 2,000 tech companies including Uber. Petricone enjoys a front-row seat in these tussles. "If you have a business model that is lucrative for you," he told me, "and somebody comes in with a better business model that is more attractive and beneficial to consumers ... and if you've been around and built up relations with regulators and you've got a chance to slow it down and stop it, it's understandable that incumbents will try." Specifically, these taxi drivers are demanding that Uber drivers play by the same rules when it comes to licensing and insurance. Many of them, in the US and elsewhere, have spent hundreds of thousands of dollars on taxi medallions only to see Uber drivers bypass the need for them entirely. Uber and its competitors argue that the old rules do not apply to them. They are not taxi companies, they claim, but ridesharing apps.

That argument did not wash with City of San Francisco and the State of California: they served Uber with "cease and desist" orders soon after it launched. Interviewed in *Inc.*, Kalanick speculated that someone from the taxi industry, "put in a call and said, 'shut these guys down'." Even London's well-functioning cab market has not proved immune to Uber's disruption. In June 2014, London's black cabs protested against the right of Uber drivers to pick up people without a license for their meter. The question turned on whether the Uber service was indeed "metered." While there is no traditional meter in the car, the fare is calculated by the app using distance and journey time. The protest saw 5,000 black cabs clog up Trafalgar Square, London's grandest square, and Whitehall, the thoroughfare at the heart of government, forcing traffic to a near standstill. *The result?* An 850% increase in Uber sign-ups. On the same day, anti-Uber protests gridlocked parts of Paris, Madrid, Barcelona, Berlin, Milan, and Rome.

This regulatory landscape is changing by the week, but in late 2014 the battles still rage. As I write, the City of Toronto is pushing for an injunction against Uber for 36 by-law infractions. In Berlin, a court placed an injunction on Uber on the grounds that it should be classified as a rental car business. In Brussels, Uber drivers currently risk fines of €10,000 for picking up passengers via the app. In Barcelona, Uber drivers risk fines of up to €6,000 and having their vehicle impounded. In France, they are subject to a bizarre "15-minute law," requiring them to wait 15 minutes in a stationary car before collecting a customer. For the most part though, Uber marches on with its hands over its ears—I used Uber in Paris during the ban and my car arrived in under 5 minutes. Even in cities where Uber has been explicitly banned, such as Madrid, users can still hail Ubers. There, as in other cities where Uber and its competitors are banned, using a ridesharing app has become a peculiarly yuppie form of civil disobedience.

However, there are signs that ridesharing is coming of age. The business model has come a long way since Lyft's early days when the voluntary fares were called "donations" to get around a regulatory loophole. A handful of cities and states are now rolling out legislation to bring ridesharing within a regulatory framework. Colorado has passed a law requiring background checks, vehicle inspections, and mandatory insurance for Uber drivers. In Washington DC, council members approved new ridesharing regulations by a 12 to 1 vote. Above all, California—which unusually has authority in the sphere of taxi regulation for the entire State—passed the US's first ridesharing regulations. The California Public Utilities Commission has issued a legal framework that, among 28 requirements, compels the startups to conduct criminal background checks on drivers and carry $1 million of liability insurance per driver. In return, Uber, Lyft, and Sidecar attain the status of "transportation network companies." While the regulations only apply to California, other localities are watching.

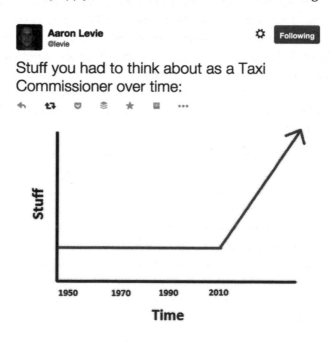

FIGURE 6.1 Tweet from Aaron Levie, co-founder and CEO of cloud storage company Box

More strife in shared transportation services

Uber may be the most high-profile transport startup to have found itself in deep regulatory waters but it is far from being the only one. In 2013,

New York State's Department of Financial Services hauled in RelayRides for non-compliance with insurance laws. The cease and desist for failing to offer what New York State deemed legitimate insurance cover has meant that the peer-to-peer car-sharing service is still suspended in New York at the time of writing. RelayRides also had to cough up $200,000 as punishment for insurance violations. Given its huge footprint, it is hardly surprising that RelayRides falls foul of some state regulations: it operates in 2,300 cities, creating incredible compliance complexities for any company, let alone a young and innovative one. As RelayRides' CEO Andre Haddad points out on its company blog, "Innovation, by its nature, does not always fit within existing structures."

In airport rentals, RelayRides competes head on with another sharing startup that has faced even stiffer regulatory opposition. FlightCar lets people "park" for free at airports by renting out their car to travelers flying into the same airport. FlightCar was sued in 2013 by the city and county of San Francisco for operating a rental car company without the required airport permits. The airport also wants the 10% of revenues and $20 per "rental" car it gets from rental car companies. Again, the question turns on old definitions: is FlightCar a "rental car company"? FlightCar calls itself a car-sharing company and argues that it should not be subject to the usual airport fees since, unlike rental car companies, its cars are parked several miles away from the airport. To transport its customers to and from the airport, FlightCar also partners with regulated limousine companies that themselves pay fees to the airports. The suit is still pending.

Books and burgers

WikiLeaks showed the world how much governments fear openly shared content. But governments can severely enforce the sharing of content that is not remotely sensitive. Aaron Swartz was a prodigiously talented programmer and political "hacktivist" who co-developed the RSS feed aged just 14. During a research stint at MIT, Swartz downloaded and released online thousands of articles from academic paper database JSTOR. While JSTOR declined to pursue Swartz, the federal prosecutors took no mercy, piling on indictments that could have left him facing 50 years in prison. On January 11th, 2013, after the prosecution had rejected a counter-offer by

Swartz and prison looked unavoidable, he was found dead in his Brooklyn apartment. Swartz had hanged himself aged 26. Speaking at his son's funeral, Robert Swartz said, "He was killed by the government." Even now— let alone in years to come—we can look on Swartz's death with collective shame for the hand that outdated and draconian legislation had in it.

Swartz knew that he had no legal right to share the JSTOR content. But we are just as constrained when it comes to sharing nonsensitive assets that we think we "own." In Finland, regulators moved to ban innocuous Finnish book rental service Bookabooka. Branded "the Pirate Bay for textbooks" for its alleged copyright infringement by the Finnish copyright lobby, Bookabooka did not even host digital content. It merely provided a website that helped students to snail-mail textbooks to their peers. In 2013, no longer prepared to risk up to 2 years' in prison for breaking intellectual property laws, the Bookabooka co-founders shut down the website. An irony not lost on them was that while their company was crushed by regulation, in that same year textbook rental company Chegg floated in the US.

This is not to say that the US is a utopia of enlightened regulation, especially when it comes to food. In many states, it is forbidden to charge money for home-cooked food without a restaurant license and illegal to sell homegrown food. Home-cooking startups like EatWith can argue that laws are outdated, but it is hard to escape the conclusion that they are frequently operating illegally. New York-based Mealku is trying to dodge this regulatory tangle by avoiding payment altogether. Mealku is meal-sharing with a radical cooperative twist. Several thousand members take turns to cook for each other with only "ku" changing hands: credits that are earned by cooking and spent by eating. One "ku" is worth something a little less than a buck, Mealku's credit system intentionally defying easy conversion into dollars to thwart the regulators. "If we can't operate," says Mealku founder Ted D'Cruz-Young, "then that's the end of bake sales. Bake sales can't exist. It's that simple. We have to kill all the grannies, because it's not safe."

Unfortunately for D'Cruz-Young, regulation can still bite even when there is no money involved. LeftoverSwap is a Seattle-based mobile startup that lets people list their leftover food on a simple app interface so that the hungry can come and collect it. Health officials were swift to condemn the startup for putting public health at risk by allowing people to offer food that is past its best. In the event of a disease outbreak, officials are also concerned about the difficulties of tracing the origin of contaminated food. "Leftover food is a huge source of food-borne illnesses and other pestilence," said Richard Lee, director of San Francisco's Health Department's environmental regulatory program when the app was released. For the LeftoverSwap founders, there is a more urgent day-to-day problem: the 40% of food that currently goes to waste.

P2P financial regulation: moving faster

Cease and desists get thrown around the peer-to-peer financial sector too. In 2008, the Securities and Exchange Commission landed one on Prosper as a result of default rates that were bobbing perilously around the 20% mark. However, when it comes to peer-to-peer finance, the relationship between platforms and regulators has been comparatively rosy. The implications of this could ultimately be enormous: debt crowdfunding will weaken the grip of retail banks in the loan market, and equity crowdfunding could lead to thousands of in effect mini initial public offerings.

Why, as a broad generalization, has the financial sector reacted so quickly to new peer-to-peer models? Partly, this is a reflection of the lack of love that most countries have for their existing financial institutions and the general goodwill extended to those experimenting with alternatives. But mostly it is a result of the financial sector having mature regulatory bodies already in place and available to work on framing up-to-date rules.

The UK and its financial regulator, the Financial Conduct Authority (FCA), is leading the way in the regulation of both debt and equity crowdfunding. From 2014, UK peer-to-peer lenders became subject to FCA regulation. Among other requirements, they need to maintain minimum levels of capital and prepare contingency plans for what happens in the event of platform failure. The UK Treasury also allows investments in peer-to-peer lenders to form part of an individual's £15,000 tax-free "NISA" private investment allowance. Equity crowdfunding has been regulated since way back in 2000. It too was updated in 2014 to reflect the growth of UK platforms Seedrs and Crowdcube. The new rules protect investors by limiting investments to 10% of their "net investible assets" in a year. Elsewhere in Europe, French financial regulators are not far behind.

In the US, debt crowdfunding is regulated and equity crowdfunding is catching up. At the time of writing, nonaccredited investors are still hamstrung by Depression-era laws that prevent them from investing in startups. But all will change in equity crowdfunding with the JOBS ("Jumpstart Our Business Startups") Act. Once the crowdfunding elements of the JOBS Act come into effect, private companies will be allowed more shareholders before triggering public company reporting requirements. Crucially, the prohibition on advertising private fundraisings will be lifted. Obama has called it a "game-changer." It may well be for AngelList and FundersClub. Moreover, it will be for the entrepreneurs who stand to benefit from crowdfunded capital. Today, venture capital favors Ivy Leaguers in Silicon Valley, New York, and Boston and is concentrated in a small number of companies: just 4,000 a year in the US. In the future, there will be more money to fund more entrepreneurs from more diverse backgrounds.

Airbnb: the NYC subpoena and fighting back

The sharing economy's climactic showdown with government involves its leading light: Airbnb. As the startup has burst into 34,000 cities and 190 countries, it too has faced an Uber-like expansion, beset with regulatory tussles. In part, cities are unhappy about missing out on hotel tax. Airbnb admits that all taxes should be collected and paid—once everyone has worked out quite how. In a handful of cities such as San Francisco, Airbnb now automatically deducts tax at source for its hosts after the city tax collector José Cisneros forced through regulations meaning that "transient occupancy" should be subject to the city's 14% hotel tax. But for the most part, earnings are subject only to income tax. Airbnb's avoidance of hotel tax is reminiscent of Amazon's avoidance of sales tax. By the time that statute had began to close the net on Amazon, it was worth some $175 billion.

However, the biggest clashes with cities involve not tax but the flouting of local planning laws restricting short-term lets in Quebec, Berlin, Miami, and Amsterdam, among many other cities. Even once these fires have been extinguished, Airbnb faces the larger challenge of finding a solution to the many tenants subletting on Airbnb: almost all leases contain covenants against subletting. At the same time as infuriating landlords by turning a blind eye to unauthorized subletting, it has also angered tenant groups who accuse it of pushing up rents. In San Francisco, Airbnb's own backyard, it has an ongoing feud with the San Francisco Tenants Union that has contributed to the passing of the "Airbnb law" that limits short-term rentals of entire apartments to a maximum of 90 days a year. Airbnb hosts are also now required to obtain $500,000 of liability insurance and to register their addresses, a move to stop illegal sublets in particular of rent-controlled apartments.

Among all these global skirmishes has been one defining battle: New York. There, Airbnb's hosts found themselves in breach of a New York law banning rentals of entire apartments for fewer than 30 days. Originally designed to clamp down on slumlords running illegal hotels, Airbnb has always denied its relevance to their hosts. But the city brought the fight to them.

Round one: May 2013. The New York regulators threatened an Airbnb host, Nigel Warren, with a $7,000 fine for contravening the by-law. Fearful of panic spreading among hosts in its biggest city market, Airbnb did not mince its words: "There is universal agreement that occasional hosts like Nigel Warren were not the target of the 2010 law," read its statement, "but that agreement provides little comfort to the handful of people, like Nigel, who find themselves targeted by overzealous enforcement officials." Warren lost the case. Then Airbnb paid Warren's legal fees to appeal and the fine was reversed. Dingaling: round one to Airbnb.

By September 2013, it was time for round two. The New York Attorney General, Eric Schneiderman, subpoenaed Airbnb for data on all of its 15,000 hosts in the city. "We are going to pursue anyone who's running illegal hotels," announced Schneiderman. He demanded all of the hosts' physical and email addresses, a list of their bookings, and the revenues that each host had made. At stake were more than just the 50% of Airbnb's New York listings that take bookings for the whole apartment rather than individual rooms: New York's ruling had the potential to set a precedent that would be followed by other cities in the US and around the world. Many disinterested observers thought the Attorney General was right to look to his State's lost occupancy and sales tax and the livelihoods of the city's 30,000 unionized hotel workers. But an alliance of critics ranging from hipsters to libertarians accused Schneiderman of pandering to the hotel lobby.

Airbnb responded with data—and not of the kind that Schneiderman had demanded. According to CEO Brian Chesky, over 62% of hosts were relying on Airbnb to pay their mortgage or rent. Airbnb also released a study detailing its contribution to the New York economy. The study trumpeted the supposed $632 million that Airbnb had brought to the city the previous year and the 950 jobs it had helped to create in the outer boroughs.[4] With case studies on New York neighborhoods like Harlem and Astoria in Queens, the report took pains to highlight how this money was reaching parts of the city that, pre-Airbnb, had received next to no benefit from tourism. Airbnb also deleted 2,000 listings belonging to the most egregious professional hoteliers on the platform like "NY Furnished Rentals" who had listed an 80-property portfolio in the Upper East Side and Midtown. Meanwhile, Airbnb's lawyers scurried to file a motion at the New York Supreme Court blocking Schneiderman.

But above all, Airbnb responded by reaching out to its community. Soon, 500 Airbnb hosts were waving placards at City Hall. The campaign gathered speed online. Douglas Atkin, Airbnb's Global Head of Community, emailed hundreds of thousands of customers—or as a politician would call them: "voters." Atkin's email evoked the language of war, "I'm writing to you on behalf of Airbnb hosts ... because our community is under attack by officials and special interests." It called on users to add their name to an online petition in defense of Airbnb, which, at the time of writing, bears over 230,000 signatures. Schneiderman's subpoena hung like a storm cloud over Airbnb until May 2014, when a state judge quashed it on the grounds of disproportionality. Schneiderman bounced back with a new subpoena and a compromise was reached. Airbnb had to share data on the number and location of its listings but with apartment numbers and personally identifiable information stripped out.

Then, in October 2014, just as this book was going to press, Schneiderman hit back with a report based on the anonymized data. In it, he argued that 72% of Airbnb's private listings could be illegal and that the startup is dodging as much as $33 million in hotel taxes in New York alone.

The fight for who can do what with some of the world's most expensive real estate continues. And the smart money's on Airbnb.

Don't mess with fire ants

Elephants in the African savanna can weigh 15,000 pounds. They have a habit of trampling vast tracts of land into devastation. *How could a plant possibly protect itself from such a huge animal?* Researchers noticed that the elephants steer clear of one species of acacia. These particular acacias are the home of thousands of fire ants. The ants form a well-organized network of bodyguards for their host trees. If an elephant touches the acacia, the fire ants crawl up its trunk, biting its sensitive inner lining with their mandibles and causing the elephant intolerable discomfort. In return, the acacias provide the ants with sweet nectar that they extrude from their leaves. The elephants learn to avoid these acacias. Just so, sharing economy businesses are defended by the thousands of customers whom they nourish. The elephants in government are learning to avoid them.

The Internet crawls with fire ants. Their mandibles are social media: a phenomenon that has allowed Internet lobbying to come of age in the last 5 years. The decisive moment when the Internet community realized its enormous political power was when it united against the proposed SOPA (the "Stop Online Privacy Act") legislation and its precursor, PIPA (the "Protect IP Act"). The acts would have required Google and other search engines to block access to websites that infringed copyrights. Many large corporates from Nike to L'Oreal, Viacom, and Macmillan (the publishers of this book) backed SOPA. But the geeks—and their line-up of companies including Google, Facebook, Mozilla, and Yahoo!—fought back. For them, it was not the role of government to impose borders on the Internet. The anti-SOPA alliance was troubled about the legislation's potential to curb the freedoms of bloggers and anyone posting user-generated content on social media.

On January 18th, 2012, Wikipedia, WordPress, Tumblr, and other major websites staged a "blackout" in protest of SOPA and PIPA. The same day, Twitter users bombarded the Twitter accounts of pro-SOPA politicians and companies with 2.2 million counts of the hashtag "#sopa." Internet plug-ins attempted 8 million calls to Senators; 10 million people signed e-petitions. Within a week, the bill was dead. As Daniel O'Connor of DisCo, the "Disruptive Competition" project that aims to give startups a voice in Washington, puts it, this was the "first Internet public policy victory for the Internet community." As the techies crowed about Internet freedom, Patrick Leahy, the Senator who had sponsored the bill, issued a statement. "Somewhere in China today, in Russia today, and in many other countries that do not respect American intellectual property," said the Vermont Democrat, "criminals who do nothing but peddle in counterfeit products and stolen American content are smugly watching how the United States Senate decided it was not even worth debating how to stop [them] from draining our economy."

The fire ants employ the same strategies when it comes to sharing economy lobbying. In Chapter 1, I defined a sharing economy company in part through its community of users who are united around a set of common values. When the platform is threatened, this community mobilizes around those values. In Washington DC, for example, Uber has long been vehemently opposed by the taxi commission. For a while, the taxi drivers had the upper hand. Council member Mary Cheh proposed the so-called "Uber Amendment" requiring the low-cost UberX cars to charge a minimum price that would have entirely removed their competitive advantage. Uber emailed its users: "It was hard for us to believe that an elected body would choose to keep prices of a transportation service artificially high—but the goal is essentially to protect a taxi industry that has significant experience in influencing local politicians." It takes one to know one. Uber did not forget to include the email addresses and office telephone numbers of the relevant council members. Just days later, the "Uber Amendment" was shelved.

Campaigning bodies

The share platforms have also come together to beef up their lobbying capacity. 2012 saw the launch of "Peers," a campaigning movement for the fire ants of sharing economy. Born out of the ideological zeal of San Francisco, Peers has since expanded to provide practical advice to workers in the sharing economy on how to find and manage their work and taxes. But it started out by inviting people to take the "Peers pledge." "I believe," went the pledge, "the sharing economy should be the biggest economic movement of the 21st century by building an economy that benefits everyone. I pledge to be part of this movement by working to grow and protect the sharing economy, whenever I can." It was a scout-like promise to support the sharing economy when it comes under attack from vested interests or governments. Peers allows its members to launch campaigns on sharing economy issues such as the one against Schneiderman's subpoena of Airbnb's New York hosts.

However, technology blogger, Tom Slee, is skeptical about whether Peers is truly as bottom-up as it claims. "A grassroots organization," he mocks, "with 40 corporate 'partners' [disclosure: JustPark is one of them], with unspecified but significant funding, formed with guidance from a set of high-profile 'thought leaders', without local chapters, and with nothing much for the grassroots to do, but with an Executive Director on day one." That Executive Director was Peers co-founder Natalie Foster, the former head of Obama's digital team at Organizing for America. The daughter of an evangelical preacher, Foster fell in love with technology as a way to scale movements. Until RelayRides founder Shelby Clark took the reins in September 2014, she ran Peers with Milicent Johnson, herself the founder of another campaigning movement for the sharing economy, San Francisco's BayShare.

I approached Foster and Johnson with Slee's criticisms. "We won't be hiring lobbyists and going in and doing the inside game," Foster told me. We were sat in a Blue Bottle café, an Oakland café chain that, in the rich waters of the West coast, has raised over $45 million of investment. "Slee's biggest concern," said Foster, "is that we support activity that involves money and that's a fundamental difference. Peers is a member-driven organization that's about things that save people money like community tool sheds and seed banks. But we are also about experiences where people are making money." Foster stressed to me that Peers is there for everyday people rather than the millionaire investors, and described to me her vision of "Peers members saying to mayors, 'Hey, I really want bikesharing in our town, let's get it here!'" According to Foster, "Sharing is the ultimate in bottom-up. We want to give people the tools to fight for it."

I asked her about what may be their greatest challenge: getting people to campaign on behalf of platforms from which they do not directly benefit. I described how the "sharing economy" and "collaborative consumption" are still abstractions in the minds of the vast majority of actual customers and will likely remain so. Very few families renting out their driveways on

JustPark would see what they have in common with people selling pottery on Etsy or designing logos in their downtime on Freelancer.com. "That's the role of Peers," replied Foster, "to make them realize that they have a home and are doing something fundamentally radical. There are common values between these different forms of behavior. They all believe in the local economy. They all believe that human interaction is an important part of a new economic model."

With a flowering of other organizations around the globe like co:NYC in New York and shareNL in the Netherlands, it is another question as to whether these startups need campaigning bodies to stick up for them. *What if the sharing economy's startups already have a dangerous amount of power?* As Paul Carr writes in *PandoDaily*, "The cult of Disruption … essentially boils down to 'let us do whatever we want, otherwise we'll bully you on the Internet until you do'." In reality, however, only a handful of startups are big enough to be bullies.

How to beat regulation: get big quickly

"When a business gets big," says Jeff Jordan of venture capital fund Andreessen Horowitz, "it's good for two reasons—firstly because of its growing revenues and also because the business develops political weight." Experience as an entrepreneur has taught Jordan that businesses that scale can get their way. When he was President of PayPal, some State regulators who had never anticipated that money could be sent by email tried to force the company to get banking licenses. When he was GM of eBay, some State regulators who never anticipated that millions of people would be conducting online auctions required every seller to get an auctioneer's license. Now on the board of Airbnb, he is watching some regulators who never anticipated that millions of people would be staying in people's homes demand that Airbnb hosts get hotel licenses. I asked Jordan if his experience of startups battling through these problems to become billion-dollar companies made him optimistic that Airbnb would also overcome them. Jordan's response: "Being in Silicon Valley makes me an optimist." In the Valley, it is assumed that successful entrepreneurs will change the world.

Fred Wilson of Union Square Ventures offers similar advice to entrepreneurs when it comes to winning the regulatory battles ahead.

"Get as big as you possibly can as quickly as you possibly can," he told me, "and make as many people's lives better as you can. If you can do that, it'll be very difficult to shut you down." Airbnb co-founder Joe Gebbia compares his company to the automobile in its ability to improve people's lives. "When the car was introduced in 1908, people could experience something more effective than a horse and cart and cities tried to outlaw cars. Of course, the law changed and the rest is history. The policy adjusted to meet the demands of the people." In Paris, where there are more listings for Airbnb than in any other city, Airbnb's popularity led to the "Bill ALUR." The March 2014 update to housing legislation now allows individuals to rent out rooms or entire homes without asking for permission from the city hall. If they can avoid scandals, startups with clout will find obstructive laws and regulations in most markets to be mere bumps on the way.

Successful startups will win their skirmishes with regulators even if it takes years for them to find themselves on a solid regulatory footing. But small, controversial startups can be crushed before they reach critical mass. Rome startup MonkeyParking and San Francisco's Sweetch launched iPhone apps that let drivers sell their on-street spot to circling cars. Sharing one's own driveway is one thing, auctioning off a city's parking spaces is quite another. San Francisco's attorney threatened to sue MonkeyParking if the cheeky primates did not pull their application from the App Store. "Technology has given rise to many laudable innovations in how we live and work," said the city attorney. "MonkeyParking is not one of them. It's illegal … and it creates a predatory private market for public parking spaces that San Franciscans will not tolerate." MonkeyParking withdrew the app. By acting swiftly, the city made sure that it did not have to deal with an 800-pound gorilla.

Light-touch regulation for a transparent world

An English coal mine in 1838. When a thunderstorm caused a river by the Huskar Colliery to burst its banks, one of the mine's ventilation shafts flooded. Twenty-six children who were working in the mine drowned, some only 8 years old. With a nation in shock, Queen Victoria ordered an inquiry. The public was outraged by the findings of Earl Shaftesbury's investigation, not least the detail that some of the impoverished girls were working bare-breasted underground. Four years later, the Mines Act prohibited all women and boys under 10 from working underground in mines. In a past where there was little visibility—literally in the pitch blackness of the mines, where upper-class feet trod for the first time compiling the government report—regulation worked slowly but surely to protect the most vulnerable from exploitation.

Many entrepreneurs in the sharing economy no longer recognize regulation as a tool to protect the vulnerable. According to them, it is now protecting established powerful interests. At the same time, they argue that the need for regulation has diminished. For while there has been no improvement in humans' propensity to exploit each other, we have made progress when it comes to increasing visibility. Our world is built ever more transparently on ever-huger amounts of data: multimedia, GPS signals, and web searches to name but a few. From the dawn of human civilization until 2003, we produced approximately five exabytes of data. By 2012, the world was producing more than that every 48 hours.[5] Data leads to transparency—and that transparency is coming not only from above, but also from below. The Internet is a broadcasting tool for everyone, forcing us into newly transparent ways of living and working.

With new transparency comes increased safety. On share platforms, participants expose their real identity through an online profile that is often supplemented with social media integrations. Transactions are time-stamped and usually geo-tagged. Reviews also provide extra visibility to a potential counter-party. "I feel safer when I ride Uber," says Michael Petricone of the Consumer Electronics Association. "You can see the driver's details and the whole thing is tracked with GPS ... It's different to a regular taxi when you have no idea who you're getting into a taxi with or where they're going." This transparency is protecting consumers and empowers the platforms to play the roles of regulatory agencies. If a chef on EatWith causes an outbreak of food poisoning, negative reviews will alert EatWith to the public health risk. EatWith is highly incentivized to ban him from the platform and could act faster than an official restaurant inspector. EatWith is also incentivized to screen members diligently in the first place. Mindful of this new transparency, Petricone says, "Certainly, there needs to be health and safety regulations. But it should be done with a light touch."

Self-regulation and exemptions

In 1979, the city of Seattle ripped up its taxi regulation in an attempt to reduce red tape and create jobs. It led to a cowboy industry with poorly maintained vehicles and drivers ripping off passengers. Five years later, Seattle would can the experiment. However, today's technology-mediated world is very different. The primary reason that we can move to a world of light-touch regulation is that—more than the startups themselves— the actual users of the platforms act as regulators. eBay was the first of many platforms to demonstrate the astonishing capacity of peer-to-peer models to self-regulate and self-police with online reputation systems of reviewing and commenting that reward good behavior and flag and punish bad behavior.

Were the Seattle taxi experiment reenacted today, each negative experience would have led to a one-star review. Bad drivers would go out of business or raise their games. On platforms like Lyft, customer service is generally impeccable. Drivers with an average star rating below four stars can be booted off but this is rarely necessary: peer-based self-regulation keeps almost everyone in check. Drivers also review passengers. Vomit in the back of a Lyft also leaves a stain on a passenger's reputation, reducing the likelihood of other drivers picking them up in the future. Self-regulation in ridesharing apps also means driver screening that they tout as more rigorous than for regular taxis. Lyft, for example, bans drivers if they have been involved in more than one accident in the last 3 years or have received two traffic tickets. Lyft also performs criminal background checks on drivers, including checking sexual offender lists across multiple States. There have been few serious incidents despite the rampant growth of ridesharing apps, although in 2014, an off-duty Uber driver hit and killed a 6-year-old girl.

There is a big difference between deregulation and self-regulation. When it comes to the latter, self-regulatory organizations, or "SROs," also have a key role. The credit crunch underlined the risks of relying on government agencies to correctly regulate innovative products. But as Arun Sundararajan argues, SROs with devolved powers already function well in various sectors through such organizations as the American Medical Association or the various Bar associations. Sharing economy startups understand this too. Zopa, Funding Circle, and RateSetter are the founding members of the UK's P2P Finance Association. The trade body requires its members to adhere to minimum capital requirements and institute contingency plans to protect investors in the event of insolvency. US crowdfunding startups including Indiegogo, RocketHub, and Wefunder have formed the Crowdfund Intermediary Regulatory Association. Self-regulation is helping startups protect the image of their nascent industries by reducing the chances of worst-case scenarios and PR disasters. At the same time, by providing their own versions of what is workable and proportionate, it lets them mold future laws and regulations.

When it comes to actual government regulation, proportionality is everything. According to Petricone, "There certainly need to be safety regulations but it's a matter of scale. If you see a city applying the same regulations to someone renting a spare bedroom through Airbnb as they do to Hilton hotels, that's clearly inappropriate and it's probably being done to protect some incumbent interests." A further distinction should be made between light and heavy users of platforms, between someone renting out their room while they are on vacation versus someone renting it out for 300 days a year. "We already make such distinctions," writes Emily Badger in *The Washington Post*. "Everyone who drives needs a driver's license. But people who drive a lot—truckers, bus drivers, cabbies—face additional training, permits and safety precautions." This is already happening. Ridesharing regulations in Chicago place stricter regulation on ridesharing startups whose drivers average over 20 hours a week.

Sharing economy lawyer Janelle Orsi wants to see exemptions for small-scale sharing, such as for her client who wanted to crowdfund $100 microloans to build a health spa without complying with securities laws, or the one who wanted to start a small cooperative without falling foul of labor laws. Exemptions are needed for small-scale, low-risk sharing. Conversely, intensively shared assets create more risk events, requiring greater regulation. Greater earnings provides greater incentives for users to jump through regulatory hoops too, such as electrical appliance testing for those renting out property, or the insurance for the part-time electrician who might carry out that testing. Governments should exempt light users from tax burdens while redoubling their efforts to recoup tax from heavy users: the sums of money are larger and the business-like activity creates a more robust case to tax them in the first place. Patterns of work and flows of money are growing more complex. Exemptions are not only common sense; they will become a practical imperative.

Regulation 2.0

When venture capitalist Fred Wilson wrote a blog post advocating regulatory reform in New York State to allow short-term rentals, he was taken aback by the backlash from his techie audience. Many of his readers did not want strangers coming and going from their neighbor's apartments. It is understandable: neighbors of Airbnb hosts see no financial upside and an increased security risk to their building. For Wilson, the correct way forward is not to make Airbnb illegal; it is to make Airbnb explicitly legal and require complete transparency from everybody in the chain of transactions. Wilson advocates that each building has a set of rules that either allow or prohibit short-term rentals. "There are people that would pay more to live in an apartment where they would be free to let out their apartment on an occasional basis," he says. Wilson continues:

> By making Airbnb illegal, you force everyone into a grey market where everyone is trying to cover up the activity … The biggest problem is not a regulatory problem or a political problem. It's the unwillingness of people to adopt a new regulatory framework which we call regulation 2.0. It's more permissive but in return for being more permissive it's also more transparent.

As an inspiration for such radical transparency, Wilson points to Bitcoin, where each transaction is posted to a public ledger known as the "blockchain." For now, there are many hurdles to Wilson's vision. In the case of Airbnb, it is the difficulty of determining short-term rental-friendly buildings, and the challenges that a principal would face raising finance for an "Airbnb-block."

But in the future, Regulation 2.0 will allow the sharing economy to be woven safely into the fabric of cities. Its transparency would give comfort to customers, most of whom do not want to operate under the radar. It would let the companies themselves lock teeth with tax legislation. It would give the public markets greater confidence to hold their stock and allow investors to price the risks of "buy-to-share" investments. Finally, it would help the businesses themselves to understand their operational risks and insure against them, key in a litigious market like the US. *If an Airbnb host with convictions for violent crime murdered his or her guest, is Airbnb liable?* It could certainly claim a defense if aspects of that rental and host had been made a matter of public record in compliance with a bespoke regulatory framework. Of course, greater transparency would help Airbnb to keep risky hosts off the platform in the first place.

Constructive engagement

In the US, the sharing economy is currently low on the President's agenda. It has been the subject of a House Committee but there is no federal legislation in the offing. Rather, the constructive engagement between the authorities and startups is happening at city level. In 2013, 15 US mayors including Mayors Lee of San Francisco and Bloomberg of New York signed a resolution in support of "Shareable Cities." The resolution advocated the creation of task forces to identify regulations that hinder the growth of sharing economy startups, and that appropriate publicly owned assets should be made available through "proven sharing mechanisms." Its preamble noted that "the placement and monetization of underutilized assets into Sharing Economy marketplaces empowers citizens to find new ways of providing jobs, housing, transportation, food, and improved lifestyles."

Unsurprisingly, San Francisco is a flag-waver when it comes to sharing. On top of its recognition of ridesharing startups, Mayor Lee has even declared "Lyft Day." The city is also trying to incorporate sharing services into its policy armory through a "Sharing Economy Working Group": when the Bay Bridge needed to close for repairs, the city's Metropolitan Transportation Commission recommended Irish carpooling app Carma to alleviate congestion. Portland, Oregon, 1,000 km due north, is even keener on sharing. Portland handed peer-to-peer car rental service Getaround a $1.7 million grant and, through the vocal support of Mayor Hales, has become the second US city after Austin to approve short-term rentals. Its regulation is indeed light-touch. The city makes an initial inspection and requires a $180 permit. Residents of homes or duplexes also need to live onsite for at least nine months a year. Airbnb—whose North American headquarters is located in Portland—also collects and remits taxes on the city's behalf.

In Europe, there is some burgeoning support at EU level. The European Economic and Social Committee (EESC), an advisory body to the European Commission, has issued a report on the sharing economy. According to

EESC member Bernardo Hernández Bataller, "Collaborative consumption can meet social needs in situations where there is no commercial interest and it can help, as a for-profit activity, to create jobs." Big-hitting Vice President of the European Commission, Neelie Kroes, vocally supports the sharing economy's disruptions. "We cannot address these challenges by ignoring them, by going on strike, or by trying to ban these innovations out of existence … We cannot criminalize a whole class of citizens, or drive tourists away from places that need money, in order to protect a few industries that think they can be exempt from the digital revolution."

Here in the UK, the sharing economy chimes with the Prime Minister's vision for a "Big Society." The flagship policy of Cameron's 2010 Conservative Party general election manifesto, the Big Society aims to improve communities through entrepreneurship, localism, and open data: key themes of the sharing economy. Frustrated by the lack of bank lending to small businesses, the UK government also injected £40 million into Funding Circle: the first time any government has used a debt crowdfunding startup. UK councils also invest in Funding Circle to channel money to local businesses and many partner with car-sharing companies like Zipcar and CityCarClub. In late 2014, the UK government even instituted an independent review of the sharing economy, chaired by Love Home Swap CEO Debbie Wosskow. Europe's other notable sharing-friendly state is the Netherlands. Amsterdam passed the world's first law for short-term rentals. Under the new accommodation category of "private rentals," hosts can rent out their homes for up to 2 months a year to up to four people at a time. The Netherlands has its own version of Peers, shareNL, and the greatest openness in Europe to shared services like high-growth Dutch goods lending app Peerby and car-sharing app SnappCar.

However, the world's leading sharing city is neither in the US nor Europe. It is Seoul, the capital of South Korea. Seoul's progressive mayor, Park Won-soon, spent three decades as a human rights activist and lawyer, and was imprisoned for protesting against Korea's former dictator, somewhat awkwardly the father of the current President. Park knows that Seoul needs to share: housing is expensive, full-time jobs are in short supply, and pollution is a menace. When I interviewed Park's representative, she mentioned Seoul's "daunting social problems," like a suicide rate that is double the OECD average and a tripling of the number of old people living alone in the last decade. But the conditions are there: Seoul is one of the world's most densely populated cities and 70% of people own a smartphone. Seoul is now implementing a 5-year "Shareable City Plan" that deals with everything from urban planning and regulation to the subsidization of sharing platforms. Today, Seoul buzzes with share platforms. Kozaza is their Airbnb. Labor marketplace Wishket is their oDesk. Kiple, a second-hand kids clothing marketplace, is their thredUP.

Liberalizing with technology

Governments should not worry about power slipping from them to the crowd: it is in their long-term interests to let out the sails. They should understand that if they fail to liberalize for a newly transparent world, they are at risk of attack from fire ants. Regulators also need to liberalize. If they do not, the same ants will question their entire reason for being. The powers that be now have an opportunity to take back the momentum. That means working towards light-touch frameworks with pragmatic exemptions that are born of consultation with startups and incumbents. Crucially, liberalizing will allow the regulators to scale alongside the startups; this is vital because they will have new and pressing work. As Arun Sundararajan of New York University perceptively notes, governments need to "expand the places of last recourse"—the support networks and infrastructure where people can turn in the event of catastrophic platform failure.

In what will be the biggest change to consumer regulation in more than a century, regulators need to borrow some startup tricks and embrace technology and data. So-called "algorithmic regulation" will allow regulators to take a more hands-off approach—until the data tells them to act. Yelp reviews, for example, can alert a city to outbreaks of food poisoning on the basis that people made ill by a restaurant are more likely to troll it on Yelp than complain to their local regulator. Indeed, St Louis, Missouri is already using Yelp data to slash the time and cost of restaurant regulation. The correct data, correctly analyzed, will allow regulators both to reduce red tape for the incumbents, thus leveling the playing field, as well as to regulate the startups. "Algorithmic regulation" is a trend we will hear much about in the coming years, especially once we fear that the benign vision of small government working on a stretched tax base has created a society under the control of programmers and computer code.

Regulators need to exploit other technologies too, like networked sensors and CCTV cameras that Sundararajan suggests could be placed inside every ridesharing car. Regulators can also tap into peer networks themselves: cutting costs by using offshored labor marketplaces and crowd-sourced solutions like the UK's FixMyStreet.com. A third-party tool built by independent developers, FixMyStreet.com interfaces with local governments around the country. I've used the app a few times to report racist graffiti, when I am only too happy to do a little unpaid work for my council. Cities can also supplement their tax bases by sharing their own assets. As April Rinne, who advises cities and policy makers on how to navigate the sharing economy, suggests, "Cities own all kinds of assets – from buildings to car fleets – that could yield additional revenues or cost savings (or both), if shared." Overregulation would also push economic activity abroad. If a country banned Etsy or Airbnb, spend in these global markets would simply shift elsewhere.

Growth and resilience

Despite the painful short-term impact on established industries, local and national governments will see a net economic benefit from this disruptive innovation: such, at least, has been the result of structural change throughout history. A ridesharing app may put local minicab companies out of business. But in time, the vast majority of drivers will migrate across, and by giving residents a cheap way of heading into town, the app will support bricks and mortar businesses. A peer-to-peer vocational skills learning platform like Skillshare can upskill the unemployed. In some places, the need is greater than others. Rockford is a small town in Illinois whose economy was battered by the decline in manufacturing. When its mayor learnt that Etsy was in fact his city's largest "employer," he worked with the New York startup to develop a curriculum called "Craft Entrepreneurship." Etsy now runs "Craft Entrepreneurship" programs in six cities in the US and UK. The work is not necessarily regular or highly paid or highly skilled but it is work nonetheless.

Share platforms can also increase the resilience of cities. When Hurricane Sandy struck in 2012 and tens of thousands of people were made homeless, 1,400 Airbnb hosts opened up their homes for free[6] (Airbnb engineers were up all night pushing code changes that would allow the hosts to rent out their spaces at 0% commission). For all of the government's resources, Airbnb could move faster. When the UK suffered severe flooding, task marketplace Taskhub released a new website called FloodVolunteers in 5 hours. Then there are the man-made stresses. I was in Washington DC during the government shutdown in 2013. Public sector workers who had been furloughed and were working without pay were turning to the sharing economy. I took several Lyfts driven by people who had started driving on the app to make ends meet. In London, a record 24,442 journeys were made on shared bicycles the day of a Tube strike.[7] Or consider how Warren Buffett reached out to Airbnb when he needed to find a way for Omaha—a city with 10,000 hotel rooms—to receive 38,000 visitors for Berkshire Hathaway's annual general meeting.[8]

Rightful caution

Regulation will not go away. Nor should it. While the free-market *Economist* comments, "If consumers want to go for the cheaper, less-regulated service, they should be allowed to do so," it is naïve to assume that consumers understand all the many risks. The photos on a home-swapping site like Knok do not reveal if the property is safely wired. Unlike tech companies that handle purely digital assets, those in the sharing economy give rise to the most profound real world risks. As Sarah Lacy from *PandoDaily* put it to me:

> The worst case scenario with Facebook is something I chose to put online being made public to the whole world. Though a ton of people would disagree with me – that's not *that* bad. The scariest scenario in the sharing economy is a dangerous stranger in my home or my children in a car with a driver who has not been properly background checked. You cannot move fast and break things in this kind of world. There are very real world safety issues.

Nor can we rely on startups to regulate themselves when, under investor pressure, they can pursue growth at all costs and sacrifice carefulness and caution for speed. An Uber driver charged with assaulting a passenger was found to have convictions for drug dealing and battery despite having supposedly been through Uber's rigorous background checks, and 14 US

States have issued warnings about flaws in Uber's insurance cover. James Surowiecki observes in *The New Yorker* that, "the companies are actually piggybacking on the trust that consumers feel in what is typically a highly regulated economy." But unless public safety is at risk, where businesses are creating economic and social capital, regulation must evolve to let their growth play out. We need more listed Cheggs than banned Bookabookas.

It will take years of debate, committees, research and lobbying to get regulation nearly right in all the many sectors impacted by the sharing economy. *Nearly right*, for by that time the world will have changed again.

Notes

1   UK government guidance in 2013 states that "The Government's view is that households should be able to rent parking spaces without planning permission, provided there are no substantive planning concerns such as public nuisance to neighbours": http://planningguidance.planningportal.gov.uk/blog/guidance/when-is-permission-required/what-is-development/#paragraph_015.

2   Riello, Giorgio, *The Rise of Calico Printing in Europe and the Influence of Asia in the Seventeenth and Eighteenth Centuries*, 2005: http://www.lse.ac.uk/economicHistory/Research/GEHN/GEHNPDF/PUNERiello.pdf.

3   Research led by Professor Eleanor Maguire from the Wellcome Trust Centre for Neuroimaging at University College London, published in *Current Biology*, December 9th, 2011. http://www.wellcome.ac.uk/news/media-office/press-releases/2011/wtvm053658.htm.

4   *The Airbnb Community's Economic Impact on New York City*, Airbnb, 2013: http://blog.airbnb.com/wp-content/uploads/Airbnb-economic-impact-study-New-York-City.pdf.

5   Siegler, MG, *Eric Schmidt: Every 2 Days We Create As Much Information As We Did Up To 2003* (*TechCrunch*, August 4th, 2010): http://techcrunch.com/2010/08/04/schmidt-data/. *Big Data at the Speed of Business*, IBM: http://www-01.ibm.com/software/data/bigdata/what-is-big-data.html.

6   *Airbnb's Hurricane Sandy Story*, Airbnb, June 12th, 2013: https://www.youtube.com/watch?v=LJgRwdIGyRs.

7   Data from Transport for London and reported in the *Evening Standard*, October 5th, 2010: http://lydall.standard.co.uk/2010/10/borisbikes-keep-23234-londoners-moving-during-tube-strike.html.

8   Das, Anupreeta, *Buffett Will Steer Investors to Airbnb to Avoid Price-Gouging by Omaha Hotels* (The *Wall Street Journal*, April 8th, 2014): http://blogs.wsj.com/moneybeat/2014/04/08/buffett-will-steer-investors-to-airbnb-to-avoid-price-gouging-by-omaha-hotels/.

A Shared Future?

The efficiency was Germanic but I could have been anywhere. Just off the orderly bustle of Potsdamer Platz in the center of Berlin, I was checking into my suite at the Marriott. Although I had never stayed there before, everything felt oddly familiar. I remember wheeling my suitcase through the revolving doors and into the church-like calm of the hotel lobby. It felt like entering a different world, an older world, where time moved more slowly.

"Good morning, Mr Stephany," said the receptionist. Even her smile felt on-brand. She processed my paperwork and wished me a pleasant stay. Indeed, it already felt pleasant in that air-conditioned lobby of marble floors and plumped-up, empty sofas. But that feeling deflated when I peered up through the Marriott's vast atrium. Above my head were 10 floors of other rooms for other guests, guests who I knew would arrive and leave as invisibly as me.

Six months later as I write this, I cannot recall what it said on that receptionist's name badge. *Why would I?* But I remember the name of the lady who welcomed me to my accommodation when I visited Germany the year before. She was a 70-year-old entrepreneur called Charlotte, with curled grey-blonde hair. A little maverick for conservative Bavaria, Charlotte was an energetic Jewish lady who ran after-school classes for schoolchildren alongside receiving Airbnb guests. She told me about her most memorable visitors, from the famous South African photographer who had documented Apartheid to the Australian who kicked her door down during the beer-swilling Oktoberfest (in defense of the inebriated Aussie, he thought his friend was ill and paid the repair bill the next day). "For a Bavarian to meet all these kinds of people from all over the world," she told me excitedly, "this is exotic. I am someone who likes people."

We have heard the stories of the entrepreneurs who founded and run these new companies. We have seen how the world's top investors and corporate behemoths like General Electric and BMW are hoping to profit alongside them. Lastly, we have seen how governments and regulators are beginning to adapt to this new landscape. But more than anything, this is an economy of people: a we-conomy.

Can we fill the gap? Clues from Ireland

Every economy needs a healthy financial sector—of some kind. In the decade between 1966 and 1976, Irish bankers went on strike three times in protest of what they deemed overly burdensome regulation. One of the strikes lasted 6 months. Each time, economists predicted mass redundancies and turmoil, and politicians feared civil unrest. Each time, the doomsayers were proved wrong. While the stock markets fell, the Irish economy was more resilient than anyone thought. People began to trade in new currencies, and pub landlords, who knew the creditworthiness of their punters as well as any bank managers, acted as arbitrators of financial disputes. In 2008, Ireland was plunged into a far more severe economic crisis as a result of its bankers' reckless overexpansion of credit.

While the Irish banking crisis showed what could be achieved by individuals acting in decentralized concert, banks are plainly necessary. Today, only banks can meet the complex financing needs of companies and governments. Clearly too, in a vastly more globalized world than that of the 1970s, a country would struggle to disentangle itself from a global financial system without becoming another self-destructing Venezuela. But new technologies have made peer networks vastly more scalable and sophisticated too. As Umair Haque, author of *Betterness: Economics for Humans*, puts it, "Banks need people a lot more than people need banks." Change is coming, even those in the most conservative of institutions agree. According to Andy Haldane, Chief Economist at the Bank of England, "Peer-to-peer finance will challenge the nation's main financial institutions … mono-banking culture is on its way out."

By 2014, the world's largest peer-to-peer lender, Lending Club, was issuing more than $250 million of loans a month. The efficiency of these new business models suggests that, sooner or later, all of the core financial products, from mortgages to life insurance, will come in peer-to-peer strains without the banks that brought Ireland to its knees. We have seen how the same disintermediation is letting us access all manner of goods and services—from yachts to graphic design—from the crowd rather than monolithic private and public sector institutions. Today, we cannot fill the gap but the gap is closing.

More people, more sharing: forced and unforced

The macro trends behind the sharing economy that we looked at in Chapter 1 are not going away. Chief among them is population growth. In 2011, demographics experts at the United Nations revised their population forecasts upwards. Instead of asserting the world's population would top out at 9.1 billion in 2100, the UN experts predicted that by 2100 there will be over 10 billion of us. Nor is urbanization a passing fad. An increasing majority of these unborn people will live in highly dense megacities where share platforms function better. We should not underestimate the impact that ever-larger cities will have on our behavior. As a study in prestigious journal *Nature* showed, there is an uncanny positive correlation between the size of a city and how fast people walk in it. The same might be true for activity on share platforms.

We will have to share. In the words of Nobel prize-winning geneticist Paul Nurse, "At present, there are no well-charted ways for 10 billion people to achieve lifestyles like those enjoyed in the most developed countries, because the only known way forward is economic growth, and that will come into collision with the finite earth." Today, study after study confirms that environmentalism does not materially drive the adoption of sharing behaviors. But they could become rapidly entrenched if they were government-enforced through bodies like the US Environmental Protection Agency, perhaps in the wake of more extreme weather patterns. To some extent, scientific opinion will move the case forward. From Professor Stephen Emmott, Head of Computational Science at Microsoft Research: "We urgently need to consume less. A lot less. Radically less."[1] And Professor Danny Dorling of Oxford University and author of *Population 10 Billion: The Coming Demographic Crisis and How To Survive It*: "It's not how many of us there are but how we live that will matter most."[2] *How important is the sharing economy?* I asked Dorling. His response: "If we don't get the sharing economy, we're done for."

Environmentalism has not been a key driver to date, largely because we are lazy short-termists. Its significance may well increase, but more as a green by-product of consumers' love of convenience. In the context of the sharing economy, this can mean the convenience of not storing, insuring, and maintaining goods. It can mean the convenience of being able to access most of our essential needs like food, shelter, and transportation from share platforms direct from a smartphone. The most powerful driver for sharing economy adoption used to be cost, just as it was for the most successful "Web 1.0" e-commerce startups that disrupted incumbents on price. Price will remain critical. Yet in the coming years, consumers will show zero tolerance for services that fail to give them what they need only when they need it. It will make consumption more efficient. And it will play into the hands of many a sharing economy CEO.

The new social web: trust and reputation

As I write, Facebook has overtaken Amazon in market capitalization, and Zuckerberg has overtaken the Google founders in net worth. For now, it appears that the naysayers on Facebook's IPO got it wrong: if anything, social media is gaining in strength. Its insatiable growth will further propel the sharing economy. Facebook's "Social Graph" is mapping in ever-greater detail an ever-greater number of lives. Third-party applications in the sharing economy and beyond will use that data on their own platforms, creating unimagined levels of trust between strangers to lubricate these marketplaces. Before getting into a shared car, users will have an uncanny understanding of each other, perhaps allowing them to break the ice with small talk about a concert that they both attended. When we feel connected to someone, our brains release oxytocin, known by "neuro-economist" Paul Zak as "the moral molecule" because it increases trust and empathy.[3] Trust is valuable: it loosens purse strings. As they loosen, many coins will drop into the bank accounts of sharing economy companies.

With the surfacing of all this information about us and the growth of these platforms, our online reputations will become more important than ever. Companies will mine this social data to market to us, sell to us, and lend to us. Meanwhile, we will become fierce guardians of our online reputation, knowing that a positive one will hold the key to unlocking goods and services at low cost. More than that, a good online reputation will mean power: to get a loan, rent an apartment, or close a business deal. Someone with hundreds of positive, verifiable reviews on a labor marketplace will be more likely to get a mortgage, and rightly so. Conversely, a negative reputation could be far more crippling than a bad credit score. Consider how a negative review of someone who damaged a host's property would make a future employer think twice. I expect the emergence of "trust tipping"—a way of publicly thanking someone online—to spread across the Internet via social networks. We will even begin to choose friends and lovers on the basis of their online reputation.

This is an opportunity that startups are just beginning to address. eRated pulls in data from marketplaces like eBay and Etsy and presents it in a percentage score on a widget. "Own your Reputation," it promises users. The market leader with 4.5 million users and most of the funding is Traity. Another reputation aggregator that pulls in trust data, it seeks to present an individual's trustworthiness in the form of a profile page with reviews and written references. Traity's mission is "To create a world where people can trust one another, enabling more transactions with strangers, more interactions and more social and economic opportunities." In theory, these new trust startups allow people to port their reputation around the Internet. It is a bigger question as to whether the platforms will let their data go: they want you to have to start from scratch if you jump ship to a competitor. Regulation may save the emerging online reputation industry. In time, Facebook will be forced to give up the stranglehold on our online reputation in the interests of competition rather than privacy.

What will this mean day to day? Increasing transparency will create a culture of extreme accountability. Our deeds, good or bad, will follow us around like school reports that anyone can read. We will have to start behaving better. On peer-to-peer marketplaces, people will behave additionally well when they are transacting with a human being rather than a company. When RelayRides started out, there was no contact between the car owner and the renters who would unlock the cars using their smartphone. People treated the cars no better than regular rental cars. When RelayRides pivoted to rely on the physical exchange of keys between car owner and renter, this human interaction led to an immediate drop in damage incidents. We have long known that being known keeps us in check: criminologists have observed that people commit less crime when they know their neighbors.[4] With the rise of peer networks, the fear of sullying our digital reputation will keep more of us on the straight and narrow.

Shifts in social value: creation and destruction

The cumulative impact of these peer networks will be the creation of massive new social capital. Couchsurfing, for example, takes the utility of getting a roof over your head and makes it about "sharing your life, your experiences, your journey, your home, your extra almonds or a majestic sunset." The individualism of selfish sharers will lead to a public good. As Adam Smith put it, "By pursuing his own interest, [an individual] frequently promotes that of the society more effectually than when he really intends to promote it."[5] This public good will be economic, as we shall see: the sharing economy is an online silk road that we can all walk. But just as significantly, it will lead to a social public good. None of the user bases of sharing economy companies will grow to rival Facebook's in size, yet the transactions on them often involve far more meaningful engagement between strangers with far more degrees of separation. By connecting people across lines of race, religion, and nationhood, the sharing economy could make the world a little more empathetic and even peaceful.

While some social value—normally of the kind that promises a financial profit—is being created, other social value will get destroyed. The sharing economy takes acts once done for free and puts a price on them. This will have two consequences. Firstly, it will underpin an ever-greater proportion of acts of generosity, hospitality, and courtesy with cash and obvious self-interest. Morality could be monetized or shrink to those anonymous acts that have no link to money or monetizable online reputation. Secondly, the number of these nonmonetizable acts could itself shrink. Fewer families will donate second-hand clothes to charity when they can easily sell them. Fewer people will let a friend stay in their apartment when they are out of town for a few days and can easily convert that idling capacity into income.

As the sharing economy seeps into our lives, prosocial deeds—those done out of the goodness of our hearts to benefit someone else—will become comparatively rarer and more cherished. *What about the poor and the weak who rely on them?* Behavioral scientist Dan Ariely has shown that once you have induced people to view acts as economic exchanges, this fundamentally alters the way that people behave. We are more likely to do unpaid work than work for a sum that we consider inadequate. In one experiment, lawyers who were offered $30 to provide needy retirees with advice refused. However, when the lawyers were asked to provide the advice for free, they typically agreed.[6] The implication is that a householder, for example, may not be inclined to lend a neighbor a ladder when he imagines himself entitled to a payment but could only command one that is too measly to be interesting. The sharing economy scales paid pseudo-neighborly deeds. But its end game will likely mean a contraction in truer unpaid neighborliness.

The sharing economy also does little to address "the tragedy of the commons." Taking its name from the problem of overgrazed common land, the tragedy of the commons is the idea that individuals acting in pure self-interest can harm their group's long-term best interests. The sharing economy provides no motivation to contribute to public goods that are not cool enough for Kickstarter and at the same time a lot costlier to build and maintain, such as sewer systems, reservoirs, highways, bridges, and so on. The commons of city streets could be improved with car- and bike-sharing. However, essential infrastructure may fall by the wayside on a narrowed tax base. In theory, the sharing economy could address the tragedy of the commons through civic crowdfunding. But crowdfunding will never be capable of financing the enormous, boring line items on every city's budget.

Sharing when the boom times come again

One of the catalysts for the sharing economy was the global recession. In Spain and Italy, they call them the "€1,000 Generation." The term refers to the minimum allowable base salary of €1,000 on which many—the lucky ones with jobs—subsist. In even less fortunate Greece, they are the "€700 Generation." Many nations will continue to feel the effect of the recession for decades to come as their spendthrift governments recapitalize at the cost of younger generations. Economic distress led the underemployed and cash-strapped to flock to freelancer marketplaces, and consumers to try cheaper models of consumption through recommerce platforms. It also helped bring the sharing economy to mass consciousness by generating countless consumer finance PR pieces. We hope that the global economy has now turned a corner. *What will be the impact on the sharing economy when the boom times come again?*

It will, for starters, take time for that level of visible prosperity to return, especially when banks remain parsimonious with consumer credit. Once it does, sharing economy businesses will be unaffected. "Ostentatious splurging," according to The Boston Consulting Group's latest Global Consumer Sentiment Survey, "has given way to more emphasis on value for money and quality,"[7] a trend that will benefit the sharing economy and outlast the downturn. Further, economic want and sharing are loosely correlated in the first place. At the height of the recession, sharing platforms found popularity with a middle class with savings and disposable income. But above all, austerity was the route into habit-forming patterns of consumption that are sticky because they are often qualitatively better on metrics like fun and convenience. The impact of greater economic wellbeing will not be platform abandonment but consumers trading up on them for more premium assets and experiences.

It remains to be seen whether the appeal of sharing economy platforms will extend to the super-rich. BlackJet brought the sharing model to the leasing of private jets: it was the sharing economy for millionaires. The logic was sound: a third of private jets are empty as they shuttle around the world to suit their owners. However, BlackJet failed to build liquidity and folded. The rich often like their own things and have no desire to share them. But others may yet succeed. JumpSeat and Wheels Up have raised tens of millions for other shared private jet businesses. For when it comes to money, wealthy people often have a shrewdness that may have got them rich in the first place, something that explains the superyacht rental and sharing markets. Wealthy people can also like showing off. By sharing your Porsche, you are claiming another form of status: to be so rich that you are relaxed about someone using your $150,000 sports car. So they crash it? *Whatever. It's a car.*

Sharing for economic growth

The sharing economy is going to grow into the larger economy come rain or shine. *Does it benefit the larger economy?* "What happens," asks Derek

Thompson in *The Atlantic*, "when millions of people spend 10% less on new things and 10% more sharing old things or getting sophisticated deals? It's easy to say that sharing is good for efficient markets. It's not so easy to say that sharing is good for a growing economy that depends on new shoppers." Pessimists would say that the sharing economy is a smaller economy. In reality, however, capital is reallocated. Decreased spend on homes, cars, and clothes finds its way into banks, where it is reborn as capital for new businesses that create jobs and keep the wheels of growth turning. Finally, popular consumer technologies create new wealth by growing the size of their markets. Far more people now take taxis because apps like Lyft have made them cheap and available within a few taps.

Ian Hathaway, a former analyst at the Federal Reserve, is confident that sharing networks will boost growth. "Doing more with less is how the economy grows sustainably over the long term," says Hathaway. Harvard Law Professor and author of *The Wealth of Networks* Yochai Benkler goes even further, arguing that collaborative projects represent that next stage of economic development. Entrenched in a growing digital economy, sharing models are already making their impact felt—on the rare occasions that we try to measure it. Analysts at Morgan Stanley estimated that the collaborative economy comprised about 16% of UK GDP in Q1 2014 up from 12% in 2007.[8] If true, the figure renders the official data about the UK's contracting economy and its supposed recession more or less useless. Arguably, the UK economy kept growing after all. But we were watching the wrong numbers.

At its root, the sharing economy helps the wider economy by increasing trust and collaboration between people. Francis Fukuyama has explored the relationship between trust and prosperity in countries like Germany and Japan.[9] Others, like UK think-tank the Legatum Institute, have found similar evidence for their strong positive correlation.[10] Meanwhile, author Matt Ridley is a self-proclaimed "Rational Optimist," studying how collaboration creates prosperity. Ridley explained to me how, "The great trend of human history is away from self-sufficiency (another word for poverty) to specialized production and diversified consumption. Growth is a collaborative enterprise and has been for more than 100,000 years." We get richer through the billions of acts of collaboration that occur at an individual rather than State level. I asked Ridley how his research informs his view of the sharing economy. "Sharing is at the heart of human endeavor," he said. "This very human habit of exchange can be trusted to drive the sharing economy and our future prosperity."

Sharing for economic stability

"If the crisis has a single lesson," says former Chairman of the Federal Reserve Ben Bernanke, "it is that the too-big-to-fail problem must be solved." For the most part, the global financial system remains a dam built out of some extremely large blocks. A mere crack in one of them spells mass alarm, and if one were to be washed away, the entire dam could collapse. A more diversified global economy that is less reliant on giant companies and banks would be a more resilient one. Everyone would benefit from the robustness of distributed networks of production such as the million-plus small businesses on Etsy scattered around the world. There is a parallel for this robustness or high "fault tolerance" in a peer-to-peer file-sharing service like BitTorrent. If someone spills a cup of coffee on their laptop while it is serving its file, the impact on the whole is highly contained as the same content is served from a "swarm" of other laptops around the world.

This distribution of economic activity helps to reduce another risk factor that contributed to the credit crunch: the risk of concentrating power in the hands of a small number of people. According to James Surowiecki's logic in *The Wisdom of Crowds*, harnessing the crowd can lead to better decisions. The sharing economy's many peer-powered platforms create diversification at this decision-making level. A peer-to-peer insurance platform, for example, allows many people to make a large number of decisions, each of which is of very little financial consequence if ultimately mistaken. Consider, by contrast, the power that traditional models gave to men like Joseph Cassano, Head of the Financial Products division of AIG. Cassano was part of a small team that insured tens of billions of dollars' worth of structured debt securities backed by sub-prime loans. The risky decisions made by a handful of people would lead to the Federal Reserve offering a $85 billion credit facility to AIG, the largest government bailout of a private company in US history.

On a micro as well as a macro level, the sharing economy will help to maintain a greater economic equilibrium. Open source enthusiast and publisher Tim O'Reilly compares an economy to an ecosystem where "if you take more out than you put in they [both] eventually fail." In the credit crunch, this "taking out" meant excessive levels of debt, however it was dressed up through derivatives. The sharing economy can reduce consumer debt by giving people access to expensive assets like homes and cars that today are usually bought on finance. It can reduce the amount we spend beyond our means and help in the urgent work of deleveraging the global economy. Of course, the sharing economy is also about "putting in" through the economic output from the many opportunities to make money. As both sellers and buyers of goods and services, the sharing economy will help to keep many of our personal balance sheets in equilibrium.

And what is good for economic stability is generally—and if not more importantly—good for political stability. Political extremism feeds on economic weakness. The Nazi Party rose in the wake of the Great Depression, and today the Far Right is rising across Europe in the wake of credit crunch. Parties like France's Front National and the virulently racist and anti-Semitic Jobbik Party in Hungary now enjoy over 20% of the popular vote. While very difficult to quantify, it is possible that in the coming years, countries with large and developed sharing economies could benefit not only from increased prosperity, but also from a moderating influence on their politics.

A new metric for the sharing economy

We should also question whether gross domestic product, or GDP—the market value of all the goods and services produced within a country—is the right metric for economic strength in the first place. Developed for a US Congress report in 1934 by Nobel Prize-winning economist Simon Kuznets, GDP has dominated our understanding of economic prosperity ever since. But the logic of GDP has become increasingly and deeply flawed. Its principal flaw in the context of the sharing economy is its failure to capture the secondary and tertiary markets for goods already in existence. If I sell my wardrobe on Preloved or my old television on eBay, this income will not be captured in GDP. Andy Ruben, co-founder of yerdle, explains it thus:

> Western and increasingly global society is based on production. We know to the fifth decimal point how many shoes are produced. But we have no

idea whether they are worn or not. This made a lot of sense after World War II to assume a pair of shoes got worn when there weren't enough shoes. It makes a lot less sense now when 80% of the things in our home are used less than once a month.

Current data also does a disservice to the "job" creation that is at the heart of many share platforms. As Arun Sundararajan of New York University's Stern School of Business points out, "eBay's impact hasn't been on the thousands of tech jobs it created for eBay but on the hundreds of thousands of sellers it created … Google comes, hundreds of tech jobs are created, and there's a lot of hoopla about these things. Meanwhile, Etsy is quietly creating massive amounts of employment, and they're not counted as jobs." "It's like an invisible economy," says Molly Turner, Airbnb's director of public policy. It is this invisible economy that the UK and every other country's economists were missing during the recession and continue to miss when it comes to economic growth and job numbers.

What is the alternative to GDP and employment statistics? GDP grew out of a bygone industrial era where factories became able to create ever-greater output through innovation after innovation, like the assembly line, bucket elevators, and bridge cranes. But the sharing economy's new version of growth concerns not increased productivity but the increased utilization of our time and the goods that we have already produced. The world's ecosystem calls for a new metric to replace GDP and output: utilization. In the decades to come, economists will develop ways of estimating and measuring value as it is created throughout the lifecycle of products. Until then, looking at GDP in isolation will lead us up some very wrong policy paths.

In the future, we will be sold on how long products will last, just like we are today when we purchase lightbulbs. Unlike with today's lightbulbs, however, this data will not be approximate. As products begin to reach the end of their useful lives, sensors embedded in them will send back real-time, geo-located data to central databases. Companies and local service providers will tap into these databases to sell new products to us. Neighbors will use them to see what they can get their hands on in their neighborhoods. Local authorities will use the databases to arrange the automated collection and recycling of goods. As we develop the hardware and infrastructure to get more out of less, the world will see a gradual and permanent decoupling of GDP and living standards.

The sharing economy losers ...

What may be good for the economy as a whole still hurts many individuals working in that economy. Think of the small-time web designer who will find himself undercut by those in the developing world in a global services marketplace. Think of the production line worker now assembling the cars that 20-somethings will buy in ever fewer numbers because they use ridesharing and car-sharing apps. For the hapless in those roles and countless others whose voices are little heard in the triumphant chorus of the sharing economy, the long-term benefits of structural change are insultingly theoretical. Some of these economic losers will happily embrace share platforms. Some will be forced unwillingly onto them. Many though will be casualties, too old or inflexible to reorientate their careers.

Yet life is not always rosy for those working on the share platforms either. It may be still less so in a shared future. We have seen how share platforms are turning ordinary people into entrepreneurs. However, micro-entrepreneurship has entrepreneurship's downsides too: hard work and uncertain rewards. Above all, not everyone is cut out for entrepreneurship. Marketplaces are unforgiving "sink or swim" places for those without the drive and talent to get on a virtuous cycle of finding work and earning positive reviews. Meanwhile, every worker, however successful, earns by the grace of the platforms and their secret algorithms. When TaskRabbit changed its business model while I was writing this book, shoe-horning its Rabbits into a few narrow categories of work, the Rabbits had to live with it—or in Brittney Bedford's case leave the platform. When UberX slashes its prices by 25% without warning, it is the drivers who take a pay cut.

For marketplaces built on labor, it is the job of those running them to push that cost as low as possible. As Martin Bryant, Editor-in-Chief at *The Next Web*, put it to me, "Workers could get trodden on by a rampant desire for efficiency." Already on Fiverr, people offer services from $5 (out of which the platform takes 20%). Many who pick up the work are desperate and working for well beneath the minimum wage. The future may look like *The Zero Marginal Cost Society* described by Jeremy Rifkin, where goods and services cost little or nothing once the infrastructure is in place. Good for the economy. Fantastic for consumers. Potentially ruinous for workers, who will, in time, unionize. As contractors rather than employees, workers also lack employment benefits. Platforms do not provide health insurance or pensions: they do not need to when the supply of unskilled labor outstrips demand. *Get sick?* Tough. *Grow old?* Simply getting by on share platforms is a challenge: good luck putting away enough money for retirement. "The employment of the future is here," quips Sam Biddell in *Gawker,* "and it's terrific for everyone except the people doing the work."

No one is forcing anyone to do any work, the platforms reply. That is true enough. The problem is ahead of us, however, when a sufficient amount of the demand for labor has migrated to freelancer marketplaces and micro-entrepreneurship ceases to be a choice. In countries with weak social safety nets, freelancing to the detriment of permanent employment will leave those at the bottom horrifically exposed. "Micro-gigging leaves people incredibly vulnerable," writes Sara Horowitz of the Freelancer's Union, an advocacy group for the US's 42 million freelancers.[11] "As we rush forward into this hyper-efficient economy, we're actually sliding back to certain aspects of the 19th century, where workers had few rights and no protections." In the coming decades, platform bosses will clash with regulators who will once again need to protect those who sink rather than swim.

… And its rich and powerful winners

Micro-entrepreneurship also comes with micro-upside compared to the entrepreneurship of the founders. While these startups will neglect the communities behind them at their peril, real wealth will remain in the hands of shareholders. Since marketplaces tend towards "winner-takes-most" monopolies, this new set of companies could be more powerful than the incumbents. Once the regulatory risk attached to Airbnb has subsided, it will IPO. *What if, under pressure from Wall Street, it and other platforms abuse their market power? Will dominant peer-to-peer marketplaces also abuse the data of their millions of users?* By then, the venture capitalists will have exited. Many investors that I spoke to aligned themselves with the moral vision of the sharing economy. But journalist Andrew Leonard is one of many who does not buy it. "Silicon Valley," he writes in *Salon,* "could start by putting a stop to pretending that the sharing economy is about anything other than making a killing."

The micro-entrepreneurs making the most money from share platforms are also the affluent ones with valuable assets worth "sweating," assets that are often rented out by similarly affluent people. It is why tech provocateur Milo Yiannopoulos slams the sharing economy as "a playground for the middle classes."[12] Almost certainly, the sharing economy will raise the living standards of the working classes by letting them affordably access goods and services and earn supplementary income. But when it comes to cold, hard net worth, the sharing economy will do little to bridge the wealth gap. It may even increase it, as the "buy-to-share" model pushes the capital cost of some assets even higher. *How much will that wealth gap matter?* We will always want savings for luxuries and peace of mind. Yet money will matter a little less when we can lead a comfortable material life by accessing assets rather than owning them. One day, net worth may even seem a slightly quaint notion, carrying, like a robber baron's mansion, a whiff of absurdity.

A new wave of online companies will emerge to whom we may look for many of our fundamental needs: clothing, shelter, mobility, and financial services. *Will these companies, the largest of which may yet to be founded, be any better as stewards of our communal welfare than 20th-century multinationals?* One route through this tangle of ideals and profit may be the B Corporation model, as adopted by Etsy and Couchsurfing. "B Corps" are for-profit businesses whose decision-making processes formally consider their impact on the environment and society. B Corps issue a publically available annual benefit report and aim to have a "material positive impact" on wider society.[13] It remains to be seen how the moral code of a B Corp may be stressed when one goes public for the first time, as will likely happen with Etsy in the next few years. Most likely, we will see a moral tug of war, with the ideals of founders and communities pitched against unsentimental public markets.

Cooperatives 2.0

Perhaps there is an alternative. *What if the communities owned the platforms?* In the next half-decade, the likes of Airbnb and Lending Club will become the incumbents, ripe for disruption by what I call "Cooperatives 2.0." Depositors will own peer-to-peer lenders. Chefs will own peer-to-peer dining platforms. Such platforms will start by crowdfunding seed capital and will invite members of their growing community to invest in future funding rounds. In fact, the crowd will own the crowdfunding platforms themselves. With employees that are salaried and driven by moral purpose rather than the hope of cashing out stock, some Cooperatives 2.0 will scale to global businesses. Unlike holders of public company stock, their shareholders will share their platform's journey and vision. Since the platform's users will normally be shareholders, Cooperative 2.0 platforms will also prove very sticky and hard to disrupt. If that sounds fanciful, consider the success of collaborative projects like Wikipedia and Linux. With Cooperatives 2.0, participants will be motivated by money as well as morals.

Most urgently, workers need to own labor marketplaces, even if that means a compulsory withholding of microinvestments from their first digital pay packets. Indeed, it is already happening. San Francisco's Loconomics is just such a Cooperative 2.0. "Loconomics is like TaskRabbit if the rabbits owned the company," says sharing economy attorney Janelle Orsi. "It's not a platform for the rich to get richer, it's a platform for reversing that." The platform gives the freelancers a stake for a $100 annual subscription. These ideas are spreading. A black cabbie in London told me that a group of cabbies are now working on their own taxi app that would be owned by the cabbies themselves. *Why not?* It would cost less than $250,000 to release a functional competitor to Uber. The real cost for Uber is in building both sides of the marketplace: passengers and drivers. A driver-owned app would be outgunned when it came to marketing to passengers. But it could have the drivers—the most important side of the marketplace in the long-term—locked in from day one.

What next? Where next?

What next? Change happens slower when the incumbents enjoy brands built over decades or centuries and are enmeshed in the political system. Such is the case with education, but it too will see similar peer-to-peer disruptions in the coming decade. With US student debt at over $1 trillion,[14] startups like Skillshare and Udemy are providing access to top-class vocational training for the price of a Harvard hoodie. Leaner new business models will also impact the old-fashioned insurance market. Berlin-based startup Friendsurance connects people to create a private insurance pool that pays out on household and consumer electronics claims. In time, the sharing economy will change other regulatory-heavy sectors like energy and healthcare, where Cohealo is now allowing hospitals to share medical equipment. Martin Varsavsky, founder of Fon, predicts the sharing economy will even reach fertility:

> For a long time, fertility has been helped by people who have been sharing their sperm or eggs but it's been done in a very restrictive way ... As the average age of people having children goes up, fertility is an area which will see a great deal of change, because of the ability to obtain embryos, eggs, sperm, surrogacy ... People don't think of fertility as part of the sharing economy, but I do.[15]

Where next? Today, while many of the companies are headquartered in the US and funded with dollars, Europe leads the sharing economy when it comes to adoption. Despite being founded in the US, more of Airbnb's top cities are in Europe. Bike-share schemes are more widely used in Europe too. As for long-distance ridesharing, BlaBlaCar and Carpooling have become common alternatives to traveling by train—and major competitors to the rail companies—while long-distance ridesharing in the US has never taken off. "U.S. drivers tend to have less trust when it comes to driving with strangers than Europeans," speculates Katie Fehrenbacher in *Gigaom*. Less trust may cause lower adoption in other verticals. Moreover, Europe is full of older, denser cities where sharing assets is more of a practical necessity. Europeans have been sharing for longer in its offline forms: it is no surprise that they take more naturally to sharing in its online forms.

In the future, growth will move outside developed nations, where less wealthy consumers are even more used to sharing costs and assets. Offline sharing habits are still more ingrained in these markets, for example in the communal washing machines that traverse *favelas* on the back of scooters, or the 1,000-plus restaurants in people's homes in Cuba known as *paladares*. Indian-born Arun Sundararajan of New York University is excited about the largest emerging markets of all. "China and India will be building cities in the future faster than any countries in history," he told me. "Sharing models will allow their citizens to do more at lower cost." His instincts have since been borne out in data. A 2014 Nielson survey involving 30,000 respondents found that while 44% of Europeans would rent goods from others, 81% of those in Asia-Pacific would, including 94% of Chinese respondents.[16]

Being born with less can be an effective spur to entrepreneurship. A disproportionate number of JustPark property owners were born on the Indian subcontinent and arrived in the UK as relatively poor immigrants. As a broad generalization, those who grew up with less space are also less precious when it comes to sharing it. In China specifically, the culture of "face" could further catalyze adoption. When I worked there teaching English, I observed how this well-documented need to show or save face was a powerful motivator of human behavior. "Face," an offline reputation system, suggests that online reputation systems will function well too. Of course, many in China have newfound wealth and want to own rather than share. But even among this segment, luxury goods sales are on the decline, hit by China's crackdown on corruption at the same time as an interest in vintage—that is say, used—goods is on the rise. The largest sharing economies will ultimately be in the "BRIC" nations: Brazil, Russia, India, and China.

Entrepreneurs and consumers in developing countries are watching the west. Every week, local versions of the major platforms spring up to meet new demand. In China, for example, Roland Berger expects car-sharing to grow 80% year on year through services like ATzuche.[17] This is, it should be said, growth from a tiny base. There is still a logjam when it comes to essential infrastructure: high smartphone adoption, developed logistics networks for the dispatch of physical goods, and, of course, the Internet itself. In 2013, McKinsey predicted that it would take until 2025 for online spend across Africa to reach a comparable level to that of the UK today.[18] But statistics do not tell the human tale. In 19th-century British slums, beds were occasionally let to three different people who had them for 8 hours each. With the price of the cheapest smartphones now $25 and falling fast, similar efficiencies will make the basics of existence affordable for countless millions of this century's poorest people.

Can sharing make us happy?

We all seek happiness; we just can't agree how best to find it. "Happiness economists" agree on the basic correlation between wealth and happiness. But after a certain point of affluence is attained, money adds nothing more to happiness or wellbeing. Without adjusting for inflation, GDP in America has soared 16-fold since 1970[19] with no comparable increase in happiness. Some of us will find it, or at least companionship, through the social experiences that sharing facilitates. Like many sharing economy platforms, the peer-to-peer city touring platform Vayable is really in the business of selling happiness. According to Vayable's website, "Happiness research shows that we get longer-lasting meaning and fulfillment from experiences than we do from stuff." It quotes Elizabeth Dunn, a psychology professor from the University of British Columbia: "It's better to go on a vacation than buy a new couch." *Can sharing even make us happy?*

The entrepreneurs think so. "Happy people share stuff," says Adam Werbach, co-founder of yerdle. "People who are into sharing are also into community and living joy-filled lives." Marieke Hart, co-founder of Shareyourmeal says, "The mere act of sharing can really brighten your day. In the case of our home cooks, this means being able to do something meaningful for someone else." Hart quotes from an email she received from one of Shareyourmeal's home cooks, Kim: "I cook for my neighbors once a week and I know even beforehand that I will go to bed that evening feeling happy." Again, there is some emerging science behind the anecdotes. In 2014, researchers at the Max Planck Institute for Evolutionary Anthropology in Germany found that levels of the molecule linking trustworthiness with happiness were elevated in wild chimpanzees after they had shared food.[20] Sharing made the group happier.

If sharing on these platforms can indeed make us happy, it is only because the human exchange that is central to the process can exist in countless different forms. *Interested in science?* Arrange a daily carpool with a scientist. *Love fashion?* Trade clothes and style tips with strangers hundreds of miles away. *Simply enjoy a bottle of beer watching your team at your local sports bar?* You might enjoy it more if you and your pals crowdfunded a giant 3D television and could drink away with the knowledge that some of the profit from your beers would flow right back to you. While convenient, cheap access to goods and services may "hook people in" as Rachel Botsman put it, it is the ability of share platforms to socialize goods and services in a limitless number of ways that will keep users engaged and change the world. A brand like Nike or Häagen-Dazs sells one or two emotions. The sharing economy is creating marketplaces for any emotion.

Day two

"An invasion of armies can be resisted but not an idea whose time has come," wrote Victor Hugo, the French author who grew up in the aftermath of the French Revolution.[21] By 2014, one in five tourists visiting Brazil for the World Cup stayed in an Airbnb.[22] BlaBlaCar was moving over 2 million people a month. Lending Club had lent out $5 billion without a bank in sight. Yet for all the seeming scale that they and others have reached, the companies of the sharing economy are still in their infancies. Many of them are just a few years old and have their growth spurts ahead of them. The fundamental advantages that they enjoy through their leaner business models and the macro trends on their side suggest that these startups will reach far larger scale and profitability—and that these disruptions are only beginning. To quote Airbnb's Brian Chesky, "It's literally day two in the sharing economy."

This is not to say that the corporate giants are going anywhere. "You can never write off the incumbents," cautions Robin Klein of Index Ventures, "which is a very unpopular view in Silicon Valley! Species evolve. Skype [an Index Ventures-backed company] disrupted the telecoms market but the incumbents are still very much there." The largest companies like telecoms and mining companies will evolve by realizing efficiencies through sharing, as airlines do today through the shared use of plane parts at airports. Once demand for peer-to-peer services grows, many incumbents will also package and offer their own versions of them. Meanwhile, for the time being, corporates give consumers what they largely desire: the same product over and over again. Coca-Cola is a hugely valuable business in part because every can of Coke tastes the same. People often say that the sharing economy's biggest challenge to growth is regulation. It isn't. It is appeasing the 20th-century's expectation of a consistent consumer experience.

To provide the necessary consistency to hit that mass market of consumers, sharing economy companies will also evolve. They will borrow from the corporate playbook of mass standardization by exerting greater control over their platforms and brands. As everyone works out which are the best business models, big companies of all kinds will begin to look a touch alike. Yet they will all be built very differently from those of yesteryear. They will cater for new norms of production and consumption in changes that will prove as significant as those brought about by the Industrial Revolution.

Unlike that revolution, however, the sharing economy is, at heart, a *counter-revolution*. Technology will let us have our needs met by trusted people rather than companies or governments, for the first time in centuries.

80% good, 20% bad

Much is promised of the sharing economy, often too much. In fact, so much has been promised that it could prove to be mostly hot air but still of enormous economic, social, and environmental consequence. We are used to dystopic visions of the future in science fiction. However, the sharing economy is a trend that posits that the 21st century could actually see more prosperity and social harmony and less alienation, needless pollution, and consumption than the previous one. For now, the sharing economy promises to be 80% good and 20% bad. That is as much as any moralist, consumer, politician, or executive could ever hope for. The threat to the commons, the monetization of neighborliness, the erosion of labor rights—these are the pitfalls to be avoided. Meanwhile, other pitfalls that we have not even thought of will appear on the road ahead, the sharing economy equivalent of Rumsfeld's "unknown unknowns."

That should not hold us back. I want a world where there are only as many cars and buildings as we need, and where it is easy for people to leave the weekly grind of their jobs and become entrepreneurs. I want a world where strangers from the other side of the world can become truer friends than those we have on Facebook. I want power to slip from the grip of multinationals and governments to people who can meet the fundamental needs—clothing, housing, work, and credit—of other people. I want communities where people are once again connected to their neighbors. I want a global economy that is less about stock tickers and more about "Ubuntu," the Bantu term for "humanness" that technology was meant to have replaced with swarms of drones and marching robots. Not so. It is time we got down to the business of sharing.

Notes

1   Emmott, Stephen, *10 Billion* (Penguin, 2013), p. 169.
2   Dorling, Danny, *Population 10 Billion: The Coming Demographic Crisis and How to Avoid it* (Constable, 2013), p. 2.
3   Zak, Paul, *The Moral Molecule: The Source of Love and Prosperity* (Dutton, 2012).

4   Shaw, Clifford R and McKay, Henry D, *Juvenile Delinquency and Urban Areas* (Chicago: The University of Chicago Press, 1969).

5   Smith, Adam, *The Wealth of Nations* (Digireads.com, 2004), p. 264.

6   Ariely, Dan, *Predictably Irrational: The Hidden Forces that Shape Our Decisions* (HarperCollins, 2009).

7   *The Resilient Consumer: Where to Find Growth amid the Gloom in Developed Economies*, based on *The Boston Consulting Group's 2013 Global Consumer Sentiment Survey*: https://www.bcgperspectives.com/content/articles/center_consumer_customer_insight_consumer_products_resilient_consumer/.

8   Charles Goodhart and Jonathan Ashworth of Morgan Stanley reviewed the growth of casual labor and self-employment since the start of the recession: http://www.ft.com/cms/s/0/777b8ae8-cc56-11e3-bd33-00144feabdc0.html - axzz3AZs4IdsX.

9   Fukuyama, Francis, *Trust: The Social Virtues and The Creation of Prosperity Paperback* (Free Press, 1996).

10 The Prosperity Index is compiled by the Legatum Institute and aims to understand the causes of economic prosperity and trace the link between social and financial capital: http://prosperity.com/ - !/innovative-entrepreneur.

11 In 2006, the Government Accountability Office released a report indicating that 42.6 million workers, or 30% of the US workforce, were independent or contingent. http://www.gao.gov/new.items/d06656.pdf.

12 Milo Yiannopoulos, *10 Reasons Why the Sharing Economy is Bollocks*, LeWeb, 2013: https://www.youtube.com/watch?v=ZeSkWeSkuSc.

13 More information of the notion of "material positive impact" in the context of a B Corporation can be found at: http://www.benefitcorp.net/business/operate-as-a-benefit-corporation/how-do-i-create-general-public-benefit.

14 2013 data from the US Government's Consumer Finance Protection Bureau: http://www.consumerfinance.gov/blog/a-closer-look-at-the-trillion/.

15 Interview with Martin Varsavsky taken from The Sharing Economy: A Whole New Way of Living, published in *The Guardian*, August 4th, 2013: http://www.theguardian.com/technology/2013/aug/04/internet-technology-fon-taskrabbit-blablacar.

16 *Nielsen Global Survey of Share Communities*, May 5th, 2014: http://www.nielsen.com/ca/en/nielsen-pressroom/2014/global-consumers-embrace-the-share-economy.html.

17 *Roland Berger study on the market for car sharing in China*, June 10th, 2014: http://www.rolandberger.com/press_releases/Car_Sharing_in_China_2014.html.

18 Manyika, James, Cabral, Armando, Moodley, Lohini, Moraje, Suraj, Yeboah-Amankwah, Safroadu, Chui, Michael, and Anthonyrajah, Jerry, *Lions go digital: The Internet's transformative potential in Africa* (McKinsey Global Institute, November 2013): http://www.mckinsey.com/insights/high_tech_telecoms_internet/lions_go_digital_the_internets_transformative_potential_in_africa.

19 Data taken from The World Bank and available by Googling "US GDP": http://data.worldbank.org/indicator/NY.GDP.MKTP.CD.

20 Wittig, Roman, and Jacob, Sandra, *The way to a chimpanzee's heart is through its stomach* (Max Planck Institute for Evolutionary Anthropology, Leipzig, January 2014): http://www.mpg.de/7717582/chimpanzees-oxytocin-stomach.

21 In the original French: *On résiste à l'invasion des armées; on ne résiste pas à l'invasion des idées.* Hugo, Victor, *Histoire d'un Crime [The History of a Crime]*, 1877; Conclusion.

22 Brian Chesky in a talk at The Aspen Institute, June 29th, 2014: https://www.youtube.com/watch?v=AGAKYeb86Oc.

Glossary of Key Sharing Economy Terms

Carpooling An alternative term for ridesharing, typically long-distance ridesharing (see below).

Car-sharing Two different models of car rental. B2C car-sharing involves companies renting out shared cars that they own and are distributed around cities. P2P car-sharing involves the rental of privately owned cars. Both present an alternative to the individual ownership of cars.

Crowdfunding The funding of companies, projects, causes, or loans using crowd-sourced capital from a "crowd" of potentially thousands of people. Crowdfunding comes in three variants, as described below.

- **Equity crowdfunding** The funding of a company through an online platform that allows a pool of investors to subscribe for unlisted shares.
- **Debt crowdfunding** The funding of a loan or portfolio of loans by a group of individuals, without the involvement of a bank.
- **Rewards-based crowdfunding** The funding of projects, causes, or inventions from backers who, instead of equity, receive rewards or perks that are usually related to the campaign and increase in value in proportion to the size of the backer's contribution.

Meal-sharing The sharing of meals between strangers in private homes, with the host charging their guests on a per seat basis.

Ridesharing Individuals offering lifts in their car to other individuals. Ridesharing comes in a short-distance and long-distance form. "Short-distance ridesharing" involves shared car journeys within cities and is a substitute for traditional taxis. "Long-distance ridesharing" involves shared journeys between cities and is a substitute for rail or coach travel.

Sharing economy (condensed version) The value in taking underutilized assets and making them accessible online to a community, leading to a reduced need for ownership of those assets.

Timebanking A system for the reciprocal exchange of services using time as a currency. An hour of time, however spent or received, usually has the same value and is held in a central repository: a "timebank."

Appendix

A Nonexhaustive Compendium of Sharing Economy Companies (in order of appearance)

Sector/Company	Headquarters	Founded	Founder(s)	CEO
REAL ESTATE Short-term rentals				
Airbnb	San Francisco	2008	Nathan Blecharczyk Brian Chesky Joe Gebbia	Brian Chesky
Roomorama	Singapore	2009	Jia En Teo Federico Folcia	Federico Folcia
onefinestay	London	2009	Tim Davey Greg Marsh Demetrios Zoppos	Greg Marsh
HomeAway	Austin, Texas	2005	Brian Sharples Carl Shepherd	Brian Sharples
HouseTrip	London	2010	Arnaud Bertrand Junjun Chen-Bertrand	George Hadjigeorgiou
Home-swapping				
HomeExchange	Los Angeles	1992	Ed Kushins	Ed Kushins
Knok	Barcelona	2011	Laura Martinez Celada Juanjo Rodriguez	Juanjo Rodriguez
Love Home Swap	London	2011	Simon Walker Ben Wosskow Debbie Wosskow	Debbie Wosskow
Other space				
JustPark (parking)	London	2006	Anthony Eskinazi	Alex Stephany
LiquidSpace (office)	San Francisco	2010	Mark Gilbreath Doug Marinaro	Mark Gilbreath

Sector/Company	Headquarters	Founded	Founder(s)	CEO
Science Exchange (laboratories)	Palo Alto, Silicon Valley	2011	Ryan Abbott Elizabeth Iorns Dan Knox	Elizabeth Iorns
Storemates (storage)	London	2011	Shaff Prabatani Ben Rogers	Bally Sappal
VEHICLES **B2C car-sharing**				
Zipcar	Boston	2000	Robin Chase Antje Danielson	Mark Norman
Car2Go	Ulm, Germany	2008	-	Nicholas Cole
P2P car-sharing				
RelayRides	San Francisco	2008	Shelby Clark	Andre Haddad
SnappCar	Utrecht, Netherlands	2011	Pascal Ontijd Victor van Tol	Victor van Tol
Getaround	San Francisco	2009	Elliot Kroo Jessica Scorpio Sam Zaid	Sam Zaid
Drivy	Paris	2010	Paulin Dementhon	Paulin Dementhon
Other vehicles				
Scoot Networks (scooters)	San Francisco	2011	Matt Ewing Michael Keating Dan Riegel	Michael Keating
Spinlister (bicycles)	Santa Monica, California	2012	Will Dennis Jeff Noh	Marcelo Loureiro
Boatbound (boats)	San Francisco	2012	Aaron Hall Matt Johnston	Aaron Hall
RIDESHARING **Short-distance ridesharing**				
Lyft	San Francisco	2012	Logan Green John Zimmer	Logan Green
Uber	San Francisco	2009	Garrett Camp Travis Kalanick	Travis Kalanick
SideCar	San Francisco	2012	Jahan Khanna Sunil Paul	Sunil Paul
Long-distance ridesharing				
Carpooling.com	Munich	2001	Michael Reinicke Matthias Siedler Stefan Weber	Markus Barnikel

Sector/Company	Headquarters	Founded	Founder(s)	CEO
BlaBlaCar	Paris	2004	Nicolas Brusson Fred Mazzella Francis Nappez	Fred Mazzella
GoCarShare	London	2009	Drummond Gilbert	Drummond Gilbert
GOODS **General**				
yerdle	San Francisco	2012	Carl Tashian Andy Ruben Adam Werbach	Andy Ruben
eBay	San Jose, Silicon Valley	1995	Pierre Omidyar	John Donahoe
Etsy	New York	2005	Robert Kalin Chris Maguire Haim Schoppik Jared Tarbell	Chad Dickerson
Peerby	Amsterdam	2011	Eelke Boezeman Daan Weddepohl	Daan Weddepohl
Freecycle	Tucson, Arizona	2003	Deron Beal	Deron Beal
Clothes				
Rent the Runway	New York	2009	Jennifer Fleiss Jennifer Hyman	Jennifer Hyman
Poshmark	Menlo Park, Silicon Valley	2011	Manish Chandra Gautam Golwala Chetan Pungaliya Tracy Sun	Manish Chandra
Threadflip	San Francisco	2012	Jeff Shiau Manik Singh	Manik Singh
thredUP	San Francisco	2009	Chris Homer Oliver Lubin James Reinhart	James Reinhart
Books				
Chegg	Santa Clara, Silicon Valley	2007	Josh Carlson Aayush Phumbhra Osman Rashid	Dan Rosensweig
BookMooch	San Francisco	2006	John Buckman	John Buckman
Dogs				
BorrowMyDoggy	London	2012	Les Cochrane Rikke Rosenlund	Rikke Rosenlund

Sector/Company	Headquarters	Founded	Founder(s)	CEO
Rover.com	Seattle	2011	Greg Gottesman Philip Kimmey	Aaron Easterly
DogVacay	Santa Monica, California	2012	Aaron Hirschhorn	Aaron Hirschhorn
Food				
Feastly	San Francisco	2013	Danny Harris Noah Karesh	Noah Karesh
EatWith	Tel Aviv, Israel	2012	Guy Michlin Shemer Schwarz	Guy Michlin
Shareyourmeal.net	Utrecht, Netherlands	2012	Jan Thij Bakker Marieke Hart	-
Cookisto	Athens	2013	Michalis Gkontas Petros Pitsilis	Michalis Gkontas
Other				
Fon (wifi)	Madrid	2006	Martin Varsavsky	Martin Varsavsky
Quirky	New York	2009	Ben Kaufman	Ben Kaufman
SERVICES **Paid**				
TaskRabbit	San Francisco	2008	Leah Busque	Leah Busque
oDesk	San Francisco	2005	Odysseas Tsatalos	Fabio Rosati (since oDesk's merger with Elance)
Skillshare	New York	2010	Michael Karnjanaprakorn Malcolm Ong	Michael Karnjanaprakorn
PeoplePerHour	London	2007	Simos Kitiris Xenios Thrasyvoulou	Xenios Thrasyvoulou
Vayable	San Francisco	2010	Samrat Jeyaprakash Jamie Wong	Jamie Wong
Airtasker	Sydney	2012	Tim Fung Jonathan Lui	Tim Fung
Instacart	San Francisco	2012	Brandon Leonardo Apoorva Mehta Max Mullen	Apoorva Mehta
Time-based				
Time Republik	Lugano, Switzerland	2012	Gabriele Donati Karim Varini	Gabriele Donati Karim Varini

Sector/Company	Headquarters	Founded	Founder(s)	CEO
Echo	London	2014	Matthew McStravick	Matthew McStravick
CROWDFUNDING **Equity crowdfunding**				
Seedrs	London	2012	Jeff Lynn Carlos Silva	Jeff Lynn
Crowdcube	Exeter, UK	2011	Luke Lang Darren Westlake	Darren Westlake
Debt crowdfunding				
Lending Club	San Francisco	2006	Renaud Laplanche	Renaud Laplanche
Funding Circle	London	2009	Samir Desai James Meekings Andrew Mullinger	Samir Desai
Prosper	San Francisco	2006	Chris Larsen John Witchel	Aaron Vermut
Auxmoney	Düsseldorf, Germany	2007	Raffael Johnen Philipp Kriependorf	Raffael Johnen
Zopa	London	2005	James Alexander Giles Andrews Richard Duvall David Nicholson	Giles Andrews
Rewards-based crowdfunding				
Kickstarter	New York	2009	Charles Adler Perry Chen Yancey Strickler	Yancey Strickler
Indiegogo	San Francisco	2008	Danae Ringelmann Slava Rubin Eric Schell	Slava Rubin
RocketHub	New York	2009	Jed Cohen Brian Meece Vladimir Vukicevic	Brian Meece
People investing				
Pave	New York	2012	Oren Bass Sal Lahoud Justin Mitchell	-
Upstart	Palo Alto, Silicon Valley	2012	Dave Girouard Mark Levin	Dave Girouard

Index

Printed and bound by CPI Group (UK) Ltd, Croydon, CR0 4YY